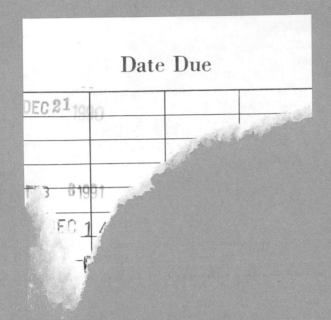

Organizational Decision Making

The Irwin Series in Management and The Behavioral Sciences

L. L. Cummings and E. Kirby Warren *Consulting Editors*
John F. Mee *Advisory Editor*

Organizational Decision Making

Bernard M. Bass
State University of New York, Binghamton

1

RICHARD D. IRWIN, INC.
Homewood, Illinois   60430

ISBN 0-256-02922-9
Library of Congress Catalog Card No. 82–82120

Printed in the United States of America

1 2 3 4 5 6 7 8 9 0 K 0 9 8 7 6 5 4 3

133355

To Ruth for her continuing patience and support

Preface

This book was prompted by a suggestion from Bert King of the Office of Naval Research that it would be useful to prepare a current state-of-the-art paper. The paper rapidly grew into a book.

In many respects, I began the effort with a somewhat naive and limited perspective about the state of the field since the seminal contributions of March and Simon (1958), Cyert and March (1963), and Thompson (1967). This was probably due to the fact that organizational decision-making has remained long on theory and short on controlled experimental evidence due to the difficulties inherent in collecting such evidence. Nevertheless, the body of theory that has emerged along with the modest amount of experimental support for it is impressive.

The classical approach has been replaced by a romantic view of organizational decision making. Instead of order and balance, we now see disorder and asymmetry. Instead of a simple, one-way causal linkage of a problem generating search for solutions, then evaluation and choice, we now see a two-way process of mutual interaction among problem, search, and choice. Instead of the causal expectations we have that problems result in search efforts and that search efforts result in evaluation and choice, we now see that the contiguity of problems and solutions may be more important.

The book is intended as a text for upper undergraduate, graduate, and professional students in management, public administration, public health, psychology, sociology, and political science. It is also intended for scholars and practicing managers interested in the subject from both a scholarly and a practical point-of-view. The expectation is that the scholar will find much food for thought as well as specific ideas about the kinds of further research needed to increase the confidence in our understanding of organizational decision processes. In the same way, the hope is that practicing administrators and managers will find important propositions about the subject which can be translated into application in their own situations. Where the study of business policy, strategic planning, and organizational design depends predominantly upon case analyses, this book may serve to supplement the systematic understanding of the decision process.

I begin with a description of the organizational decision process as we have come to know it. It is less orderly than prescribed by classical management theory. For purposes of exposition, we examine the phases of the process in separate chapters: Problem discovery and diagnosis in Chapter 2; search for and design of solutions in Chapter 3; evaluation and choice in Chapter 4; and authorization and implementation in Chapter 5. Achieving agreement about what to do in each of these phases is discussed in Chapter 6. This process is subject to many social, political, and behavioral constraints, which are described in Chapter 7. Decision supports are detailed in Chapter 8. I conclude with an integrating model and a discussion of needed research in Chapter 9.

There are independent bodies of knowledge about human decision making, decision making in small groups, and organizational decision making. The limited space available for examining organizational considerations and the social, psychological, and political aspects of the individual decision maker within the organizational context prevents us from investigating most of the body of information available on the subject in operations management, statistics, and economics. Statistical inference and utility theory can be fundamental tools for the sophisticated organizational decision maker, but we must assume that the reader will go elsewhere for the details of these approaches.

As can be seen by the large reference list, I am indebted to a wide array of scholars for many of the ideas presented. Especially important also was Professor John A. Miller's review of the final manuscript.

Particular appreciation is owed to Mrs. Mary Bean and Mrs. Marie Duffy for typing the manuscript under trying conditions.

Bernard M. Bass

Contents

1. **The organizational decision**   1

   Importance. Problems and decisions. The process. The unit. Ill-structured rather than well-structured problems. Organizational rather than personal goals. Substantive sources of difference in the organizational decision process. Organizational and human decision processes.

2. **Methods and models**   21

   Prescription versus description. Methods: *Mathematico-deductive methods. Empirico-inductive methods.* Theories and models: *Role of theory. Economic theory of the firm. Behavioral theories of the firm.*

3. **Problem discovery and diagnosis**   39

   Problems and dilemmas. Discrepancy as trigger. Scanning and screening. Goals and objectives. Displacement. Diagnosis. Participation and involvement in the decision process.

4. **Search and design** 53

Organizational search as seen by Cyert and March. Further conceptualizations about the stimulation of search. Search is ubiquitous and dynamic. Search as anticipatory behavior. Heuristics of search. Search or design? The design of innovative solutions. Terminating search and innovation processes. Information systems and the search and design process: *Availability. Relevance of information. Reliability of information. Distortion of information. Cost of information. Economic theory of teams.*

5. **Evaluation and choice** 69

Preclosure evaluation of the anticipated benefits and costs of alternatives: *Criteria for evaluation of alternatives. Anticipated utility of outcome: The model of complete rationality. Satisficing outcomes: The model of bounded rationality. The ideal as anchor: The model of the displaced ideal. Political solution: The model of accommodation and adaptation. Strategic striving: The model of objectives orientation.* Dealing with uncertainty: *Risk and uncertainty. Reducing uncertainty. Response to uncertainty. Risk, uncertainty, and subjective probability.* Choice and commitment: *Policy capturing with linear regression models. Making inferences and applying rules to make choices. Authorization.* Justifying the chosen alternative. Evaluation of obtained outcomes: *Implementation. Criteria for evaluating obtained outcomes. Postdecision cost-benefits analysis.*

6. **Dealing with conflict** 99

Sources of conflict. Resolving conflicts in decision making: *Authority and power. Persuasion. Coalition formation. Joint problem solving versus negotiating.*

7. **Constraints on organizational decision process** 115

Environment, goals, and tasks as constraints: *Definition of constraint. Sources of constraint. Environmental constraints. Organizational goals as constraints. Tasks and technology as constraints.* Organizational structural constraints: *Multiple impact. Organizational structure. Role expectations as constraints. Bureaucratization. Centralization versus decentralization. Controls. Formalism as a constraint.* The immediate group as a constraint: *Types of teams. The risky shift.* The individual as a constraint: *Explicit values and premises. Implicit values and premises. Perceptual and cognitive biases. Personality and competence. Effects of role. Interactions among constraints.*

8. Decision aids and support systems   151

Fully structured aids: *Modeling. Model types. Sensitivity analysis. Applications. Implementation.* Partially structured aids: *Supports for the decision process as a whole. Supports for problem discovery and diagnosis. Supports for search and innovation. Supports for evaluation and choice. The uses of contrived conflict. Impact of education and training.*

9. Unanswered questions and unresolved issues   171

Methods and models. Problem discovery and diagnosis. Search and design. Evaluation and choice. Conflict and authorization. Constraints. Decision aids and support systems.

References   193
Index   213

1

The organizational decision

What are the processes of organizational decision making? What is the state of theory and research in the area? What efforts are being made to improve it? What is known and what needs to be known? What are the variables of consequence involved in the pathology of decision making in organizations? What can the practicing manager learn about it that may help to improve his or her performance?

To answer these questions, we will explore organizational antecedents and intermediate dynamics to describe and understand effective decisions made by the individuals and groups in an organizational matrix. We will emerge with a substantive model of organizational antecedents, location, focus, processes, and outcomes that affect decision quality. Improvements will be sought by making the organizational decision-making process more explicit. As we shall see, many of the approaches to such improvements are efforts, made as the decision process unfolds, to move to the surface of the decision makers' awareness what now tends to lie at subconscious or deeper levels (Kast & Rosenzweig, 1970).

Importance

Concentration on organizational decision making is seen to be of particular importance to furthering our understanding of organizational behavior in general. It is what holds organizations together and makes them progress. The goals, tasks, and choices determining the organization's activities are highlighted, broadly illuminating the dynamics of organizational life (Cyert & March, 1963). Furthermore, focus on organizational decision making provides the meeting ground for concepts from economics, quantitative methods, and behavioral science (Dill, 1965).

There are many concepts and theories about the individual decision maker and about group decision, but those that are appropriate in the organizational context remain mostly unverified and unapplied to improving our understanding and management of organizational decision making. Yet a majority of the really crucial events of the world are a consequence of the organizational decision-making process rather than isolated, individual decision making. It is impossible to attribute the decision-making process in the American hostage crisis in Iran solely to one Iranian, or only to President Carter, or just to one short-lived occurrence. Hindsight review suggests that the Iranians slipped by unintended incremental steps from student demonstrations to militant kidnapping officially sanctioned by the Iranian government. Jimmy Carter's decisions, beginning with those concerning the Shah's medical problems, seem to have been strongly affected by a mix of medical misinformation, pressure groups, and his own personal predilections (*New York Times*, 1981). The Watergate coverup dynamics appeared to be accounted for by: (1) little immediate public concern; (2) the psychological homogeneity of the principal decision makers, who shared an amoral view of the situation and consequently a tendency to reinforce each others' misperceptions; and (3) an inadequate grasp of information by the decision makers of both the legal aspects of the situation and public opinion (Gouran, 1976). The delayed decisions by Detroit auto manufacturers to switch to production of small cars can only be understood in terms of consumer attitudes toward the small car (fostered by a generation of advertising), the gasoline crises, political support for continued low gasoline prices, differential profitability of small and large autos, short public memory, and long lead times for investment turnarounds. Seeing the failure of Detroit's decision making during the 1970s as due to management Neanderthalism is gross oversimplification of the organizational decision-making problem. But the question that remains is whether understanding of better organizational decision processes could have produced better decisions in this situation.

Problems and decisions

A problem exists requiring decision making if there is a barrier between a current and a desired state of affairs. Something blocks the attainment of a goal. Ordinarily, in organizational problems, the desired state is a steady state. If a deviance occurs and obstacles prevent return to the steady state, a problem is perceived. Again, a problem arises if the organization cannot automatically move from a current steady state to a more preferred one. A problem will be sensed if the current state is judged undesirable even if no goal or desired state can be discerned.

Organizational decision making is problem solving, where the problem is sensed, solutions are sought, evaluated, and accepted or rejected for authorization and implementation. The decisions refer to the judgments directly affecting the courses of action involved in the problem. Although problem solving and decision making are often used interchangeably, they are not synonymous. Solving one problem may involve many decisions (Shull, Delbecq, & Cummings, 1970). However, smaller decisions may be encapsulated in larger ones, so the distinction may not be important.

Decisions are action oriented. They are judgments which directly affect a course of action (Griffiths, 1958). But the decision process involves both thought and action culminating in an act of choice. Thought-oriented decision making can be defined in terms of information acquisition, information processing, and communication. The process then is seen as a matter of widening or narrowing the decision maker's information set (MacCrimmons, 1974). On the other hand, action-oriented decision making defines it in terms of resource acquisition, resource allocation, and commitment (Stricklin, 1966). The process is described as a widening or narrowing of the decision maker's resource set. Both the information processing and the resource processing modes are relevant when trying to understand organizational decision making.

In organizational decision making, alternatives of choice are likely to be complex and characterized by multiple attributes and multiple objectives (Zeleny, 1981). Organizational decisional situations contain at least two dilemmas which must be solved simultaneously: the problem itself, and a set of viable organizational arrangements, compatible with the problem solution and organizational interrelationships (Stricklin, 1966).

Fully programmed machines, or technical measurements of utility followed by mechanical search, are illustrations of automatic organizational decision making (Zeleny, 1981). In the same way, decisions may be fixated by habitual effects (Simon, 1960). Based on empirical analyses of decision processes, Feldman (1981) for example, concluded that to the degree that observed behavior is consistent with expectations, "it is noted and stored automatically. It is only when a behavior departs from expectations, or when the task is somehow changed, that conscious attention and recognition processes are engaged" (p. 129).

Our fundamental task will be to examine the nonautomatic decision processes of discovery and diagnosis; search and innovation; evaluation and choice; authorization; and implementation in the context of extraorganizational, organizational, team, and individual variables that modify the process.

The process

In the past half-century, a variety of increasingly jaundiced views have emerged of the organizational decision process as it is and as it should be. The classical ideal of clearly perceived goals is now usually seen as the exception rather than the rule. The classical requirement of complete search is seen as infeasible, if not impossible. Classical choice with complete information is seen as a chimera. A disorderly rather than an orderly process is discerned. Even means-ends logic is seen as only one possibility. Ends may justify the means, not be a consequence of them. Means and ends may be linked because they happen to appear at the same time and location. But it is not an either/or matter. Rather, we must deal with the amount of order or disorder, sequencing or contiguity, completeness or lack of completeness, and forward or backward linkages, as variables in designated decision processes in our search for regularities and generalities. (See p. 175 for a model representing this view.)

As idealized by economists and classical management theorists, decision making is a series of logical steps beginning with identifying a goal; measuring the gap between the goal and the current state of affairs; searching exhaustively for solutions; and choosing the single optimal solution which maximizes benefits or minimizes costs. As first idealized by behaviorists, decision making is an orderly process beginning with the discovery by the decision maker of a discrepancy between the perceived state of affairs and the desired state. This desired state is usually between an ideal and a realistically attainable state. Alternative actions (usually just a few of those possible) are selected or invented. One of these alternatives emerges as the action of choice followed by justification for it. Then comes its authorization and its implementation. The process cycle is completed with feedback about whether the action resulted in movement toward the desired state of affairs. If the perceived and desired state of affairs have not narrowed sufficiently, a new cycle is likely to commence.

Lindblom (1959) and Soelberg (1967) put the emphasis on recycling, on the small incremental changes in the final choice, as successive alternatives are compared with an early favorite.

A person may be following some sort of generalized guidelines when making judgments in ill-structured problems, but he or she would probably regard the experience as unique. However, Soelberg (1967) suggested that an observer would see that:

The decision makers applied few special purpose rules when arriving at their choice.

The decision makers might not be able to specify, in advance, the nature of an ideal solution to their problem.

A number of the decision criteria that they wished to apply were not operational before they tackled the problem.

Many of their choice alternatives were unknown when they began.

Information about the merits and consequences of alternatives were not immediately available from the task environment.

Realistic pictures of the process were captured by Zeleny (1981) and MacCrimmon (1974):

> Decision making is . . . complex, redolent with feedback and cycles, full of search detours, information gathering, and information ignoring, fueled by fluctuating uncertainty, fuzziness, and conflict. (Zeleny, 1981, p. 333)

> In real decision situations, one seldom observes . . . clear, step-by-step process. . . . Steps in the process proceed simultaneously, some steps are skipped some are repeated. . . . There are obvious interactions, feedbacks, and cycles. Also, decision situations intermingle; decisions are imbedded in decisions. All these complications are quite real and usually quite rational. (MacCrimmon, 1974, p. 446)

And a five-year study of 25 strategic organizational decisions by Mintzberg, Raininghani and Theoret (1976) concluded that:

> . . . a strategic decision process is characterized by novelty, complexity, and openendedness, by the fact that the organization usually begins with little understanding of the decision situation it faces or the route to its solution, and only a vague idea of what that solution might be and how it will be evaluated when it is developed. Only by groping through a recursive, discontinuous process involving many difficult steps and a host of dynamic factors over a considerable period of time is a final choice made. This is not the decision making under uncertainty of the textbook, where alternatives are given even if their consequences are not, but decision making under ambiguity, where almost nothing is given or easily determined. (Mintzberg et al., 1976, pp. 250–251)

Thus, to the logical search directed by previous objectives must be added the possibility that alternative objects may be discovered in the process of search. Organizations that focus too narrowly on achieving only present objectives miss opportunities of uncovering new, more important objectives. Some organizational foolishness—search activity not justified by current objectives—is needed (March & Shapira, 1982).

Coming a full 180 degrees from the classical, orderly, purposive view of organizational decision making, March and Romelaer (1976) see that what may be more important to the process is the contiguity in time and place of problems, available solutions, and decision makers. They agree that the organizational decision process tends toward the disorderly. Policies fail to be implemented. Solutions seem to have vague links to problems. "Decision makers seem to wander in and out of decision arenas." Their participation is erratic rather than continuous. Proximity to each other of problems, solutions, and decision makers may be more important to understanding a decision process than the logical means-to-satisfy ends.

Contiguity is also an important consideration because many other organizational events that may affect the process and be affected by it, are occurring along with the decision process.

Decision processes offer the time and place to fulfill or violate role expectations and earlier commitments; to define virtue and truth; to examine what is happening to the organization; to declaim on what justifies its actions; to distribute recognition and blame; to challenge or reaffirm friendships and informal relationships; to discover and express self-interest and organizational interest and to obtain satisfaction from participating in the process.

The loosely coupled actions of different decision units depends considerably on these considerations of contiguity resulting in a "shifting intermeshing of the demands on the attention and lives of the whole array of actors." To appreciate what problems will draw attention and which will be ignored becomes a matter of studying how attention is focused in a situation of multiple, changing claims on attention (March & Olson, 1976).

Although logic (consistency), self-interest, and organizational purpose may underlie much of organizational decision making, allowance must be made for accidental and random causation in organizational decision making in all of its stages. Serendipitous discovery of problems and solutions are common. A consideration initiated by two executives who happen to meet in the corridor may ultimately lead to decisions or actions by one or another's organization which never would have occurred if they had not met. Contingency planning must allow for the completely unexpected (Bass & Ryterband, 1969).

It is suggested that coin tossing may be a sensible way to deal with certain kinds of decisions about allocating available resources, or about schedules when there is no rational way to give more weight to one alternative than another. In the same way, lotteries may be a good way to make distributive decisions; drawing straws, the best way to select a whipping boy.

These iconoclastic views of the organizational decision process may help to explain Stagner's (1969), Bing's (1971) and Mintzberg, Raisinghani and Theoret's (1976) survey results.

Stagner's (1969) survey of 217 executives from 109 firms involved in corporate decision making concluded that rough estimates were made of anticipated costs and profits which might result from a decision; that company image often outweighed cost considerations; and that considerable importance was placed on company traditions.

Despite the academic availability of a variety of complex optimization routines for investment decisions, most financial executives surveyed (Bing, 1971) tended to use only the one or two simplest ones rather than the more rigorous analytical procedures. Even with quantitatively-trained-and-oriented project engineers in the aerospace industry, when accuracy is critical and the customer is the Federal Government, subjective bases for decisions were mentioned over three times as frequently as sophisticated methods of analysis such as PERT, linear programming, and other decision supports. Many never mentioned using any sophisticated tools in making their important decisions.

Mintzberg, Raisinghani & Theoret (1976) called attention to six disturbances in the 25 strategic decision processes they analyzed which detracted from the ideal, orderly process of discovery-diagnosis-search-design, evaluation/choice-authorization/implementation. These were: (1) interrupts (caused by the environment); (2) scheduling delays; (3) timing delays and speedups (due to the decision maker(s)); (4) feedback delays; (5) comprehension cycles; and (6) failure recycles inherent in the decision process itself.

Interrupts cause changes in pace or direction of the decision process and are due to meeting unexpected constraints, political impasses, unexpected new options, and discoveries. They are most common in high pressure environments and public institutions.

Scheduling delays are due to the need to factor complex decisions into manageable tasks. The managers, faced with a multiplicity of other tasks as well, introduce scheduling delays to attend to them.

Timing delays and speedups are frequent. As Martin and Sims (1956) have noted, managers may time their announcements to when they believe they are likely to do the most good. Managers may purposely speed up or delay a decision process to take advantage of special situations, to await support, to mesh actions with other activities, to bring about surprise, or merely to gain time. Managers try to time the initiation of decisions to facilitate their smooth execution.

Where competitiveness, distrust, and disagreement are high, a greater incidence of timing speedups and delays are expected. In crisis decisions, Schwartzman (1971) found that managers used delaying tactics of stalling, bluffing, or finding temporary solutions to reduce pressures.

Feedback delays were due to the need to await the results of previous steps and the reaction to them.

Comprehension cycles involve cycling back to earlier phases in the decision process and is seen as the norm. The decision process is circular, not linear, resembling biochemical fermentation rather than an assembly line (Pfiffner, 1960). The manager

> may cycle through a maze of nested design and search activities to develop a solution; during evaluation, he may cycle to understand the consequences of alternatives; he may cycle between development and investigation to understand the problem he is solving (Diesing, 1967); he may cycle between selection and development to reconcile goals with alternatives, ends with means. The most complex and novel strategic decisions seem to involve the greatest incidence of comprehension cycles. (Mintzberg, Raisinghani, & Theoret, 1976, p. 265)

Failure recycles are observed. Faced with the inability to find an acceptable solution, the decision makers may delay further consideration or change criteria. Unable to defeat the stronger British Navy outright with the Dutch fleet that was available, John de Witt adjusted his goals to suit his means (Rowen, 1978). Mintzberg *et al.* found typically that organizations faced with failure to find or design an acceptable solution cycled back to the development phase. The decision processes either returned to a special design branch to remove a constraint, developed a new solution, or modified an existing one. Sometimes, a previously rejected alternative was reintroduced under the new conditions. Faced with failure of a solution, decision makers try to remove constraints, modify the solution, develop a new solution, or accept what was previously unacceptable as a solution to the problem, adjusting the criteria of acceptance.

Distribution of activity. Activity is concentrated at the beginning and end of the course of a decision process. It is not uniformly distributed over the length of the process. Witte (1972) completed an unusual documentary analysis of 233 decisions by German organizations to purchase electronic data processing equipment (EDP). Documents in the manufacturers' files formed the basis for the study. Each decision involved from 2 to 452 distinct operations such as information-gathering, communication, evaluation, and direction. The mean number of operations was 37.7. The total time required for a decision ranged from four days to more than six years. The mean length was 14 months. For each decision, the total time was divided into 10 equal intervals and the following distribution of the 8,788 operations over the intervals was obtained.

Time Interval	Number of operations	Total operations (percent)	Cumulative percent
1	1,066	12.1	12.1
2	513	5.8	17.9
3	568	6.5	24.4
4	592	6.7	31.1
5	549	6.2	37.4
6	530	6.0	43.4
7	656	7.4	50.8
8	917	10.4	61.3
9	1,036	11.8	73.1
10	2,361	26.8	99.9

The emerging pattern is interesting. After an initial flurry of activity in the earliest interval, a diminished flat level of operations follows for over half the course of events. There is some pickup in the seventh, and more in the eighth and ninth intervals, but over one quarter of all the operations, as documented, appear in only the last interval! Almost half of all operations occur in the last three intervals. There may be implications here that much of the inertia seen in large organizations is to be expected. Following initial interest in a project, a lengthy time for digestion is needed before the final push occurs for closure.

Although a sequence of activities was expected such that more information-gathering would be seen in early intervals and more evaluation in late intervals, such was not the case. Little difference in the mix of these three types of operations was observed in early, rather than middle, or late intervals. The implication was that a recycling, not-too-orderly process was the rule rather than the exception. Only 4 of the 233 decisions could be found where there was the expected sequential development of recognition of the problem, information-gathering, development of alternatives, and choice. Although these four orderly decisions were expected to be faster, more thorough, and more free of conflict, such was not the case.

Importance of power and politics.   Power, coalition formation, and conflict resolution were seen to be paramount in the policy-decision processes in the federal bureaucracy in one of the few empirical studies available about the process of organizational decision making (Gore, 1956).

Interviews were held in each of 18 federal field offices about a variety of decisions concerning budgeting, personnel, procedures, programs, and structure. A total of 33 case histories were completed. Policy decisions were differentiated from operating decisions. Policy decisions dealt with tradition, custom, legality, or some new principle. The decisions involved power centers outside the field office. They substituted a new for an old program or function, restructured the formal organization of the office, substituted new for old procedures, or selected top level personnel. Need for change in policy was instituted by the demands of clientele, politicians, the press, and the central office. This outside pressure did not automatically lead to search or choice of remedial actions. Often it led to complete resistance to further action. Those offices which resisted any change rationalized the demands as due to unfair clientele or legislators. Even responsive offices were reluctant to change. They complained of a vacillating higher leadership unwilling to protect programs from a fickle public.

Some of the resistance or responsiveness was prompted by informal communication channels. Sometimes these were more important than formal channels in circulating relevant information. This informality in turn caused variations in whether information from the central office was withheld or disseminated by agency heads. Also of consequence was the fact that some personnel concentrated on collecting information from the central office and outside the agency; others on transmitting and distributing it.

If there was perceived a need for change in policy in a field office, diagnosis, generation of alternatives, and choice-making followed. But along with the means-ends rationality of the situation, political considerations figured heavily in each of these phases. In addition to attempting to match possible policy changes with internal agency objectives, public approbation for the choice and competitive advantages were sought as well as consistency with other decisions currently under consideration. The benefits to the agency of a proposed change were weighed against the costs. Tangible possible actions emerged from earlier detections of vague discrepancies between current and desired states of affairs. Then programmatic and policy discrepancies were seen. There were three forms of tangible action: actively resist change; wait and see; or change policy.

If active resistance was to follow, then the next steps were to develop countermoves and to form or strengthen alliances with other agencies, higher authority, or clientele. If change in policy was to be effected, then its implementation had to be planned. Either case (to resist or to change) required mobilizing power in a leadership clique to plan for successful action by monitoring what others were doing, by sending up trial balloons, by consulting above and below, and by engaging in speculative discussions. Success depended on negotiating with centers of power in the larger system, either persuading them to go along with what was or was not to be done, or compromising with them. If a change in policy was the consequence, the change was formalized in rewriting the relevant regulations and manuals based on commitments of support received for the change all along the decision process.

As can be seen, with acceptance from many outside parties critical for the change or resistance to it, political support played a continuing role of importance to the overall process.

The unit

The decision-making unit can be a fully programmed machine, a man and machine, a small face-to-face group, a committee, a task force, or a project team embedded in a larger formal organization of such units. As the unit is part of an organization, the unit's decision, whether the unit is a machine, an individual, or committee, is subject to organizational constraints. Such constraints are requirements or limitations imposed (or perceived) on the focal unit's decision making. The constraints may arise from the organization's environment, goals, policies, the behavior of other units in the organization, or individual attributes within the unit.

Organizations imply a charter, implicit or explicit, and norms and roles that transcend the composition of any single decision-making unit. Persistent communication patterns exist between the decision-making units of the organization. The character of such networks also strongly affect the unit and the subsequent decisions to be made for the organization as a whole.

Within the organization as a whole, numerous units are involved in decision making to accomplish the organization's objectives. But a decision made by a particular unit may commit the entire organization to a certain course of action. More often decisions committing the organization are made by several units, reviewed at several levels in the formal structure, and eventually authorized by the chief executive or the top administrator (Carter, 1971).

The supervisor as decision-making unit. When the decision-making unit is an individual supervisor operating as a member of a formal organization, he or she is faced with a bipolarity of aims as old as civilization. Is humanity inherently evil, in need of control by higher level decision-making in order to do good? Or, is humanity inherently good—needing organizational autonomy to self-actualize—so that control by higher authority is likely to inhibit accomplishment (McGregor, 1960)?

Closely related are the dilemmas in locus and focus of supervisory decision making. Will the locus for making the decision be the supervisor (as in directive supervision) or in the subordinate (as in participative supervision)? Will the focus be on the work to be done, productivity, the task at hand or will it be on the subordinate's needs and satisfactions? Much of the answer will depend on organizational antecedents and consequences (Bass, 1981).

The cascade. Based on dissatisfaction with his current location, the army commander decides to cross a stream. Subordinates recommend where to cross. The commander authorizes the crossing. Or, as a consequence of stoppages and breakdowns, a lower level management committee agrees on the need for new equipment. They next convince a higher level manager who authorizes the expenditure. In each instance, the organizational decision is said to be cascading or multistaged. This is usually, but not always, the case when the decision units are embedded in a formal organization.

Thus, ordinarily, more than one decision-making unit is sequentially involved in the process from onset to completion. Krouse (1972) constructed a model whose key aspect was the explicit treatment of the decision-making concept as a sequence of choices by which the organization makes a commitment to tentative resource allocations, then enacts experiments to gather information for future decision making. In this sequential process, the organization revises its decisions and policy goals, rather than as conventionally implied by the single-step analysis. It is a sequence of adaptive moves.

Ordinarily, what culminates in the decision made by, say the firm's president, is likely to have been the accumulation of many decisions by many people in the organization. According to Rice and Bishoprick (1971), it is useful to conceive an organizational decision as an actual conclusion. The conclusion is based on a premise or a number of premises which in turn are based on information received by particular decision units through their communication channels. A decision of one unit may be the decision premise of another. Hence there is a growth from many smaller decisions serving as premises for larger decisions, until the final decision takes place. The flow follows functional rather than hierarchical channels.

The organizational decision usually involves an upper management with problems arising from organizational objectives and from feedback from operations and the environment. The management is responsible for planning, direction, coordination, and control of lower management. Lower management, in turn, is responsible for planning, direction, monitoring, and control of operations. Such operations generate problems in the flow of supplies to be transformed into outputs of goods and services. Feedback is obtained on whether objectives are being met (Shull, Delbecq & Cummings, 1970).

Ill-structured rather than well-structured problems

It should be clear that we are dealing here with ill-structured problems that do not lend themselves to easily programmed decisions rather than well-structured problems that can be easily programmed. Most problems faced by managers are ill-structured for at least five reasons. Usually, there is considerable ambiguity and incompleteness of information about the problems. The problems are continually being redefined. Programs of desired outcomes are unavailable. More than one person is likely to influence what is happening. Finally, the decision process is likely to extend over a lengthy period of time (Ungson, Braunstein & Hall, 1981).

The usual way of making decisions for dealing with ill-structured problems has been by "seat of the pants" judgment, intuition, and experience. Managers have trouble explaining what techniques they use in making these decisions because they are not consciously aware of how they make them. Executive "intuition" is a very elusive decision-making technique (Luthans, 1973). According to Simon (1958), well-structured problems can be formulated explicitly and quantitatively. As a consequence, they then can be solved by known and feasible computational techniques. For ill-structured problems, the essential variables are symbolic or verbal rather than numerical. Goals are vague and non-quantitative. Computational algorithms are unavailable. Most practical problems and decisions that executives face every day, particularly the most important ones "lie much closer to the ill-structured than to the well-structured end of the spectrum" (p. 3).

It also follows that the higher in hierarchical level a manager is in the organization, the more likely he or she is to face ill-structured rather than well-structured problems.

As noted by Mitroff and Emshoff (1979), organizational ill-structured problems ordinarily involve more than one person in their formulation, solution, evaluation and implementation, and include one or more additional characteristics:

1. The problem may be clearly stated but there is no agreement by those dealing with it about an appropriate solution.
2. There is no agreement on a methodology for developing such a solution.
3. There may be no agreement on a clear formulation of the problem, its objective, controllable variables, and uncontrollable variables.
4. Problems are likely to be mixes of *highly interdependent important ones that cannot be formulated, let alone solved, independently of one another.* These are what Ackoff (1967) terms *messes*.

The programming possible with well-structured problems deals with usually less important decisions which are repetitive and routine. Definite procedures are worked out for handling them. They are not treated as a completely novel situation each time they occur. For the routine, repetitive, programmed decisions, the specific processes for handling them traditionally have been habitual, clerical routines, standard operating procedures, mathematical analyses, computer simulations and electronic data processing. Or use has been made of an organizational structure of common expectations, agreed-upon and well-understood subgoals, and well-defined channels of information. On the other hand, decisions remain unprogrammed when there is no routine for handling the novel or ill-structured problem because it is new, or because its precise nature and structure are elusive or complex, or because it is so important that it must be given special treatment (Cyert, Simon, & Trow, 1956). Rather, the programmed decisions—"one shot," ill-structured, novel, policy decisions—are handled by general problem-solving processes. Traditionally this has meant processes of judgment, intuition and creativity, rules of thumb, and selection and training of executives. Modern technology can also apply heuristic, "rule of thumb" computer programs and heuristic training of human decision makers (Simon, 1960).

Whether nonprogrammed decision processes will require judgment, compromise, and/or inspiration depends on whether the sources of ill structure are due to disagreements and vagueness about the means to solve the problem or the ends to be served (Thompson, 1967).

In the dynamic organization, the decision maker makes mainly unprogrammed decisions for which a high level of judgment and creativity must be exercised (Tosi & Carroll, 1976). Supporting this contention, Friedlander (1970) found that the ratio of unprogrammed decisions to programmed decisions is higher in R&D organizations in which there were many changes and where the tasks tended to be nonroutine and complex.

Unprogrammed decision making calls for different kinds of individual and group decision makers than does programmed decision making. Unprogrammed decisions require greater training, competence, and experience. Also, decision-making groups mainly involved with unprogrammed decisions are organized differently. Thus, Duncan (1971) studied 22 decision groups in three manufacturing and three research and development organizations and concluded that decision units organize themselves differently for making routine and nonroutine decisions under different conditions of perceived uncertainty and perceived influence over the environment.

For well-structured problems, computational or algorithmic routines may be available to guarantee a solution. For ill-structured problems, lacking quantitative definition and alternatives susceptible to mathematical analysis, more judgment and creativity are required. But even here, as already noted, heuristic solutions can be worked out building on "rules of thumb," and finite, standard steps to achieve the objective. Heuristic programs can be prepared.

With well-structured problems, a search for an appropriate algorithm is reasonable. But with ill-structured problems, algorithms can rarely, if ever, be obtained. On the other hand, even for well-structured problems, heuristics that provide satisfactory solutions can be worked out rather than spending the extra effort on algorithm generation and operation. Heuristics lie between routinized responses and *de novo*, creative responses (MacCrimmon, 1974).

Heuristic programming can assist decision makers in a wide range of problems. Although the concepts—such as means-end analysis and breadth versus depth search—underlying heuristic programs are quite general, the heuristics themselves are usually particular to a specific decision problem at hand. Thus, although it is difficult or impossible to locate or discover an algorithmic solution or computational formula for ill-structured problems, it is still possible to write computer program solutions based on step-by-step heuristic rules which can substitute reasonably well for the real-life human decision maker. Since so much of management decision making is ill-structured, heuristic computer programming is making an increasing contribution to management decision making (Newell & Simon, 1972).

Organizational rather than personal goals

Once gripped by organizational considerations, the individual decision maker is faced with what is officially required and what is personally desired (Aram, 1976). Observers such as Barnard (1938), emphasized the importance of distinguishing between personal and organizational goals. Barnard felt decisions for organizational ends were more likely to be logically made than those serving self-interests. Nevertheless, personal choice figures in the organizational decision process: whether or not one will participate, and, if one participates, to what degree self-interest will take precedence over organizational purposes.

Ordinarily, one cannot delegate personal decisions to others as one can organizational decisions.

> For example, what may be called a major (personal) decision by an individual may require numerous subsidiary decision (or judgments) which he or she also must make. A similar important decision by an organization may in its final form be enunciated by one person and the corresponding subsidiary decisions by several different persons, all acting organizationally, not personally. Similarly, the execution of a decision by

one person may require subsequent detailed decision by him as to various steps, whereas the execution of a similar decision in an organization almost always requires subsequent detailed decisions by several different persons. (Barnard, 1938, p. 187)

The importance of self-interest to organizational decision making is attested to by Patchen (1974) who provided a conceptual framework taking into account self-interests which better described the purchasing decisions in business firms and what influenced them than did French and Raven's (1959) bases of power: coercive, expert, legitimate, reward or referent. Argyris (1964) saw the need for integrating individual and organizational goals while Culbert and McDonough (1980) examined the importance of awareness, openness, and the need to legitimatize consideration of both. More will be said about this when we deal later with conflict in organizational decision making.

Substantive sources of difference in the organizational decision process

In a panel study of 240 finance departments of county, city, and state governments' promotion decisions, Halaby (1976) obtained evidence that the analysis of the decision process remains incomplete without a consideration of its substance.

Strategic, policy-making decisions are likely to emerge from different processes than tactical, operational decisions. Strategic decisions deal with the long-term health of the enterprise. Tactical decisions are concerned with the day-to-day activities necessary for efficient and smooth operations. For Selznick (1957), critical decisions must be distinguished from noncritical decisions. Critical decisions concern the goals an organization should pursue and the outputs required to achieve its goals. Tactical decisions are decisions about communication channels, work simplification, personnel selection, morale-building techniques, team organization, and conference methods. For Katz and Kahn (1966) policy decision making is separated out for special consideration and includes

> . . . those decisions within an organization which affect the structure of the organization. Policy making is therefore an aspect of organizational change—the decision aspect. Policy making is also the decision aspect of that level of leadership which involves the alteration, origination, or elimination of organizational structure. (Katz & Kahn, 1966, p. 259).

Three basic dimensions are considered of consequence to policy decisions: the level of generality or abstraction of the decision; the amount of internal and external organizational space affected by the decision; and the length of time for which the decision will hold.

This leads Katz and Kahn to distinguish among four types of decisions:

1. Policymaking as the formulation of substantive goals and objectives.
2. Policymaking as the formulation of procedures and devices for achieving goals and evaluating performance.
3. Routine administration, or the application of existing policies to ongoing operations.
4. Residual, ad hoc decisions affecting organizational space without temporal implications beyond the immediate event.

Decision processes clearly differ with the different kinds of organizational activities or functions. Parsons (1960) categorized organizational activity into technical, managerial, and institutional. The technical core of the organization operates its technology to achieve desired outputs rationally. The criteria for technical decision rationality are the extent to which activities result in desired outcomes and avoid unnecessary costs. To facilitate the attainment of technical rationality, decisions in the technical core are aimed at eliminating uncertainties and providing closure. Such closure is much less possible in the managerial or institutional cores for they must deal with the less controllable external environment. This, in turn, makes it difficult for the technical core, interlocked with the managerial and institutional, to avoid some uncertainty.

> Nevertheless, persistent attempts are made to attain an environment of certainty within the technical core. To the extent that such shielding is attained, the sources of uncertainty are principally confined to the technology itself, and decisions focus upon maintaining and improving the operation of the transformation processes. (Ebert & Mitchell, 1975, p. 36)

The managerial core involves overseeing the technical core, determining its scope, and facilitating its interactions with the environment consistent with changing requirements introduced by the institutional core. The management core mediates between the technical and institutional cores. The managerial core tries to facilitate the closure for the technical core by producing buffering units (such as inventories), smoothing input and output transactions (such as discounts to customers during off-seasons), by anticipating needed changes requiring technical adaptation (e.g., maintaining forecasting units) and by rationing scarce resources (e.g., setting priorities) (Thompson, 1967).

The institutional core is responsible for establishing the organization's identity in relation to its economic, physical, and social environment. Thus, it is most affected by environmental fluctuations and change. It is designed and oriented toward coping with environmental uncertainties rather than being shielded from them.

The organization's legitimacy—its ability to maintain employee compliance, its ability to attract investment capital vital to achieving its goals, and its ability to influence its prospective clients and customers to accept its goods and services—depend on the institutional core's flexibility in dealing with societal codes, laws, norms, values, and interests. Thus, the institutional core is responsible for setting and adjusting the organization's goals reflecting the environmental influences and interests of its various dominant organizational constituencies.

As concluded by Ebert and Mitchell (1975), decision making among the three cores of the organization is interdependent. This is seen in its flexible dealings with the external environment and its making commitments to, and placing demands on, various elements of the managerial and technical cores. Yet it depends upon the technical core to meet these commitments, providing the relative certainty in which the technical core can operate efficiently. Mediation and balance between the institutional needs for adaptability and the technical core for certainty are provided by the managerial core. An example is the managerial role of expeditor who tries to handle special rush orders from customers without unduly upsetting the production line.

Organizational and human decision processes

The dynamics of organizational decision making parallel those of the individual decision maker. Thus, organizations appear to use strategies in complex problem-solving situations that are functionally similar to strategies employed by individuals (Simon, 1960). However, organizational decision making, as such, requires much additional exposition. The differences from individual decision making must not be underestimated. For instance, ordinarily, since it involves transactions or influences between people, organizational decision making is more open to observation and cross-checking than is isolated human decision making (Barnard, 1938). Nevertheless, in the following chapters two streams of research will be considered: organizational decision making, which has been primarily theoretical; and human decision making, which has emphasized experimentation.[1] Organizational analyses have been mainly collections of simple ideas and metaphors aimed at understanding and interpreting naturally occurring organizational events. Research on human cognition and choice is mainly carried out in laboratory settings to provide empirical tests of a small set of propositions about inference and information processing. Yet much communality has been noted (March & Shapira, 1982). Both will contribute to understanding of the various

---

[1] See for instance, Hogarth (1980) for a review concentrating on the psychology of the individual decision maker.

phases of the decision process in organizational settings which we propose to examine: problem discovery and diagnosis, search and innovation, evaluation and choice, conflict and authorization, constraints on the process, and supports for it. But first we need to examine the methods to approach the examination.

Organizational decision making is an imporant, if not the most important, aspect of organizational life. But it is a messy rather than an orderly process, particularly if the problems for which decisions are needed are ill-structured rather than well-structured.

A way to capture the qualities of the process is to break it up into ideal phases even though, in reality, the separation between phases may be fuzzy. Furthermore, phases may be skipped, appear out-of-order, or reappear.

As we now shall see, the two approaches to understanding the process mainly have been either economic and mathematical or political, social and behavioral.

2

Methods and models

We now turn to considering the methods to study organizational decision processes, the models to guide our data-gathering, and the theories to interpret what has been discovered.

Prescription versus description

"Knowing how the decisions are made can teach us about *how* they should be made; the reverse causal linkage, unfortunately, does not follow" (Zeleny, 1981, p. 322). Thus, take two decks of playing cards and exchange the hearts and spades so that one deck has three black suits and the other has three red suits. To maximize success in predicting which suit will turn up in the three-fourths black deck, the prescription is to always predict black. But decision makers actually predict black only three fourths of the time (Taylor, 1965).

While mathematicians and economists wrestle largely with formal prescriptive models based on deductions from postulates on how things should be if one was, and could be, completely rational and consistent, behavioral research on organizational decision making is mainly descriptive. It has been concerned primarily with how, in fact, do managers and administrators actually make decisions? Normative models that can be constructed from such information are likely to focus on those aspects of decision-making behavior that economic decision models usually ignore or minimize (Simon, 1960).

All prescriptive effort need not remain only an academic exercise. Rather, normative theory can be formulated concerned with prescribing courses of action that conform most closely to the decision-maker's beliefs and values. Description of these beliefs and values and how they are incorporated into the decision-making process must precede the development of normative theory that can be externally validated. In the past, superficial comparisons were obtained between actual behavior and normative models. Now we concern ourselves with the psychological dynamics underlying observed decision-making processes.

Normative models will have a better chance of mirroring reality if they are based on psychologically sound axioms (MacCrimmon, 1968; Slovic & Tversky, 1974). For example, the paramutual betting and options markets indicate that people in general favor the long shots. Above and beyond this there are wide-ranging individual differences in preferences. The existence of stock market trading in massive frequencies and amounts attests to the extent to which—in the same overall environment—thousands of traders reach diametrically opposite decisions to buy what thousands of others are offering to sell. The traders differ in objectives, differ in their access to information, preferences for risk avoidance and choice strategies. To understand and predict their decision making requires careful description of the overall process involved. It becomes important to start with assumptions that are closer to reality than those upon which the purely economic theories are based. Economic utility theory still can only say that the utility for a completely rational gambler is the same when wagering $10 to win $1 with 9 chances in 10 to win, as when wagering $1 to win $10 with one chance in 10 to win.

Normative models which provide employment officers with optimums in deciding whether or not to hire a prospect can be constructed if various parameters can be fixed by previous experience, such as the known accuracy of judgment (the validity of the predictors against the criterion for performance), the base rate of occurrence of successful outcomes, the selection ratio, the costs of errors in making choices, and the pattern of successful and failing outcomes. Prescription can follow from adequate description.

METHODS FOR STUDYING ORGANIZATIONAL DECISIONS

Mathematico-deductive methods

Computational decision making has been most appropriate for the classical models of organizational decision making. Problems are well structured; alternatives are exhaustive and utilities are quantified. But generally as Zeleny (1981) has pointed out, in engaging in organizational decision making, managers do not duplicate "rather recondite mathematics . . . to maximize utility" as would be called for by most economists and many management scientists. Although considerable effort has been expended to apply simple mathematical rigor to decision making, it has generally been inadequate to capture the realities of decision making. The rigor has often been without relevance. The axioms upon which deductions have been derived often are not reality based.

This is not to say that we lack useful specific applications of mathematical analysis to better structured problems or to well-structured parts of the decision process, even when they have required simplification of reality in order to deal mathematically with the data at hand. For example, Ashton (1976) has shown that linear models in general, and linear regression models in particular, are superior to humans in terms of decision performance even when estimated from previous decisions of the individual. As we have already noted, human decision makers make systematic and random errors in the weighting and utilization of information which errors are exacerbated and compounded in organizational settings. The linear regressions can detect and adjust for these errors.[1] Indeed, as Slovic and Lichtenstein (1971) concluded:

> . . . much of what we call "intuition" can be explicated in a precise and quantitative manner. When this is done, the judge's insight into his own cognitive process is often found to be inaccurate. (Slovic & Lichtenstein, 1971, p. 724)

Many more specific examples will be cited and the significance of mathematical decision supports will be discussed at length in Chapter 8.

Nevertheless, it is not surprising to learn that practicing production managers avoid making use of the decision supports provided by complex operations research techniques, and practicing finance managers avoid complex mathematical models in favor of a few simple rules in investment decision making (Bing, 1971). Part of the problem is that the mathematical, deductive effort has been to prescribe the rules when we still remain unable to fully describe what goes into an effective decision.

---

[1] See Chapter 5 for brief descriptions of linear, nonlinear, and multiple regression.

Only if the mathematics follow reality-based axioms, is much progress likely here.

Mathematical structures need to be sought which describe decision-making behavior when organizational considerations infringe dramatically on the effectiveness of decisions and their outcomes as actually observed in real life. As they stand now, elegant mathematical models of preferences fail to mirror decision-making reality. In reality, organizational decisions are based on a progressive comparison of the preference systems of multiple actors in an unstable environment, evolving through interactions under the influence of different political and power systems. The preferences are fuzzy, incompletely formulated, nontransitive, and often incoherent and conflicting. They differ from one actor to another; they change with new circumstances and during the decision-making process (Roy, in press).

Futhermore, Zeleny (1981, p. 331) notes that alternatives are seldom specified in advance but creative generation of alternatives is ordinarily important. Preferences and trade offs are constantly changing. Further, rational, human choices fail to remain systematic, transitive or consistent. Single index numbers seldom capture the values in incommensurate performance measures. To employ a single, quantitative, objective function as the one and only criterion for the decision process is an "unscientific reduction of reality."

For an adequate mathematical account, we need to begin with behavioral approaches, then proceed in another direction, culminating in quite different mathematical descriptions which will more closely match reality.

Empirico-inductive methods

As we noted in Chapter 1, in certain senses it is easier to study organizational decision process *in vivo*, than individual human decision making. Organizations have external memories, computational aids, and resources permitting the identification of more alternatives, and the collection of more data on their outcomes. More quantitative criteria are available (Behling & Schriesheim, 1976). At the same time, it is obviously much more difficult to undertake controlled experimentation with organizations than with individuals.

Traditional methods.   Field methods for the study of organizational decision making have included the case history based on interviews with the key members of the organization, content analysis of available documents (memos, reports, news accounts, letters, minutes of meetings), and participant observations by the key members. Also use has been made of verbal protocols, diaries, time logs, sociometry, communication and information flows, and responses to questionnaires.

Multiple sources of information may be combined to trace the decision process longitudinally from start to finish. Heller (1982) observed decision-making meetings and examined their agenda and minutes to determine the key persons and agencies involved in a decision process on whether to build a third London airport. Subsequently, the key persons were individually interviewed to retrospectively trace the whole decision process.

Finally, some controlled laboratory experiments, and to a lesser degree, field experiments also have been employed, along with simulations such as business games.

Innovations. More recent innovative methods have included studying the organization as metaphor, organizational mapping, in-basket techniques, and interactive human-computer systems. Information-seeking has been studied by asking participants to select or purchase available information (Payne, 1976). Eye-movement paralleling decision processes have been examined by Russo and Rosen (1975).

A fruitful example of a simulation for studying decision making is the Tactical and Negotiations Game (TNG). Participants make complex military decisions in responding to experimenter-controlled information. Although the participants believe that they are playing against another team of decision makers, all information that they receive is preprogrammed to suit research interests. TNG permits assembling individual decision makers or decision-making groups and exposing them to a military environment representative of the model to be simulated. Since a decision-making unit can be continuously involved for eight hours or more without interruption, a real-time characteristic for the simulation is achieved. (What has been found, for example, is that highest levels of risk are reached after approximately six hours of decision-making activity. Risk levels tend to stabilize somewhat at that point) (Streufert, 1970).

Through controlled introspection, participants may be asked to build and validate their own networks of concepts and categorizations. In addition to traditional introspective methods of thinking aloud while making a decision, interviews with decision makers after-the-fact may be employed. Such interviews can be structured by stimulated recall. Bloom and Broder (1950) used tape playbacks asking participants to describe what they had been thinking about during the original problem solving. Videotaped playbacks of decision-making meetings could also be used for increased stimulation of recall.

Dependence on memory. Much of the study of organizational processes depends on some form of retrospection and recall. Hence, a critical issue concerns the reliability and validity of memory, the schema in which memories are encoded, and the extent to which they are sources of distortion.

Phillips and Rush (undated) summarized some of the relevant findings:

1. When asked to recall an event, humans often have difficulty distinguishing the objective character of that event from schematic information. Their descriptions, therefore, tend to be biased in the direction of their intuitive expectations, making their recall of the event more consistent with their schema than it actually was.

2. Information that is irrelevant to one's schema may fail to be stored. Even when such information has been stored, it may not be recalled since it is not integrated into relevant schema.

3. Current feelings and beliefs about an event can significantly distort memory of it. Cognitive bolstering of a previously experienced event results from our tendencies to selectively attend to, or encode and remember, information which strengthens our current stereotypes and expectations.

4. Factual information can be systematically distorted through the introduction of new information embedded in questions. Cues embedded within new information may activate certain schema, which serve as retrieval cues for other encoded information.

Thus, there can be serious impairment in the data based on recall of organizational decision processes. When asked to recall such processes, managers are likely to respond depending on their own already-established schemas and stereotypes. The very questions posed by the inquiring investigator will affect what is recalled and how.

More field research sought.   Browning (1977) calls for more field study and less laboratory study because real organizational groups are influenced by external expectations and membership changes that make them function differently from model groups. Mintzberg, Raisinghaini and Theoret (1976) agree with Browning seeing the typical controlled laboratory group decision study as inadaquate since they believe that the:

> . . . structure of the strategic decision process is determined by its very complexity. Oversimplification in the laboratory removes the very element on which the research should be focused. (p. 247)

Although they can cite exceptions (Snyder & Paige, 1958; Witte, 1972), for field work, Mintzberg et al. argue in favor of interviews with key members over extended periods of time rather than depending on documents as the best source of data, for they believe that strategic decision processes "seldom leave reliable traces within the files of the organization" in documentation. Nevertheless, as noted in the preceding chapter, Witte (1972) was able to complete a documentary analysis which revealed the concentrations of effort that occur early and late in the organizational decision process.

THEORIES AND MODELS

Role of theory

Models are simplified representations of the decision-making process: Theories are explanations of the process. The theories usually postulate memories, information processing, and a hierarchy of decision rules. Applications of these theories turn these postulates into testable hypotheses by specifying in detail the contents of the memory and the information processes as well as the content and order of the required decision rules (Clarkson & Pounds, 1963).

Theories of organizational decision making deal with human decision making embedded in organizational contexts, data banks, information processing, and decision rules. In contrasting the individual decision-making manager standing alone to the decision-making manager embedded in an organization, Sayles (1964) sees needed conceptualization becoming more dynamic. Decision making, as such, becomes shaped as much by the pattern of interaction among managers as by the contemplation and cognitive processes of the individual manager. Sayles rejects as inadequate the static conceptualization of the individual manager with a certain amount of authority that permits him or her to make certain types of decisions, to be carried out by subordinates who have the responsibility to follow instructions:

> This conception of administration and the manager's role produces the neat organization pyramids with their unquestioned hierarchical characteristics and, in the process, deludes many observers into condemning the monolithic structure. (Sayles, 1964, p. 208)

Although synthesis among theoretical explanations have been attempted (Schaefer, 1971), it is difficult to pull together the different theoretical approaches to organizational decision making. Ebert and Mitchell (1975) suggest why. The field is a highly interdisciplinary one. Also, the theories vary in their level of abstraction and whether they are broad or specific.

Economic theory of the firm

According to McGuire (1964), the economic theory of the firm most widely accepted by economists includes the following tenets: (1) the firm has a goal (or goals) toward which it strives; (2) it moves toward its objectives in a "rational" manner; (3) the firm's function is to transform economic inputs into outputs; (4) the environment in which the firm operates is given; and (5) the theory concentrates particularly upon changes in the price and quantities of inputs and outputs.

The economic theory of the firm is operated by an economic man who is completely informed as to alternative actions and outcomes facing him, infinitely sensitive to what alternatives are involved, and rational in making decisions (Edwards, 1954). He has a set of utilities that permits him to rank all sets of consequences according to preference and to choose the alternative that has the preferred consequence (Cyert, Simon & Trow, 1956; Simon, 1959). This ability to identify all decision alternatives means that we are dealing with a closed system.

Fundamental to using closed systems is utility theory. Axiomatic is transitivity (if $A > B > C$, then $A > C$) and that decision makers prefer one of two outcomes, or are indifferent. To construct a utility index according to Alexis and Wilson (1967) requires:

1. A set of mutually exclusive and independent events.
2. A procedure for assigning numerical values to each outcome.
3. A procedure for assigning probability measures to each outcome possibility.
4. The assumption that the decision maker is a maximizer.
5. The assumption that the decision maker is willing to gamble. (p. 155)

With closed systems, given an objective function and known constraints, we can determine the complete set of feasible solutions through using utility theory. For highly-structured routine problems, with effective management information systems, coupled with powerful computers using problem-solving algorithms, we can literally compute mathematically optimal solutions. Probabilistic methods, which deal adequately with incomplete information, are also available for such closed systems to fill in the missing gaps.

Problem-solving algorithms and systematic computing generate and order feasible solutions to permit the selection of an optimal solution. Closed models make it possible to apply linear programming, often with very powerful and useful effects to solve inventory storage, scheduling, and other types of important managerial problems.

Again, mathematical game theory depends on a closed system of clearly defined goals, a given number of alternatives, and players who can estimate the consequences of their choice as determined by their own choice and the choice of others. With a closed system we can be completely rational. We can identify alternatives, order them, and select the best one to attain predetermined goals.

Decision aids abound for closed systems, as will be discussed in Chapter 8.

Compatible with the economic theory is the machine model of organizations (Rice & Bishoprick, 1971). The organization is deliberately designed and constructed to accomplish a purpose. Humans within the organization are components of the machine. Decision making is limited to management. All needed information and wisdom rests with the boss. Labor is treated as a factor in production. People are economic and rational, directed toward the single objective function of maximizing money income. Decisions must travel top-down in accordance with a number of universal principles such as the chain of command, span of control, and division of labor.

Criticisms of the economic theory of the firm. Barnard's (1938) descriptions of how organizations really made decisions were a far cry from what was required by economic thinking for closed systems. Stimulated by the criticisms of Barnard (1938) and Simon (1955), Cyert, Simon, and Trow, (1956) completed an observational study suggesting that understanding of organizational decision making required treating the ill-structured problems of the world of business as open, not closed, systems of variables. Cyert, Dill, and March (1958) published four case studies suggesting that none of the required economic assumptions were valid descriptions of the organizational decision-making process.

In contrast to traditional economic theories, they noted that the search for alternatives was not continuous. Rather it occurred when stimulated by a significant environmental change or a crisis in the organization. Human perceptions of these events played an important role in initiating action. The search for decision alternatives was highly restricted and was far from exhaustive. Simple and objectively unevaluated guidelines were used to narrow the range of alternatives that were considered. Proposed solutions were not determined by examining all alternatives on an economic basis; rather, they were actually recognized as the preferred actions for many organization members long before the decision problem arose. The decision problem appeared to present an opportunity to implement an already preferred course of action. (A well-known tendency among executives is to call decision-making meetings primarily to announce and to sell decisions they have already made).

Contrary to the assumptions of economic theory, estimates of costs and returns for the preferred alternative were vague and expressed ambiguously. Only after the decision had been made were detailed cost estimates obtained. Early cost estimates for alternatives were over-optimistic. Only after a time were the cost implications of the decision examined more carefully. Perceptual and motivational biases dominated evaluation and choice. Staff analysts prepared a recommendation for the alternative they believed to be preferred by management. As environ-

mental conditions changed, other problems came to dominate organizational activities, and the implementation program was abandoned.

Alexis and Wilson (1967) further noted that:

> Suboptimization is more typical of organizational decision making (than
> optimization). The decision maker acts on the basis of the decision frame-
> work and information available to his particular unit or department in the
> hierarchy. He makes decisions from a local point of view. Such decisions
> may not be optimal for the organization as a whole. The organization is
> affected by the total set of effects; a department may not be. Decisions
> beneficial to one department may create difficulties elsewhere in the
> organization which are much greater than the benefits received by the
> decision maker's department. (p. 157)

More often, suboptimization is the rule (even for decisions that lie
wholly within the organizational unit involved), for the decision maker is
constricted by a limited perspective, possesses limited computational
skills, is seldom privy to complete information, is subject to a multitude
of errors and systematic bias in the process of discovery, search, evaluation, and choice. Reality is simplified in order to be able to deal with it
to fit with the capabilities and needs of the decision maker. It is seldom
possible to weigh all the alternatives. For example, when U.S. firms
decide to expand production facilities abroad, they do not consider 160
countries as possible locations, then optimize the choice from among
them. Rather, they tend to focus on one country because they have
already had trading experience in it, exporting has become a problem,
and now they estimate whether a correct investment in that country will
be more satisfactory than continuing to export to it. Time and costs
prevent the kind of search called for by traditional economic theory
(Bass, McGregor, & Walters, 1977), although if time and costs of search
are taken into account, a constrained search among several countries can
be economically rational.

Soelberg (1967) offered a number of other criticisms of traditional
economic theories of decision making which depend so heavily on the
concepts of single-objective functions based on the utility of alternatives
and probability estimates.

1.   Decision value attributes are usually multidimensional; they are
not compared nor substituted for each other during choice. Stable utility
weight functions cannot be elicited from decision makers prior to their
selecting a preferred alternative. Such weights do not ordinarily enter
into decision processing. The noncomparison of goal attributes during
screening and selection of alternatives also negates the decision maker's
need for a multidimensional utility indifference map. Nor is there any
point in postulating the existence of one.

2.   Probability theory does not represent how decision makers perceive and deal with uncertainty during unprogrammed decision making.

Probabilities which even highly-trained decision makers provide are neither additive nor cardinally scaled. Decision makers do not normally think of their choice alternative in terms of multiple consequences. Rather, they think of each alternative as a set of noncomparable goal attributes. Uncertainty is usually going to depend on the decision maker's personal evaluation of an alternative's uncertain attributes.

The simplicity of information processing computations is a far cry from representing the conditional probability distributions for each alternative which, according to distributive probability theory, decision makers should be associating with each multiconsequential, multivalued alternative.

3. Often, several alternatives are considered by decision makers at one time rather than as suggested by sequential search models. Yet, evaluation proceeds in steps; at each step, new information is collected and evaluated about a subset of attributes of each alternative. Thus, search within alternatives is as important a process to understand formally as the search across alternatives.

However, in all fairness to the economic theory of the firm and its economic man, multiobjective functions are now taking on increasing importance in management science. And, as Luthans (1973) has noted:

> Most economists do not claim that economic man is a realistic descriptive model of modern management decision-making behavior. They use economic man primarily for certain theoretical analyses. On the other hand, some aspects of economic man can be useful in describing actual decision-making behavior. For example, a survey of "excellently managed" firms by James Earley (1956) found that short views, innovative sensitivity, marginal costing, and marginal pricing were all preponderant among the respondents. Yet, except for the few indirect exceptions, the economic man model is not realistically descriptive of management decision-making behavior. (p. 194)

Although such economic principles do make a contribution to rationalizing the work place for well-structured and routine work and to organizing for crises, the failure to consider the socioemotional elements of organization, and the impossibility of complete rationality in dealing with most problems (particularly ill-structured ones), resulted in the construction of behavioral models and theories to more closely represent the realities of organizational decision making.

Behavioral theories of the firm

Nonroutine decision making in organizations follows a pattern better dealt with by the psychology of problem solving than by an elegant optimization calculus (Hogarth, 1980). The problem itself may not be adequately sensed or defined. Alternatives may be vague. Search may be avoided because of the costs. The consequences of various choices can only be guessed. The required judgments and estimates are filled with a wide variety of human errors and systematic biases (Cyert, Simon, & Trow, 1956).

Formal models. Formal models of the behavioral approach to organizational decision making abound. As will be seen, their similarities are much greater than their differences, despite the passage of 25 years in which they have been surfacing with steady elaborations and some shifts in emphasis.

Simon (1955) pioneered in fashioning a formal model for unprogrammed decision making containing three phases: intelligence (finding occasions for making a decision); design (finding, inventing, developing, and analyzing alternative courses of action); and choice (selecting a particular course of action from those available). In the same vein, Cyert and March (1963) formulated a behavioral theory of the firm to more adequately portray the realities of organizational decision making. For them, aspiration levels, not predetermined objectives, are the stimulus to search and choice among alternatives, but the relations between alternatives and outcomes can remain unspecified. Only a relatively small number of alternatives are considered rather than an ordering of all possible alternatives. The effort is to find a satisfactory solution to meet aspiration levels, not the maximization of benefits-to-costs.

With reference to organizational goals, overall goals such as profit, are too general to have any operational effect. Operational goals originate as a consequence of bargaining among coalitions in the firm. What is viewed as important depends on who belongs to the relevant coalition at the time.

> New participants enter or old participants leave the coalition. . . . operative goals for a particular decision are the goals of the subunit making that decision. . . . goals are evoked by problems. Aspiration level(s) (depend on) . . . the organization's past goal, the organization's past performance, and the past performance of other "comparable" organizations. (Cyert & March, 1963, p. 115)

As the price of their continued participation in the coalition, members exact from the organization money payments as well as side payments such as policy commitments. Under prosperous conditions, these exactions tend to rise above the minimum level necessary for the participants to be kept in the coalition. (Such payments above the minimum required are illustrative of organizational slack.)

Operational goals are multiple. Several are likely to be involved in any one decision. Each such goal is more clearly identified with some coalition members than with others. The sales manager is more attentive to the effects of the decision on customers; the production manager, on employees. And each goal imposes an additional constraint upon the decision. That is, the alternative finally chosen must meet the diverse goals of the coalition.

It is not unusual for these multiple goals to be in conflict with each other. Such conflict among them is likely to be only partially resolved through decentralization of decision making. They may be dealt with in sequence rather than giving them simultaneous attention.

Organizational expectations depend on drawing inferences from available information, on hope, and on previous experience. The firm continues to operate under the standard decision rules it has used successfully before.

The intensity and success of the search to meet expectations will depend on the extent to which goals are achieved and the amount of organizational resources and slack in the firm. The direction of search will depend on the nature of the problem stimulating the search and the location in the organization at which it is focused.

Organizations concentrate on observing selected short-run feedback that will indicate whether current goals are being met. Such search results in short-term readjustments on the basis of available knowledge and is a way to maintain avoidance of uncertainty. Short-run feedback indicates that aspiration levels are being met. Unmet goals are the stimulus for search, search that is simpleminded and biased by the hopes and expectations of the decision makers. It is simpleminded in the sense that it concentrates efforts in the neighborhood of the problem symptom and current solution before going further out.

Choice usually settles on the first acceptable alternative although maximization rules may be applied to select among alternatives if several have been generated or found. If no acceptable solution appears, aspiration levels are lowered.

Organizations learn. Behavior that is successful becomes codified into rules for attention, search, and choice to be followed in the future. When these rules no longer work, they will be modified.

Figure 1 shows a complete model derived primarily from Cyert and March's theory. They validated their model by using it to generate price and output decisions with data supplied by a department store and investment decisions from data supplied by a trust department. The price and investment decisions they generated matched quite well the real-world decisions actually reached by the firms. The organization decision processes as seen in Figure 1 according to Cyert and March involve four phenomena: quasi-resolution of conflict; uncertainty avoidance; problemistic search; and organization learning. Each of these will be discussed in more detail in later chapters.

FIGURE 1 Organizational decision process in abstract form

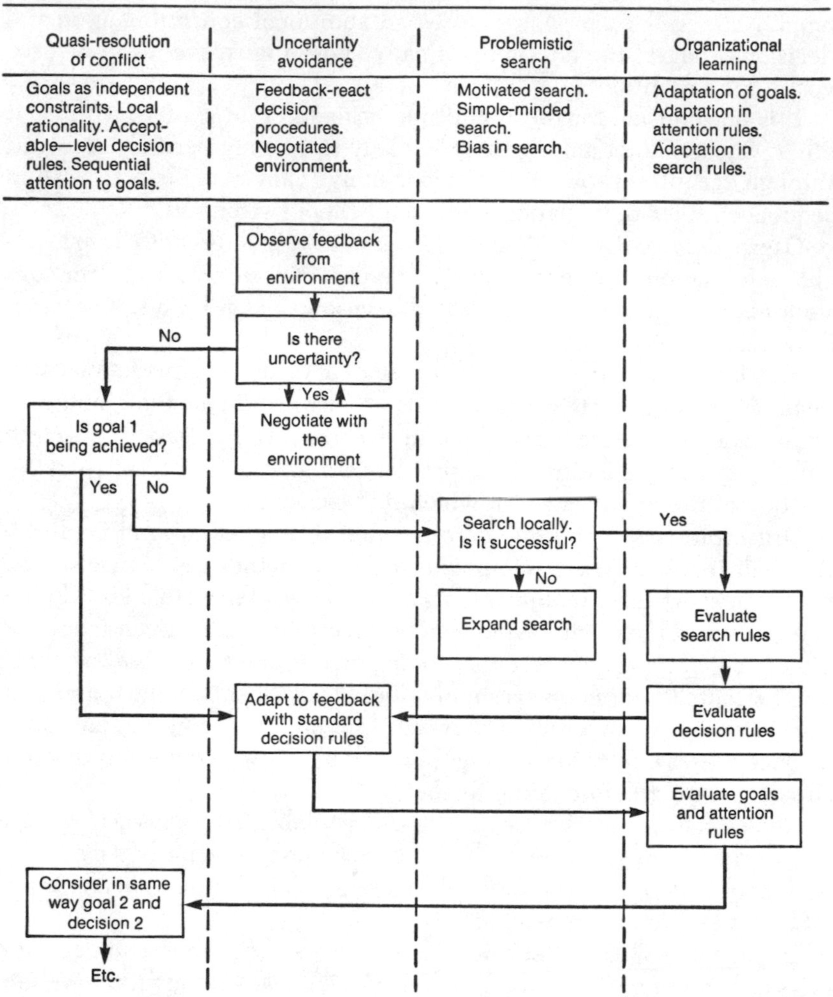
Quasi-resolution of conflict
Uncertainty avoidance
Problemistic search
Organizational learning
Goals as independent constraints. Local rationality. Acceptable—level decision rules. Sequential attention to goals.
Feedback-react decision procedures. Negotiated environment.
Motivated search. Simple-minded search. Bias in search.
Adaptation of goals. Adaptation in attention rules. Adaptation in search rules.
Observe feedback from environment
Is there uncertainty?
No
Yes
Negotiate with the environment
Is goal 1 being achieved?
Yes
No
Search locally. Is it successful?
Yes
No
Expand search
Evaluate search rules
Evaluate decision rules
Adapt to feedback with standard decision rules
Evaluate goals and attention rules
Consider in same way goal 2 and decision 2
Etc.

From R. M. Cyert and J. G. March, *A Behavioral Theory of the Firm* (Englewood Cliffs, N.J.: Prentice-Hall, 1963), p. 126.

Incrementalism. Lindblom (1959) offered a number of amendments to the basic behavioral model of limited search and goal modifications to make the problem manageable. Pragmatism rather than idealism is the value that dominates the process. Rather than attempting a comprehensive survey and evaluation of a wide array of alternatives, the decision maker focuses only on those which differ incrementally from existing policies and practices. Furthermore, there is no one decision or "right" solution but a "never-ending series of attacks" on the issues at hand through serial analyses and evaluation. Thus, decision making is remedial, geared more to the alleviation of current imperfections than to the attainment of future goals.

Soelberg (1967) elaborated on Simon and Lindblom. Intelligence was expanded into a diagnostic activity in which the decision maker defines operationally the problem he or she intends to solve. Such problem definition may involve: (1) a description of differences between current status and goal on one or more attributes; (2) a description of the strategy associated with a previously encountered problem with a similar stimulus configuration; and (3) a prescription of an ideal solution to the encountered problem.

The diagnosis includes an investigation of the task environment. This is followed by an attempt to develop an appropriate set of classifications of events to formulate and test hypotheses about the apparent cause-effect relationships in the environment. Such hypothetical cause-and-effects help generate solution alternatives. Mintzberg et al. (1976) likewise found it particularly important to attend to this diagnostic phase.

In the search and choice phases, in agreement with behavioral models, in general, Soelberg argued that unlike what was called for in the traditional economic model, decision makers do not estimate probabilities to attach to a set of mutually exclusive consequences associated with each alternative. Instead, decision makers search within each alternative until they feel they have sufficient information about each important goal attribute of that alternative, or until search resources are exhausted. If the alternative is not rejected, decision makers assign some value, or range of values, to each goal attribute. Choice then follows of one of the alternatives.

Mixed scanning. Rejecting both the traditional economic and the incremental models, Etzioni (1967) proposed a behavioral but prescriptive model in which several levels of scanning for problems and solutions are maintained. Truncated or full review of different sectors of the environment are maintained depending on the costs of missing out on an option by failing to fully examine for it. Sporadically, or at set intervals, broad and narrow perspectives are pursued so that the decision maker neither remains stuck with an errorful, incremented approach nor loses sight of necessities by being overly abstract. With mixed scanning, fundamental decisions are made by exploring the main alternatives seen in view of perceived goals. At the same time, details and specifications are omitted so that an overview is feasible. Incremental decisions are made also but within the contexts set by fundamental decisions.

The environment, organizational level of the decision maker, and the capacities of the decision maker are seen to affect the appropriate mix in mixed scanning. In stable environments, more incrementalism is expected to work better. But in rapidly changing situations, fundamental efforts are required.

> In some situations, the higher in rank, concerned only with the overall picture, are impatient with details, while lower ranks—especially experts—are more likely to focus on details. In other situations, the higher ranks, to avoid facing the overall picture, seek to bury themselves . . . in details. (Etzioni, 1967, p. 391)

With more capability, more all-encompassing scanning is possible; with less capability, the decision-maker may be better off relying mainly on incremental approaches.

Other behavioral models. Numerous other assumptions have been employed to build behavioral models. For example, according to Roth (1974), members of an organization have their own subjective interpretation about what is good for the organization. A single investment strategy of the organization can be seen to emerge from the attitudes toward risk and the authority of each of the different members. When individuals are dissatisfied with the organizational investment, they will attempt to extend their authority to exert a greater influence upon the investment decision. A rule about authority may be subverted by willful individuals. On the other hand, individuals may acquiesce to a decision they consider suboptimal for the organization in order to avoid becoming involved in the decision process.

Alexis and Wilson (1967) also begin with a problem as stimulus and emphasize a dynamic, adaptive, aspiration level as fundamental to a model of organizational decision making. The decision maker begins with an idealized goal structure and defines one or more action goals as a first approximation to his or her ideal goal. Action goals are representative of the decision maker's aspiration level. As shown in Figure 2 the individual engages in search activity and defines a limited number of outcomes and alternatives but does not attempt to establish the relations rigorously. Analysis proceeds from loosely defined rules of approximation. The alternatives selected or created establish a starting point for further search toward a solution. Search among the limited alternatives aims to find a satisfactory solution, not an optimal one, to reach a modified adaptation level.

Zeleny's (1981), Cohen, March, and Olsen's (1972) and March and Romelaer's (1976) models of the organizational decision process are further elaborations of the behavioral approach. Zeleny sees that organizations strive to do more than just satisfy aspiration levels, yet do less than maximize. For Zeleny, the process begins with a complex interplay between the individual's current beliefs and desires, the currently perceived courses of action, and the means to provide a fuller understanding of his or her goals, objectives, and alternatives. An initial set of feasible

FIGURE 2   An open decision model

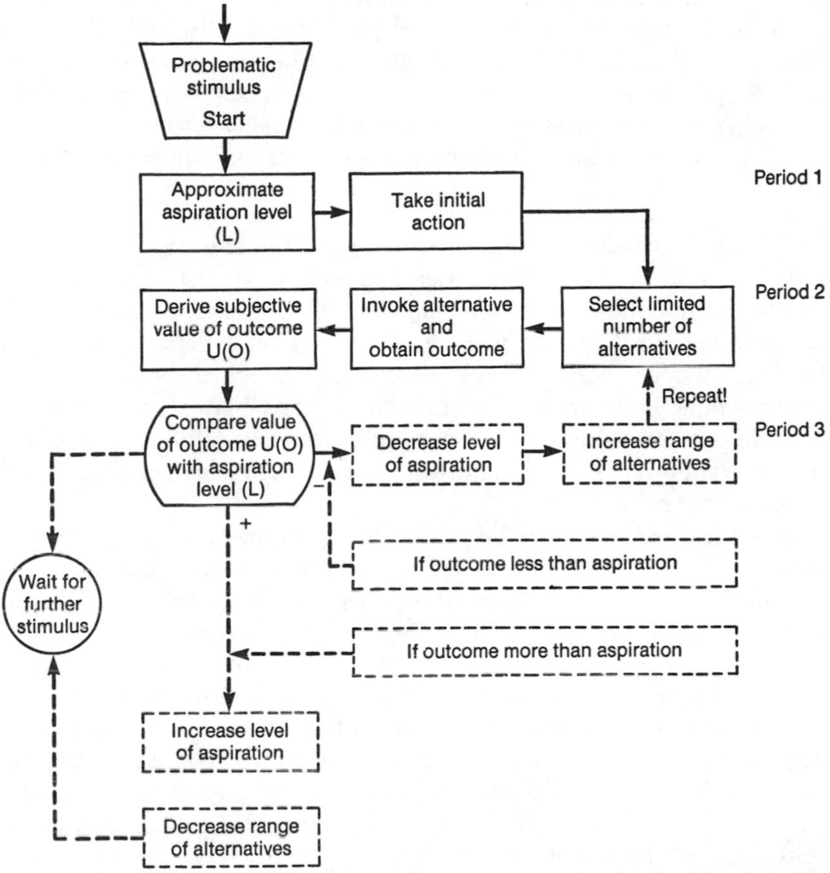

Adapted from M. Alexis and C. Z. Wilson, *Organizational Decision Making* (Englewood Cliffs, N.J.: Prentice-Hall, 1967), p. 160.

alternatives emerges in parallel with currently salient evaluative criteria. This gives rise to predecision conflict as the decision maker realizes that his or her ideal alternative is not feasible. As a consequence, a search for additional alternatives is initiated. At the same time, the ideal alternative is further displaced. Conflict is increased. Evaluative criteria are changed. Search is begun but will diminish if the ideal displacement becomes smaller. Eventually, the ideal and the criteria are stabilized. Conflict is reduced. Partial decisions are made to abandon inferior alternatives. The ideal moves closer to the potential solutions. Justifications and postdecision regret for lost opportunities increase. Information and criteria are modified and new information is sought (biased in favor of the remaining alternatives) with the ideal stabilized in its newly displaced location. But a last displacement of the ideal alternative occurs when it merges with the finally chosen alternative.

In the Garbage Can model of Cohen, March, and Olsen (1972) and for March and Romelaer (1976), contiguity in time and place of decision makers, problems and solutions is more important than causal links between problems and solutions. The decision makers wander in and out of the process. Similarly, problems and solutions may appear and disappear.

Criticisms of behavioral models. Despite the empirical support for some of the behavioral models, Learned and Sproat (1966) pointed to a number of limitations. They see behavioral theories as incapable of dealing adequately with strategic decision making since behavioral models fail to allow for superordinate goals precise enough to be operational. Further fault is found in that decision-maker's biases are limited to self-interest and aversion to uncertainty. They are fallible information processers. Moreover the administrative climate in which organizational decisions are made is ignored.

Too much attention may be paid to things as they are, rather than as they could be. What training can do to improve decision making is possibly underestimated. More attention also needs to be focused on the costs and benefits of systematic, orderly approaches to problem discovery, problem diagnosis, search, evaluation, and choice in contrast to the haphazard attack so often conducted in behavioral approaches. Nevertheless, once we understand the rules of the game as it is currently played, we can determine what changes in the rules could improve the success, effectiveness, and efficiency of the process. To this end, we now move to a more detailed, mainly behavioral consideration of each idealized phase of the organizational decision process starting with how it begins in the discovery of a threat or an opportunity and what to do as a consequence.

We have concentrated on the differences between the economic and behavioral theories and models of organizational decision making. This is a familiar and useful dichotomy. Nevertheless, the boundaries between the two approaches are not distinct anymore. Management scientists and economists wrestle with fuzzy, multiple objectives and rationalization. At the same time, behaviorists worry about the costs of search.

Whether the economic or behavioral approach is pursued, the process, as idealized, culminates in evaluation and choice, ostensibly based on the discovery or invention of possible solutions. But first an organizational problem must be sensed for which a solution is needed.

3

Problem discovery and diagnosis

The questions arising here include the following: What prompts notice that objectives are not being met? What screens are in place to detect such discrepancies? What limits effective screening? What determines whether individual organization members will become involved in the decision-making process? What factors shape the diagnosis of what needs to be done? How will goals be adjusted and how will such adjustments be made operational?

Problems and dilemmas

Whether we are ready to diagnosis a situation depends on whether we discern that we are facing a problem or a dilemma. A problem can be solved in the frame of reference suggested by its nature, by past precedents for dealing with it, or by the application of existing policy. On the other hand, a dilemma is not soluble within the assumptions explicitly or implicitly contained in its presentation; it requires reformulation. Often if we approach a mechanical puzzle with all our customary preconceptions about the nature of the problem, we can never solve it. We must abandon our habitual set and find a new way of looking at it (Rapoport, 1959). While many organizational difficulties are problems which can be solved in their own terms of reference, other discrepancies between current and desired states of affairs are dilemmas. They call for innovative and creative appreciation of what is wrong that needs to be put right (Katz & Kahn, 1966).

In classical management theory, discrepancies arise out of the failure of operations to meet standards set in planning as determined by the control function. Or, current operations may be seen to be unlikely to match the forecasts of the future, based on strategic planning. Or, conflicts between individual values and organizational needs form gaps in the system (Roberts & Hanline, 1975).

Discrepancy as trigger

Decisions are needed when a problem exists, when something is not as it should be. A process is initiated in which a change is consciously made to bring about a more acceptable state of affairs. Thus, the organizational decision maker must be able to describe two states: *what is*, and *what should be*. *What should be* is a standard, an objective, or a criterion against which alternatives can be evaluated.

If the discrepancy between the two states is unacceptably large, efforts will be made to change *what is* to *what should be*. The causes of the problem must be identified to reduce the discrepancy (Kepner & Tregoe, 1965).

The performance standard of *what should be* may not be explicit. It may be objective or subjective. Subjective performance standards vary among executives depending upon their current and past assignments as well as their motives and personality. As a consequence, if standards are subjective, differences of opinion will arise about the existence and severity of problems. On the other hand, objective performance standards make it easier to agree about them and to gain acceptance organizationally that a problem exists (Tosi & Carroll, 1976).

For Zeleny (1981), the discrepancy between *what is* and *what should be* generates a sense of conflict. The dissatisfaction with the current state of affairs provides the decision-motivating tension. There are no suitable alternatives automatically available. Zeleny sees that what really triggers the onset of the process is the *infeasibility of the ideal alternative*. The decision maker perceives how much of each attribute of the desired end can be obtained. For example, it is easier to identify from among a list of products, the one with the lowest price, with the highest quality, or with the highest reliability. It is more difficult to identify which is the best product overall that would provide the best price, quality and reliability.

According to Mintzberg, Raisinghani, and Theoret's (1976) study of 25 organizational decision processes, many different precursors actually trigger recognition that a discrepancy exists and needs to be considered. Opportunities appear to be set off by a single stimulus. They may lie dormant in the mind of one executive until he feels ready to take action. Then, he may act quickly when there is a clear match between an opportunity and a perceived problem. On the other hand, threats, again resulting from a single stimuli, require immediate consideration. But ordinarily, problems involve multiple stimuli calling for diagnostic analyses before moving ahead.

The discrepancy must be above some minimal threshold to be perceived (Lewin, 1946). Attention will shift sequentially among gaps of different thresholds, from one gap to another (Cyert & March, 1963). The threshold is higher for opportunities than for threats (Drucker, 1963) and for gaps based on communications from subordinates rather than superiors (Barnard, 1938). That is, organizational decision makers are slower to react to opportunities than alarms. They pay more attention to their superiors than to their subordinates.

The perceived discrepancy depends on how validly and realistically we have defined both *what is* and *what should be*. The perceived gap or problem may be truly nonexistent except for our misperceptions. The description of the problem may identify superficial symptoms rather than underlying causes. Diagnosis will be faulty. If the search for solutions is instituted based on defining a problem in terms of its symptoms rather than its causes, the problem will reappear with new symptoms (Flippo, 1966). Taxes did not cause the American Revolution. In 1776, the true gap for Americans was between the liberties they had enjoyed as colonists and the threatened loss of their freedoms. Objectively, they remained in a favored position compared to Britons at home. Most Englishmen were not represented in British Parliament either. The total annual taxes paid to Britain by Americans was about $1.50 per capita (4 percent of what Englishmen paid in taxes at that time). "Taxation without representation" was but one element in the overall feeling of Americans that they were being treated as second-class citizens, about to be politically relegated by the British aristocracy to the same servile status as the Irish peasantry. It was the fear of a threatened loss of status and downgrading by the British government, rather than tax and property issues as such, that generated the willingness in a sufficient number of colonists to fight a long war for independence. There also was a mistrust in the likelihood that the results of negotiations would be faithfully observed (Fleming, 1975).

Scanning and screening

The earlier that symptoms are detected of *what is*—such as falling sales volume or cost overruns—the earlier that actions to correct the problem can be contemplated (Behling & Schriescheim, 1976). Indeed, most managers would like to be more proactive than they actually are (Bass & Burger, 1979). Etzioni's (1967) mixed scanning model begins with this monitoring function. Feedforward controls (to be discussed later) are a way of facilitating this phase of the decision process. For Etzioni, mixed scanning is the appropriate way for managers to remain vigilant to both smaller, immediate problems as well as larger, remote ones. Some resources need to be invested in a broad "camera" covering all parts of the organization and its environment, while other resources concentrate on detailed examination, in depth, of selected sectors based on what the broad camera reveals.

We can trace a sequence of levels of vigilance from peripheral awareness of a problem accruing from wide scanning, to the monitoring of the problem with a narrow scan, to the placement of the problem on the organizational agenda (Arrow, 1974).

Categorization.   Potential problems are screened by categorization. A hypothetical threshold of discrepancy is reached between *what is* on the basis of an initial categorization and *what is expected*. The decision process is initiated when what is detected and categorized does not easily match available prototypes—primary exemplars of what will serve for later copies of the same condition. Decision processes are initiated when categorization cannot proceed automatically (Feldman, 1981).

Once the current state of affairs is categorized, its reorganization is biased toward the general characteristics of the category. Falling demand for a product may fit into the category of a sluggish market, and little can be done until the market turns around. Yet, in fact, the falling demand may really be due to a surge by a successful competitor. The search for solutions will depend on which category of explanation is selected, i. e., how the problem is diagnosed.

Goals and objectives

What should be obviously depends on the organization's goals and how clear they are to decision makers. Goals may be explicit; more often they are implicit. For a given decision, they are likely to be multiple and interdependent rather than singular. They may be nested in a hierarchy with some as subgoals of others. They may be complementary, compensatory, or in conflict. A firm may specify its targeted rate of return on investment. Implicit in this are complementary goals and subgoals to provide stockholder and management satisfaction.

The institutional core, dealing as it does with the outside environment and the interests of dominant constituencies within the organization, sets the broad goals which are the premises for setting objectives at the managerial and technical cores. At lower hierarchical levels, objectives need to be operationalized consistent with the goals set at the higher levels. In turn, this promotes stability at lower levels. Each lower-level goal becomes a means to a higher order goal. Acceptance of subgoals at lower levels coincide with higher-order organizational sanctions and inducements to meet individual member personal values and needs (Simon, 1965).

Stability and change of goals. Once set, subgoals become stabilized by the higher cost of innovation, sunk costs, and sunk assets (such as investments for equipment, which cannot be easily changed) again curtailing the ability to optimize individual preferences and needs (Simon, 1965).

But performance outcomes affect goals, just as goals affect subsequent performance. Zander, Forward, and Albert (1969) contrasted the goal setting views of repeatedly successful and repeatedly failing United Fund Boards. (As might be expected, central board members were more deeply involved in setting the funds' goals each year than were peripheral members.) Previous success was seen to prepare the ground for future success; failure, for future failure. Forward and Zander (1971) followed this up with an experiment using goal setting four-member teams of high school boys. Goals set were affected by the apparent previous success of the team, prior previous success of the larger organization (their school) and external pressure raising group levels of aspiration.

The impact of the goals set on subsequent effort continues to be a subject of theoretical controversy and mixed empirical outcomes. Since performance depends on the probabilities of obtaining valued outcomes (Vroom, 1964), effort should be enhanced by easy goals. But empirically, Locke (1968) found that effort is enhanced by the setting of hard goals. And Atkinson (1964) sees that for achievement-oriented participants, goals of moderate difficulty—both challenging and obtainable—are optimum. Shapira (1975) may have helped to clear up the confusion by showing that hard, challenging goals are best where participants are intrinsically interested in the work to be done, and easy, readily obtainable goals are best when only extrinsic payoffs occur from performance.

Operational versus nonoperational goals. March and Simon (1958) distinguished between operational and nonoperational organizational goals. Operational goals make possible means for testing actions to choose among alternatives. Promoting goodwill is not operational, as such. It is related to specific actions only through the intervention of subgoals. Subgoals become operational by being substituted for the more general nonoperational goals of an organization. In general, the limited objectives and subgoals lend themselves more readily to using operational criteria for decision making. Where operational goals are shared, differences about *what should be* can then be resolved by rational, analytic processes. Where shared goals are not operational or where the operational subgoals are not shared, differences must be adjusted through bargaining. The outcome becomes a compromise to achieve internal harmony rather than overall organizational objectives. (See also, Thompson & Tuden, 1959.)

Goal clarity. The determination of *what should be* requires clarity about the organization's goals. For Katz and Kahn (1966), consideration of organizational goals may be instituted: (1) to sharpen and clarify organizational purposes and to exclude irrelevant activities; (2) to add new objectives; (3) to shift priorities among objectives; or (4) to shift the mission of the organization.

Goal and subgoal consistency. Many examinations of goals come about also to clarify the major organizational mission, or to achieve consistency between it and subgoals which have developed in the organizational structure. Individual units within the organization may develop a logic of their own. The larger system must redress the resulting imbalance in its functioning. Thus, a university may find that its intercollegiate athletics program has become so professional that it is in open conflict with its educational objectives. The leadership must reaffirm its basic mission and bring athletics into line, or have its goals altered by the deviant athletic program subsystem. Such persistent imbalances will lead to external difficulties, precipitating organizational actions to define or redefine organizational goals (Katz & Kahn, 1966).

Katz and Kahn along with Blau (1955) see a tendency for executives to pursue a broadening of their missions. Limited directives are expanded over time. "Empire building" is seen as a common attribute of bureaucrats.

Multiplicity of objectives. As Cyert and March (1963) found, the coalitions of interests that make up the firm's membership (owners, managers, workers, suppliers, clients) result in objectives that are multiple including profitability, employee satisfaction, growth, maintenance of satisfactory operations, client satisfaction, and so on (Dent, 1959; Pickle & Friedlander, 1967). The goals often are hierarchical (i. e., growth, then profitability) and complementary (maintenance of satisfactory operations and employee satisfaction) but they can also be in conflict (supplier versus employee satisfaction). Thus, as they become operationalized as objectives, in the cascade downwards in the organization, they generate multiple interactive objectives which initiate decision processes. When making decisions, the manager of the finishing department of the large manufacturing firm needs to bear in mind the multiple requirements for efficient production and customer satisfaction, as well as requirements for maintaining good relations with subordinates, peers, and superiors.

Even if one starts at the top of the organization with a particular single goal—say, profitability—the subgoals that will be operationalized will be difficult to match up as we move from the sales to the manufacturing departments. And given disparate subgoals which may be in conflict with each other, the operational goals that do emerge will be based on bargaining between the different units involved (Cyert & March, 1963). The purchasing department may want to minimize prices of supplies; the production department is more concerned about reliability to meet its goal of quality output. A compromise will be found, satisfactory to both departments.

Organizational goals as sets of constraints.   As Simon (1964) has concluded:

> In the decision-making situations of real life, a course of action, to be acceptable, must satisfy a whole set of requirements, or constraints. Sometimes one of these requirements is singled out and referred to as the goal of the action. But the choice of one of the constraints, from many, is to a large extent arbitrary. For many purposes it is more meaningful to refer to the whole set of requirements as the (complex) goal of the action. (p. 17)

Simon doubts that organizational decisions are ever directed toward achieving a goal. Rather, they are concerned with discovering ways to deal with a whole set of requirements. It is the set of requirements that is the goal of the actions.

If any of the requirements are selected for special attention, it is because of their relation to the motivation of the decision makers, or because of their relation to the search process that is generating particular actions. The constraints that motivate and guide decision makers (to be discussed in more detail in Chapter 7) are sometimes viewed as more "goal-like" than those that limit the actions they consider to those that test whether a potential course of action is satisfactory. Whether all or only some of the constraints are treated as goals is largely a matter of linguistic or analytic convenience.

Displacement

The broadly-stated goals of an organization (such as, to make a profit) must be made into operational objectives (such as, to increase new customers by 10 percent this year). In the course of operationalization, displacement often occurs. The goal of making a profit may be operationalized into winning a seat on the board of directors by the vice president of marketing. The vice president subsequently makes decisions calculated to win him a seat, not necessarily to win new customers. As Behling and Schriesheim (1976) have noted, organizational purposes are subject to displacement as they become operational. In mutual benefit associations, this may take the form of catering to the interests of the paid professionals of the organization. In the large publicly-held corporation, this often means emphasizing the interests of managers at the expense of the stockholders. In service organizations, the organization may come to serve staff interests instead of those of the clients. The military coup is a displacement where the legal monopoly of armed force is used to give control of the government to the military. The apocryphal late-night drunk, asked why he is searching for his lost keys under the lamp post, answers that there is light under the lamp post. Objectives are sometimes set not because of the orginally described goals, but because successful actions can be completed to obtain the displaced objectives. The original goal of the bureaucracy of maintaining quality service may be subverted to the objective of maintaining a good public image by heavy investment in good relations with the press.

Organizational controls are instituted to minimize displacement. The vice president must present quarterly reports on gains in new customers. Individual decision units are given responsibility for reaching the objectives. Division heads are given quotas of new customers to obtain. Account files are audited.

Aspiration level. Classical models of decision making dealt with absolute discrepancies between *what is* and ideally *what should be* as the initiative for stimulating decision making. Behavioral and neoclassical decision making posit both an ideal condition of *what should be* as well as an aspiration level likely to be at variance from the ideal. Various neoclassical models introduce additional elements. The aspiration and the ideal become a gap of consequence. Aspiration level is subjective and modified by incremental learning as to what is possible and what to trade off. All relevant variables are now subjective matters. Ideals are also modifiable although generally less so than aspirations (Zeleny, 1981).

It is the perceived, not the actual, current state of affairs that counts. To the extent the perceived state is at variance with the true state, erroneous directions in search and choice will emerge. Thus, learning and motivation of individuals at various levels in the organization are important dynamics in how goals are set, how problems are defined, and how diagnoses are made. March and Simon (1958) provided a model showing how one's aspiration level depends on expected values of re-

wards to be obtained from search instituted by dissatisfaction. By searching the environment and his or her past experiences, the individual is
able to assess the likely rewards which accrue from various actions. The
actions are attractive to the extent they fit the individual's values and
aspirations. Satisfaction and level of aspiration will increase with increases in the expected value of the rewards. Anticipated satisfactions
are what stimulate the initiation of the decision process. As Katona (1953)
concluded, aspirations levels are dynamic, growing with achievements
and declining with failures. Also, they are affected by various influences
such as the performance of one's peers and reference groups. Filley,
House, and Kerr (1976) set forth and provide the experimental support
for the proposition that:

> . . . continued failure to achieve a minimum standard of satisfaction results
> in the successive lowering of the standard until an acceptable compromise
> is reached; conversely, easy success tends to raise minimum standards.
> (p. 125)

Much qualification is needed. They note that aspiration level is likely
to be raised more by a given amount of success than lowered by a given
amount of failure.

Other factors need to be taken into account. For example, the familiar
"doubling up of one's bet" was seen by Levi (1981). After initial failures,
the decision to escalate aspirations or curtail them could be accounted for
by one's evaluation of sunk costs in the first decision and one's resources
still available after the initial failure. If a lot was invested in an initial
failure but there was still enough money left for further investment,
escalation was more likely to occur than curtailment as an attempt to
"catch up."

Diagnosis

Antecedent information, beliefs, and motivation about an opportunity, a problem, or a threat lead to attributions about their causes. The
attributed causes, in turn, determine anticipations and the onset and
direction of search and innovation (Kelley & Michela, 1980). If the cause
attributed to low worker productivity is worker motivation, search for
improvements will take different directions than if the cause is attributed
to worker inability or faulty equipment.

For well-structured situations, the situation is identified and its main
characteristics are defined. A model is then constructed to provide the
basis for estimating possible outcomes of the decision over a range of
possible conditions. Finally, there can be a determination of quantitative
measures of costs and benefits appropriate to the situation under consideration. Uniform measurements are sought to facilitate subsequent com-

parisons among the alternatives proposed to deal with the recognized problem (Radford, 1981).

Certain aspects of ill-structured problems can also be modeled. For example, people tend to be consistent when diagnosing cause-effect relations. They seem to have preferences from among relational "operators" which systematically bias their diagnoses and subsequent search efforts. Programs can be constructed to model these operations (Newell & Simon, 1972).

Faced with an ill-structured dilemma, we first need to try to reformulate it to make it recognizable in terms of characteristics with which we are more familiar. We may also need to remain prepared for qualitative rather than quantitative comparisons. The danger exists in this reformulation that we will try to solve a really new and distinct problem with methods that worked primarily on an older, really dissimilar, problem. We must be willing to accept the inability to completely define the problem in advance, since we lack complete information. So we move on to search and to make a trial choice. However, we may cycle back to the definition phase several more times as additional information becomes available during the search and trial choices. Indeed, Maier & Hoffman (1960) found that going back a second time to the same problem already solved improved the quality of the final decision.

Brunswik's (1955) probabilistic functionalism was applied by Filley, House, and Kerr (1976) to account for a manager's anticipatory perceptions. According to Brunswik's theory, we subjectively evaluate the probable occurrence of events by associating patterns of actions, sequences, or events learned from past experience with patterns seen in the current situation. We then continuously search for confirmation or disproof of our evaluations and modify our anticipations as new information is acquired and as success or failure is experienced. At the same time, stray, contextual variables will also be affecting our attention and awareness and what we will do in an ongoing process.

The initial stimulus might be the announcement that the firm is losing money. Ways to increase revenues or reduce costs might be considered. Decisions would be made and orders given. The production department would be ordered to cut back inventories and the marketing group to raise prices. These decisions would be based on the executives anticipation of near-future market demand, the inability to increase sales through special efforts, and so on.

> Because no market is static, the manager may be faced with the same decision sequence six months later. Forms of feedback, such as weekly sales reports and monthly accounting statements, will be in operation. The manager will make predictions based on past performance, but other variables will also be considered. The manager will be called upon to anticipate the most likely of a wide variety of possible future events, and

to alter plans and activities accordingly. Much of the manager's behavior will operate at an unconscious level and will be affected by personal needs and desires. However, as experience is gained in evaluating the unique variables in an enterprise, the manager will typically become more proficient in the art of prediction. (Filley, House, & Kerr, 1976, p. 128)

Participation and involvement in the decision process

Once a problem has surfaced, which positions in the organization and which persons participate further in the decision process depend on a number of factors. Where psychological investment is greater, more participation will occur. The vice president for production is more likely to become engaged in deciding on a new plant location than would a small investor. Social visibility will make a difference. The town mayor may be asked or required to participate on a problem about a government loan; the telephone operator will not. Control of resources will make the president highly likely to be involved in budget decisions which will not concern the salesman. Being inside rather than outside the organization will make a difference. The production planner will be involved in decisions of no concern to the customer. Frequency and speed of response to apparent needs for decisions are obviously slower for production planners than for telephone operators (Starbuck, 1976).

But when should one participate in decisions? The screen indicates that a problem exists. Should the executive do something about it? Should it be brought to someone else's attention, or ignored? Should the executive participate directly in the appropriate next steps of searching or inventing solutions to the problem?

Barnard (1938) first articulated answers to the questions of when one was responsible for making decisions and when one was well-advised to avoid such action. He felt that an executive had to be clear about the boundaries of his new responsibilities so that he would be able to adequately care for his own domain; otherwise, he could be drawn into other areas and overburdened by other executives who shirked their own responsibilities.

Barnard identified three types of cases requiring an executive to initiate the decision process: higher authority, subordinates, and self. Requests from higher authority, dealing with interpretation, application, and distribution of instructions, require an initiative by the executive although some of the activity can be delegated. Serious dilemmas may be faced if the instructions violate one's ethical sense, or are perceived to be harmful or impossible.

Cases about subordinates stem from the incapacity, the uncertainty of instructions, the novelty of conditions, conflicts of jurisdiction or in orders, or failure of subjective authority. Barnard suggested that executives make these "appellate" decisions when they are important or cannot be delegated. Others should be declined.

The self-generated case is the perceived discrepancy between organizational objectives and current states of affairs which need attending. The executive's ability and initiative and the organization's adequacy of communications will provide the sense of something needing correction. Nevertheless, "there is much incentive to avoid decisions but the executive must decide on those issues which no one else is in a position to deal with effectively." Barnard's famous lines are still worth quoting:

> The fine art of executive decision consists in not deciding questions that are not now pertinent, in not deciding prematurely, in not making decisions that cannot be made effective, and in not making decisions that others should make. (p. 188)

Other ways of questioning whether or not to become involved have been posed by Shull, Delbecq, and Cummings (1970). Can the would-be decision maker do something about the problem? Are a real set of alternatives likely to exist? How much are some of the variables of consequence under his or her control? Will his effort have a favorable impact? Can the would-be decision maker influence some future state of affairs or even just become better prepared for the future? Will it pay to take foresightful action?

Unfortunately, much of the American public avoids voting on the basis that their one vote is irrelevant in determining who is elected. One is much more likely to participate in the decision process when a particular future event of importance is seen to depend on one's involvement. Self-interest is a critical factor. A manager will volunteer to be a member of an ad hoc committee to decide on activity schedules in the belief that the costs of participation are less than the costs of an undesirable schedule which might be developed in his or her absence. A manager will avoid engaging or being identified in a decision process if high risk of the penalties for failure are seen to outweigh the benefits of success.

Increasingly, worker participation in the organizational decisional process is the subject of inquiry. Bass and Rosenstein (1977) suggested and Heller (1982) confirmed that while immediate superiors, organizational climate, or legislated industrial democracy may or may not encourage worker participation, by themselves they will not produce worker involvement. The decision problem also has to be an operational or shopfloor issue rather than a strategic question. If given the opportunity, workers become involved in problems of safety but not in how to finance a company loan. They must have relevant reasons to become involved. They must feel some sense of control in the situation. Once involved, they proceed to survey their task environment—those elements of the larger world which are relevant to goal setting and goal attainment (Dill, 1965).

Control. Whether or not one should become involved in trying to solve the perceived problem, will depend on the results of categorizing the perceived discrepancy as controllable or uncontrollable (Mac-Crimmon, 1974). For a particular manager, locating lower price suppliers may be controllable; dealing with higher interest rates may not be controllable. Partially controllable factors can be decomposed into their controllable and uncontrollable elements (Howard, 1971).

In the same way, one conclusion reached from the diagnostic phase may be that the problem is insolvable, and that there is unlikely to be a feasible solution (MacCrimmon, 1974). A construction firm faced with seriously declining demand for its houses may find no solution but to file for bankruptcy due to the firm's inability to control what appears to be the causes of declining demand—high land prices and high mortgage rates.

Priorities. Roberts and Hanline (1975) suggest that priorities can be established for those decisions with which to become involved. Such priorities can be based on the anticipated gains from involvement in dealing with each problem. A decision-making schedule is envisaged based on "intuition, logic, and mathematics." The important point here is that the executive is exhorted to consciously decide to engage or not engage and to set priorities for doing so. If priorities cannot be ordered quantitatively, they can be handled qualitatively (Ansoff, 1965). Care must be exerted to avoid attaching too high a priority to short-term expediencies which may detract from long-term strategic capabilities (Radford, 1981).

According to Radomsky (1967), managers' thresholds shift continually depending on their current work load and the number of decisions with which they are currently involved. When putting out a fire, a manager is unlikely to be actively alert for new opportunities. For the manager needs to feel the time and resources are available to examine the opportunities, and also to search for ways to take advantage of them.

Wide and narrow scanning lead to thresholds of awareness that discrepancies exist between current and desired states of affairs. The desired states, the attainments of goals, are displaced when aspirations fail to be achieved.

Problems are revealed and diagnoses made depending on who, as persons, participate in the process, and what roles they are expected to play. This, in turn, affects the initiation, mobilization of resources, and directions for the search for solutions that follows.

4

Search and design

The completely rational view of decision making involves the search for or innovation of all possible alternatives before moving on to choose the best from among them. But as we have already noted, only limited rationality is possible in how decision makers actually proceed. Search and innovation processes tend to be bounded (March & Simon, 1958). Unaware of all the possible alternatives, Simon's (1957) "administrative man" cannot possibly know all the consequences of choosing one alternative over another. The complexity of a problem is reduced to the level at which his limited knowledge and judgment can make the decision. Administrative man responds to the perceived, not necessarily the real, problem. The generation of alternatives is further constrained by organizational and individual factors to be discussed in Chapter 7.

Organizational search as seen by Cyert and March

As already noted in Chapter 2, for Cyert and March (1963) search is stimulated by a problem; depressed by a problem solution. Search is

53

simpleminded, based on a simple model of causality until driven to a more complex one. Search is biased. Perceptions of the environment and considerations within the organization involved in the search are affected by the individual goals and competencies of the involved participants. Search begins by considering obvious solutions and problems, then moves on to other alternatives only if the obvious solutions are deemed unsatisfactory. This sequential effort is guided by heuristics, which reduce the number of alternatives to a salient few. The small number of possibilities examined in the entire problem space are accounted for by two rules: search in the neighborhood of the problem symptom and in the context of the current approach to the problem. Other possibilities are ignored. As Simon and Newell (1971) suggest this actually makes good sense when one considers what "all possible alternatives" implies. (The decision tree for the game of checkers has 10^{40} alternative paths.)

Some theory or policy, explicit or implicit, guides and limits the search for solutions. This decides the time, place, methods, and approaches that will be considered. Unfortunately, there often is need for counter theories and counter policies to generate a different array of alternatives among which may lie a better solution (Feyerabend, 1975). The policy of containing Communism lay behind all seriously considered alternatives from 1945 onward for U.S. policy makers dealing with North Vietnam. Trying to convert Vietnam into another Yugoslav-type ally was never entertained.

Further conceptualizations about the stimulation of search

As seen by Thompson (1967), search by organizations is stimulated by the effort to reduce uncertainty, to increase closure. The greater the amount of uncertainty present, the more intensive the search is likely to be. Search will continue until uncertainty is reduced to tolerable levels (Driscoll & Lanzetta, 1965).

Again, as seen earlier, deviation from level of aspiration, a function of the decision-making unit's previous successes, failures, and expectations of the future, is conceived as the stimulus for starting the search activity to reduce a discrepancy between the current and desired state of affairs. The level of aspiration is also a basis for terminating search activity for it provides the criteria for evaluating the alternatives which have been found (Alexis & Wilson, 1967). In addition to aspiration levels, search is also initiated by internal curiosity, conflict, and recognition that problems exist. External information can do likewise. Search can be instituted as a consequence of criterion checking, repetitive procedures, policy statements, and other organizational stimuli. Deviations of performance standards signal possible problems whose solutions are likely to be searched for locally, only to be expanded if localized search fails

(Ference, 1970). Localization of search will depend on the nature of the criterion checks. They may be clear and highly instrumented so that search can remain narrow. Or they may be more ambiguous so that search has to be broader (Thompson, 1967).

Activities or periodic, recurrent events in the organization also generate problems, again usually to be dealt with locally rather than by policy statements with broader organizational implications requiring broader innovative efforts.

Managers usually do not independently look through their own portfolios for problems needing attention. Rather, they are most often stimulated by others inside and outside the organization. Managers acquire information about alternatives from those over whom they have some control, such as subordinates, consultants, and salespersons (MacCrimmon, 1974). Such search efforts can be initiated by the manager but Lacho (1969) found in 14 case studies of food brokerage firms that search for additional products was passive. The executives waited for manufacturers' representatives to present products. They made inquiries of manufacturers only after they heard of a promising account. They made inquiries of broker friends when convenient. Aggressive search for new product lines was uncommon. Even such search, which occurred when faced with a severe goal deviation, was limited to familiar rather than unfamiliar sources.

As seen in the multitude of communication network experiments (e.g., see Shaw, 1964), whether one will be the recipient of search-stimulating information or will have to seek it out from others will depend on whether one is located at the center or periphery of an information network. At the center, one may easily be faced with search-stimulating overload; at the periphery, with underload.

Who gets what search-stimulating information from whom is a key question for understanding the organizational decision process. Blocking, bypassing, and intentional and accidental distortion of information is commonly found as the informal communication structure deviates from the communication system prescribed by the organization (Rice & Bishoprick, 1971).

Search is ubiquitous and dynamic

For the sake of exposition, we have focused on search as a discrete stage in the problem discovery-search-choice process. In fact, search itself can occur in all phases of the decision process. Search may be instituted to recognize and define decision problems. The environment may be scanned to maintain an awareness of the occasion for a decision. Search may be instituted to determine the decision rules to apply to the choice situation, to operational criteria, to the consequences of alternatives, to the worth of alternatives, and to the nature of "ideal" search generators (for instance, asking salesmen to be looking for new sources of supply) (Soelberg, 1967).

Search is seen to be conservative by Cyert and March (1963) in that it unearths relevant information by focusing on what is "nearby." But as MacCrimmon (1974) suggests, such "conservative focusing" is likely to be inefficient. A more adventurous "focus-gambling" strategy is preferred for quick decisions. Whether search will be instituted, conservative or adventurous, will depend on what the decision maker anticipates.

Search as anticipatory behavior

To become involved in the search process implies that the decision maker can do something about the continuing problem-generating discrepancy to bring about a more desired future state of affairs or to be better prepared for it. Ordinarily, this will direct search toward past events relevant to predicting the future and efforts to anticipate relevant relationships (Shull, Delbecq, & Cummings, 1970). Estimates of the effects of alternatives will be drawn up. These, of course, will be subject to various limitations and biases. Administrative, legal, social, or physical constraints place arbitrary upper and lower limits on what is possible. Estimates are biased by motivational factors. Cyert, March, and Starbuck (1961) discovered that participants in simulated budgeting, when engaged in cost analyses, protected themselves by overestimating costs. However, when they engaged in sales analyses, they underestimated sales. In both instances, error would be more likely to enhance appraisals of their performance and actual costs proved to be lower and actual sales higher than estimates.

Other characteristics of the search process are captured in the most commonly observed heuristics.

Heuristics of search

The most generally employed heuristic is means-ends analysis. We start with a goal to be achieved and, through incremental shifts (Office of the Chief of Military History, 1959) or successive approximations (Barnard, 1938), discover the means to reach the goal. As we go along we refine purposes and discriminations using cues, techniques, analogies, and rules of thumb based on past experience to both generate and limit what means will be tried (Shull, Delbecq, & Cummings, 1970). The search is pragmatic in that it sees what will work. This is in contrast to the algorithmic effort to determine what is logically true or best.

Alternatives are reduced by working forward toward subgoals and working backward from the desired end state to the starting point of the search. Many human, legal, social, and administrative constraints further severely restrict what alternatives will be considered (Feldman & Kanter, 1965).

But the ends are not really as firmly fixed as this would imply. When routine, previously workable answers are not available, or don't work, limited search is initiated along familiar, well-known paths until the first satisfactory, not optimum solution, is found. As will be seen, what standard is set for determining a satisfactory solution is part of how the situation is defined. When solutions are easy to find, standards are raised. When alternatives are hard to find, standards are lowered. According to Perrow (1972), the organization rather than the individual tends to control these standards. (Although, work group collusion against standard setting by "rate busting" management is a well-documented phenomenon.) The organization can manipulate individual expectations about the ratio of inducements to contributions. So to a considerable degree, search activity is a function of problems as defined by the organization and choices as guided to meet organizational standards. Consider how much search is likely when the organization indicates you must replace a secretary within three days or lose the position in the next budget.

Dealing with problem complexity. Alexis and Wilson (1967) suggest that as cognitive strain increases due to greater problem complexity, search rules are simplified in order to cope with the problem. When first faced with a problem, simplistic search rules are employed. How were similar problems handled in the past? What are immediate solutions? The "immediate neighborhood of the problem symptoms" is searched for alternatives (Cravens, 1970). Variables within the individual's control are examined before those outside the individual's control (Emory & Niland, 1968). Failure to find or design acceptable alternatives leads to a search for clarification by reexamining the estimated consequences of alternatives that have been considered. Continued failure to find or develop a successful alternative will then lead to a reduction in the level of aspiration (Cyert, Feigenbaum, & March, 1971).

Dealing with problem uncertainty. Search is more likely and more intensive the greater the organization's environmental uncertainty. Ebert and Mitchell (1975) argue that the scope of search will be greater in organizations facing dynamic, unstable environments. Focus will be on searching among those segments of the environment that are controllable rather than uncontrollable, as was seen in a study by Kefalas and

Schoderbek (1973). This is consistent with Lanzetta's line of investigation (e.g., Driscoll & Lanzetta, 1965) demonstrating that uncertainty results in search to reduce it. Again, Levine and Samet (1973) allowed judges to purchase information from three fallible sources until they could decide toward which of eight possible targets an enemy was advancing. Information seeking was greater when conditions were more uncertain.

Search or design?

Little innovation, invention, and creativity in the system as a whole is possible at any one time. Many factors restrict and limit efforts to deal creatively with organizational problems. There is specialization of activities and roles so that attention is directed to restricted sets of values. There are attention directors that channelize behavior. Rules and programs reduce what can be considered. The locale confines the range of stimuli and situations to narrow perceptions. Training and indoctrination enable the individual to proceed as preferred by the organization—uncreatively. Goals and tasks form semi-independent programs, again limiting the scope of action (Simon, 1960; Perrow, 1972).

A statistical analysis of innovations in hospitals was completed by Kimberly and Evanisko (1981). The innovations were improvements in treating respiratory diseases. Technological innovations such as introducing a new drug or surgical procedure occurred more frequently in larger, more specialized, but departmentally decentralized hospitals. At the same time, administrative innovations such as applying computer data processing to medical records were more common in larger and more specialized hospitals in which the hospital administrator was cosmopolitan in outlook and the departments were more functionally differentiated.

Mintzberg et al. (1976) found that in 22 of the 25 cases they studied the greatest amount of decision-making resources were consumed in search for a single satisfactory solution. Only when no such single alternative could be discovered was the design of a custom-made solution or the modification of an available one undertaken. Thus, only when previous experience or standardized solutions, or other available alternatives cannot be found, will invention or creativity be attempted, bringing something new into existence (Luthans, 1973). Such creativity will be facilitated or constrained by a variety of organizational factors. Obviously, this shift toward creativity, in itself, will depend on organizational history and policy. Consider the many organizations that reject alternatives invented externally. Creativity for them is required once solutions cannot be found within their own boundaries. Conversely, firms that practice industrial espionage lack appropriate ethical standards and may face legal difficulties but they do reduce the need for creativity.

Zeleny (1981) has provided a model which includes contingencies likely to shift the process from search to innovation. Questions whose answers determine whether a shift from search to innovation may occur include: Is the organization closed technologically? Can its current technological limits be extended? Is it promising to extend the limits? Can there be "purposeful challenging and extending of . . . habitual domain(s)"? Can goals and decision criteria be reformulated? Can additional resources be provided for innovation?

It may be that the behavioral emphasis on description rather than prescription has focused more attention on search rather than innovation (Alexander, 1979). More important, innovation may be hindered because of conflicting interdepartmental interests in an organization. Each department sees only the possibilities of its own local, habitual solutions to an organizational problem. The conflict may be allowed to fester as a source of continued irritation, or it may be seen as an opportunity for constructive innovation. Organizations can profit from the invention of new, concrete solutions to deal with such conflict (Barnard, 1958).

The choice process awaits the discovery of a feasible alternative. When there are no feasible solutions awaiting discovery, they have to be designed or created by associational or Gestalt (patterning) processes. But search and creative design are not necessarily mutually exclusive. Creativity involves search and adoption as well as invention. The associational approach to creativity links insight with search (Rothenburg & Hausman, 1976). Complexity-reducing creativity involves systematic search through a problem space. The direction of the search affects its creative possibilities (Marquis, 1969).

The design of innovative solutions

The process of design itself is seen by Mintzberg, Raisinghani, and Theoret (1976) to follow certain regularities depending on whether it is a custom-made solution or a modification of already available alternatives. The designers begin creating the custom-made solution with a vague image of some ideal one. They pursue a sequence of nested design and search cycles, working their way through a decision tree. The decisions at each successive node became more narrow and focused. Failure at any node leads to cycling back to an earlier node. A solution takes shape as the designers move along developing their solution without really knowing what it will look like until it is completed.

In solving 20 of the 25 decision-making cases studied in which designing of innovative solutions was required for lack of already available alternatives, only one custom-made solution was fully designed. Modifications of known alternatives were created usually. When search coupled with modifications of existing alternatives was required, more than one solution might be developed and compared.

Terminating search and innovation processes

Complete search is infeasible, if not impossible. Designing of alternative solutions cannot go on forever. But search and design processes usually stop too early for achieving the levels of effectiveness possible if search had continued or additional creativity had been attempted. Understanding what contributes to premature termination and what could stimulate further search or innovation will ordinarily serve to improve the quality of the solution finally chosen.

When involved in a sequence of decision making, with the option to stop the process if an outcome is achieved that satisfies the decision maker, termination is likely to occur prematurely and further from optimality, when options are actually increasing in value. This is particularly so just after a large jump occurs in the value of an outcome (Corbin, Olson, & Abbondanza, 1975). Contrarily, decision makers may erroneously continue searching long after options have begun decreasing in value (Brickman, 1972). This seems especially true when the individual decision maker or decision-making groups are insecure, face resistance (Fox & Staw, 1979), and feel personally responsible for the negative outcomes that have occurred before (Giuliano, Appleman, & Bazerman, 1981). However, when sequential outcomes of options vary randomly, stopping is close to optimal (Rapaport & Tversky, 1970). Alexander (1979) built a rational two-dimensional theory to explain preemptive closure inhibiting continued search (or design) which would promote higher quality outcomes. The continued search and generation of additional options were seen to be limited by various constraints of knowledge, time, resources, costs, and power differences.

The search or design phase of the decision process may intensively interact with the preceding problem discovery and diagnosis phase, and with the choice and evaluation phase which follows it. Such continuing interaction implies that preemptive termination of search or design will be avoided. On the other hand, if there is little continued interaction and feedback of the search or design phase with the diagnostic phase and the choice phase, complete closure and termination will be premature. Avoidance of premature closure permits continuing means-ends interaction. However,

> . . . some closure is necessary to establish a framework for the synthesis of options, but too much closure, such as rigidly predetermined goals or a problem diagnosis locked in by oganizational or disciplinary predilections,

may inhibit the emergence of potentially optimal alternatives. (Alexander, 1979, p. 387)

In addition to previously mentioned constraints, Alexander suggests that closure is increased when problems are defined at one institution and plans made in another. Available methodology, as well as theory and ideology, also promote less-than-optimum closure, unduly limiting the range of alternatives. In addition, disciplinary biases, perceptual filters, and personal propensities force premature closure of the gap between diagnosis and search or design. The biased diagnosis calls forth the favored design and closes out other possibilities.

On the other hand, if choice and evaluation processes too readily affect search or design options, valuable opportunities may be lost. (One sees this most often in the untrained group which proceeds to spend much of its total time evaluating just the first option mentioned).

Alexander was able to account for three complex decision-making cases in terms of the above conceptualizations: U.S. Vietnam policy (Donovan, 1970), siting of a third London airport (Lichfield, Kettle, & Whitbread, 1975), and retrenchment of personnel in the University of Wisconsin system. In all three cases, high closure prevented the development of more creative outcomes. Solutions to the Vietnam dilemma were constrained by the dominant and highly accepted domino theory. The ultimate suspension of the third London airport project was attributed to premature closure of siting options, as well as failure to fully consider timing and need for a four-runway airport. In the Wisconsin retrenchment case, organizational constraints were brought to bear before any options were sufficiently elaborated for formal evaluation.

These are only some samples of the many case examples that can be cited of the failure to create effective solutions to problems which might have been possible if the decision-makers had been willing to fully explore possibilities. Rather, decision-makers terminated exportations as soon as a most favored solution had been reached. They never considered more remote, unusual, and unorthodox alternatives.

INFORMATION SYSTEMS AND THE SEARCH AND DESIGN PROCESS

A key to understanding organizational search and innovation processes is to understand the organization's information system. For example, keeping good records was seen as fundamental to effective search and choice efforts by boards of directors (Tropman, 1980; Heller, 1969). Again, committee effectiveness has been strongly associated with the quality of secretarial service provided (Heynes, 1950). According to Vaidya, Lloyd and Ford (1975), proper message summarizing and message routing are important elements of effective organizational decision making.

Alexis and Wilson (1967) suggested that the ready availability of information to decision makers, its content, relevance, reliability, and freedom from biases is particularly important. Ungson, Braunstein and Hall (1981) add concreteness, distinctiveness, saliency, and lack of diverting redundancies. Effective decisions depend on the quality and quantity of available information.

Availability

The availability of information or its accessibility to a decision unit, the ease of obtaining information, and the speed with which information flows in the organization, are determined primarily by the form of the organization's communication structure as well as the extent to which the organization has an open, trusting climate. Needless to say, the quality of electronic data processing, retrieval capabilities, input-output, and display features will also be highly important.

Information overload. Too much information may be available. The system of information is likely to be a grid "made up of overlapping, often contradictory and elusive channels . . ." (Pfiffner, 1960, p.129). Particularly with the advent of computerization, decision makers can be surfeited with an overload of information. The volume will drive up the costs of storage, screening, and retrieval for searching.

Completely rational arguments would suggest that organizations spend money and effort for information up to the point where added information to solve a problem will be of greater cost than the benefit of the information to improving the effectiveness of discriminating among alternative solutions to the problem. In fact, March and Shapira (1982) declare that the truth lies elsewhere.

Organizations actually gather much information which they never use. Much obtained information is irrelevant to the decisions. They ask for even more, then ignore it. Often, decisions are made first, then information is sought to support it. Problems may be identified only after solutions for them have surfaced. Why? Feldman and March (1981) and March and Shapira (1982) suggest it is because managements monitor as much as they can about what is going on rather than selectively seek specific information to deal with a specific problem. Furthermore, highly-regarded advice is often bad advice for an organization. "Advice givers typically exaggerate the quality of their advice." Much of it is bolstered by social supports and biased by conflicts of interest and advocates such that the information requires fine filtering. "Organizational information is rarely innocent; thus rarely as reliable as an innocent would suspect." It is more difficult to evaluate the final outcomes of decisions than to evaluate the extent the decision makers used the proper search procedures. So one of the ways that organizational decision makers compete for reputations is by producing information. The result again is overproduction of information. Still another influence contributing to the collection of too much information is the tendency for redundancy to breed overconfidence. The decision maker's confidence increases with the increasing information even though usually beyond some relatively early point in the information-gathering process, a limit in the usefulness of information is reached. Nevertheless, confidence in one's decisions continues to climb steadily as more information is obtained. Thus, toward the end of the information-gathering process, most people are overconfident about their judgments.

This can be seen if our accuracy of predictive decisions about personnel depends on a multiple correlation. After the first few predictors have entered the regression equation, adding predictors, is likely to mainly add redundancy. Yet decision makers continue to feel more confident about their predictions with the additional data, particularly if they are redundant, that is, if they are correlated with the earlier-obtained predictors. In fact, uncorrelated, nonredundant additions would be more helpful to augmenting the accuracy of the multiple prediction.

Thus, there is an excessive craving by organizational decision makers for more, not better, information. Management information systems often may increase management confidence without improving the quality of their decisions (Zeleny, 1981). And yet too much information will clog the system even when it is relevant (Campbell, 1968). Miller (1956) found that for accurate short-term retention seven chunks of information was the ordinary limit as an individual decision maker worked through a problem. However, greater loads could be processed and retained for ready recall by the decision maker by grouping the information into new chunks and arranging them hierarchically (Simon, 1969).

Streufert (1978) concluded from a series of simulated complex military decision experiments where the load and timing of information input was controlled by the experimenter (ignoring the costs of the information), the best complex decision making was obtained when one item of information was received by the decision-making unit every three minutes. Information received as rarely as every 6 minutes or as frequently as every 2 minutes produced severe decrements in decision-making quality.

O'Reilly (1980) completed a survey of over 1,500 organizational members showing that perceived information overload was associated with lower performance of decision makers than was perceived information underload. When overloaded, subjects were found by Halpin, Streufert, Steffey and Lanham (1971) to underestimate the relevance of information. When actual relevance of information to total amount received was low, relevance was overestimated.

Broadbent (1971) discovered that individuals overloaded with information filter and pigeonhole it for action or delay into the familiar and the unfamiliar. Available special vocabularies, standard operating procedures and information channels affect how the information is filtered and pigeonholed (Perrow, 1972).

Relevance of information

Information will be relevant to the extent it serves a particular task and supplements the prior knowledge of the decision maker. Thus, Wotruba and Mangone (1979) found that the quality of management decision making was dependent on the effectiveness of the reporting by salespersons of relevant marketing information.

It is obvious that up to some optimum, the more relevant the information received by the decision-making unit, the better its decisions. Nevertheless, the overproduction of information already noted results in executives receiving too much irrelevant information (Ackoff, 1967). Computer systems can make saturation with irrelevant information a manager's nightmare.

Unfortunately, there are strong tendencies to use irrelevant information. Tversky and Kahneman (1975) asked subjects to decide the probability that a personality description belonged to one of 30 engineers or one of 70 lawyers. A second group was assigned the same task except that they were told that there were 70 engineers and 30 lawyers involved. The descriptions actually contained no information that discriminated between engineers and lawyers. Without information they made the expected judgments of .3 and .7. But when given worthless information, they moved to judgments of .5. Zeleny (1981) concluded that we tend to utilize whatever information is available—even though it may be erroneous or irrelevant. Thus, overloading with irrelevant information is a serious deterrent to effective search and innovation. In the absence of relevant information, gaps are filled with naive rationales often at odds with reality.

Irrelevant information detracts from decision performance, in both level and consistency. Performance here can be improved by a mechanism to filter irrelevant information from the environment. Experience with a decision task is crucial for such intuitive filtering (Ebert & Mitchell, 1975; Ebert, 1972; Kleinmuntz, 1968).

Filtering is one among several procedures for simplifying what is being received. When overloaded by a too complex environment or too much relevant or irrelevant information, the individual decision maker can ignore it temporarily by processing the information for error (error checking); by putting it into a queue for delayed processing; by using fewer categories and less precision to process the information; by using multiple channels (i.e., several units instead of one unit) to process the information; or by ignoring the data input altogether (Miller, 1960).

Reliability of information

The reliability of available information will depend on how information is screened and transformed by the many decision units prior to its immediate application. Reliability can be increased at the cost of increasing redundancy. For example, an organization can arrange for parallel multiple channels of communication.

Unreliability of information may be endemic in organizations because such a large proportion of it is informally distributed. This is the rule rather than the exception. Informal rather than formal channels of information are used more frequently. For example, in a survey of a large, light industrial firm, Klauss & Bass (1982) found that about 85 percent of the information used by project engineers to make decisions came from oral communications and face-to-face contact rather than written documents. And Aguilar (1967), in a study of top management noted that personal sources of information played a greater role than impersonal information. As sources of information outside the organization, documents and meetings were less significant than personal contacts. For inside information of consequence, superiors were a poorer source than subordinates. (Nevertheless, as we have noted earlier, managers pay more attention to communications from their superiors than from their subordinates.)

As Ference (1970) has noted, information sources are selected more on the basis of the substantive aspects of the problem than by procedures prescribed by the organization. Information will be sought from sources where bargaining and time lags are not involved (Ebert & Mitchell, 1975).

Distortion of information

Perhaps because so much information dispersion is informal—as well as for numerous other reasons—bias of information is also endemic in organizations. It is present in all available information (Alexis & Wilson, 1967). Organization members hear and see what they expect to hear and see based on "scripts" they have learned from previous experience so that new information is misperceived as some of the same old information (Abelson, 1976).

As information is passed downward through the departments of a system, receipt, interpretation, and further transmission will be modified in terms of each decision-making unit's own needs. Each department will be looking for, and sensitive to, different kinds and amounts of information; each will filter what it takes in. The resultant transmission to other departments will be systematically altered (analogous to the parlor game for systematically modifying a rumor passed by whispering from one participant to the next). Transmission will be simplified, and particularly of consequence to the decision process, uncertainties will be absorbed (March & Simon, 1958).

MacCrimmon (1974) agrees that information tends to lose some of its uncertainty as it moves through several decision units. It becomes more precise—but the precision is specious. Units further along do not appreciate the uncertainty that really exists (Woods, 1966). More attention will be paid, and more weight given, to information that is polarized. Neutral information is undervalued, as is information inconsistent with what has already been received (Filley, House & Kerr, 1976).

A major source of error emerges when decision makers have to aggregate different pieces of information to make a single decision. Marshak (1965) advised organizations to avoid too much aggregation of data for storage (for example storing annual stock price changes rather than monthly data). One can always aggregate, but it is very difficult to disaggregate when more detail is needed. How much detail to store obviously depends on anticipated needs. That form of data for storage and processing should be pursued which yields the greatest gain from the information keeping cost considerations in mind (Marshak, 1968, 1971).

Other sources of error lie in fallacious statistical inferences. Samples may be treated as if they were truly representative of the total population. Correlations may be seen where they do not really exist, or they may be misinterpreted when they do.

Cost of information

Information overload and irrelevancy greatly increase the cost of search. But if the problem is well-structured, complete information can be obtained about it, and we could precisely price the cost of adding information to make it so, then a zone of cost effectiveness can be determined—for typically, as one gains additional information, redundancy increases. At any one time during the search process, information for choice still remains incomplete. But the cost of additional search may add less in benefit than its cost. Harrison (1981) argued that the cost of continually trying to add information rises exponentially at some point, as shown in Figure 3, the value of additional units of information declines "precipitously."

At first, as search continues, the cost curve rises rather slowly, because the initial units of information often require relatively little effort. As the search for information continues, it becomes increasingly difficult to obtain.

FIGURE 3   The cost of additional information

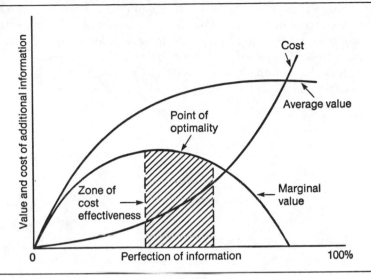

Source: E. F. Harrison, *The Managerial Decision-Making Process* 2d ed. (Boston: Houghton Mifflin, 1981), p. 34.

The marginal-value curve in Figure 3 reflects the value of an additional unit of information. A zone of cost effectiveness is suggested around the point of optimality.

Economic theory of teams

Another normative rationale has been provided by Marschak and Radner (1972), an economic theory of teams, to deal optimally with three aspects of organizational search and information acquisition. This theory is also based on the highly unrealistic premise that the organization's members are all in complete agreement. It proposes how organizational members should acquire information from the uncertain environment; what communication channels and messages should be utilized to communicate this information to other members; and what actions members should take based on the information they receive. Information is acquired and communications sent, but optimality is achieved only when the recipient of the information can use it.

Despite its unrealistic assumptions, team theory can be used to generate the same information processing errors for study in simulation found also in real systems (MacCrimmon, 1972). It also can provide the economic structure for designing management information systems (Emery, 1967).

In this chapter we have seen how the search phase is energized and directed. We have looked at the conditions under which search for available solutions gives way to the design of new alternatives. We have enumerated what may be of consequence about the flow of information from multiple sources to multiple recipients: information availability, relevance, reliability, distortion, load, and cost. In Chapter 7, we will explore how this search phase is affected by various constraints imposed by the organization. But before this, we proceed to the evaluation and choice phase.

5

Evaluation and choice

The search process is terminated by an evaluation and choice among the discovered or invented alternatives. This requires a comparative assessment of the alternatives to estimate which one is most likely to close the gap between the current and desired state of affairs. What underlies such judgments has been the subject of considerable analysis.

Evaluation can be haphazard or orderly. It appears more profitable to be orderly. Yet, more often than not, decision makers make a choice from among alternatives on a fairly haphazard basis. Failure to be orderly results in accepting choices on vague feelings about their rightness.

Evaluation and choice are difficult to clearly separate. Ordinarily, once an alternative that seems reasonably satisfactory comes along, it is accepted. Criteria for choice and their relative importance are not considered explicitly. But decision makers should be more systematic. In fact, many strive to approach optimal decisions, although optimality, itself, as we shall see, is a chimera.

If we consider what should be done, criteria upon which evaluation will be based need to be established. Weights may be attached to each of these criteria. Risk preferences need to be explicated. Outcomes yielding as much gain as possible with the least risk of loss are sought. The consequences of implementing each alternative are estimated as well as the potential new problems generated by each alternative (Bass & Ryterband, 1979).

What emerges from the search process can make the choice process more difficult or impossible. Two equally attractive alternatives may have been uncovered in the search. The decision maker may be overloaded with acceptable alternatives. Or, it may be now understood that no single discovered or invented alternative will solve the problem. Or, anticipated side effects may force abandoning any choice from among the available alternatives. In some of these instances, choice may be better left to the toss of a coin; or objectives may have to be revised or the search renewed (Harrison, 1981).

Ideally, five constituents can be conceptually distinguished in the overall evaluation and choice process. Zeleny, 1981; Mintzberg et al., 1976. First, there is evaluation of the anticipated benefits and costs of available alternatives. This takes place before closure occurs and one of the discovered or created alternatives is finally chosen to close the gap between the current and the desired state of affairs. Evaluations are made of the extent rival alternatives will be likely to close the gap. Benefits and costs in this regard are estimated for each alternative. A second preclosure constituent deals with estimates of the risks and uncertainties that the various competing alternatives will succeed or fail to close the gap. The third constituent is closure—commitment to one alternative to close the gap. With closure, a process of authorization begins, described in detail by Mintzberg, Raisinghani, and Theoret (1976). This was found in 14 of the 25 longitudinal decisions they observed. The fourth constituent is concentration justifying the choice. The fifth constituent is an evaluation of outcomes resulting from implementing the chosen alternative. It is a follow-up of the degree to which the chosen alternative did in fact succeed in closing the gap and to what extent it did so. Were objectives met? Were goals reached? Thus, the five ideal constituents are evaluation of alternatives, risk estimation, commitment, justification, and evaluation of outcomes.

Although experimentally, one may be able to arrange to focus on any one of these constituents exclusively, as Mintzberg et al. (1976) observed, it is impossible in real life to isolate these constituents from each other. We do so here for purposes of exposition. While reevaluation, of necessity, must come late in the process, the other constituents are not necessarily likely to appear in any one order. Also a cycling back and forth among them is likely. Furthermore, we have noted earlier that evaluation and choice interact with the search process. Evaluation and choice also interact with the goal setting which occurs in diagnosis. As Behling and Schriesheim (1976) concluded:

Organizational objectives do change, though much of what is considered to be change is actually expansion of the domain of the organization. Changes occur under three circumstances: (1) when the organization is extremely successful in accomplishing existing objectives, (2) when it is depressingly unsuccessful, and (3) when it is subject to substantial pressure from elements of the task environment. (p. 188)

Just as objectives first set in problem discovery and diagnosis guide the direction of search, and just as search experience results in lowered levels of aspiration and readjusted goal settings, search processes also uncover alternatives that guide what evaluations are feasible. But at the same time, evaluation may hinder the scope of the search. Moreover, objectives and needs may force premature evaluation foreclosing on needed search. Evaluation and choice may bring on alterations and reinterpretation of objectives and diagnoses. Ordinarily, evaluation and choice follows search, but more search for justification may follow choice than precede it. Evaluation of alternatives in later search may be distorted by prematurely early choice.

EVALUATION OF THE ANTICIPATED BENEFITS AND COSTS OF ALTERNATIVES

Criteria for evaluation of alternatives

An important aspect in evaluating whether or not a particular alternative may be the desired solution to a problem involves establishing the criteria, implicit or explicit, upon which the judgment will be based. The source, timing, and nature of criteria were seen by Stricklin (1966) as important dimensions for understanding organizational decision making.

The judgment of adequacy may pursue a *minimax, maximin* or *mixed* strategy. With the minimax, we will accept that decision which is likely to yield the least ill effect if the worst happens. The least amount of loss is risked for an acceptable gain. With the maximin, we strive for the greatest gain fixing on the amount of loss we are willing to accept. Probably most frequently employed is a mixed strategy of striving for a reasonable gain avoiding undue risks.

Standard setting. The level at which the standards are set—the surrogate acceptable alternative below which alternatives are unacceptable—affects the chances of locating acceptable alternatives. MacCrimmon (1974) suggests that it may work out to start with lower standards, then to gradually tighten up.

The earlier diagnosis of the problem often determines the formulation of the criteria set up to be matched against its possible solutions. The factors of consequence listed in the diagnosis suggest criteria and result in attending to the same or similar criteria in the evaluation. Concern in the diagnosis about product quality and price to stimulate sales will reappear as criteria of quality and price in the evaluation.

The criteria usually suggest a desired level and direction. The level established may be feasible and therefore be able to serve as a standard. Or, the level may be an ideal—say, the lowest possible price at which a profit can be made.

If a feasible level is set, then alternatives found or invented in the search process are compared against it as a standard. If the criteria concern an ideal level, then alternatives are compared with each other to ascertain how close they each come to the ideal. An alternative that is better than the others on each of the criteria is sought and chosen. If, as is often the case, such an alternative cannot be found or created, criteria may be considered as compensatory. For example, a deluxe quality product is abandoned in order to achieve a feasible price. A lower value on one dimension is offset by a higher value on another. Linear weighting is such a compensatory approach (see footnote 3, page 91).

Following Barnard (1938), Koontz and O'Donnell (1968) suggest for effective choice in planning, the need to sort out the more important from the less important criteria.

> In choosing from among alternatives, the more an individual can recognize and solve for those factors that are limiting or critical to the attainment of a desired goal, the more effectively and efficiently he can select the most favorable alternative. (p. 153)

Quality versus acceptance. Maier (1963) emphasized two criteria of effective decision making: quality and acceptance. Vroom and Yetton (1973) built a leadership model around these criteria. An acceptance-dominated solution is more likely to be implemented subsequently because it has attained such acceptance by those involved. A quality-dominated choice implies comparisons with a technical standard or specified objectives. Katz and Kahn (1966) suggested that decision makers close to organizational operations will be more concerned with the solution that can be put into acceptable operation easily, not necessarily with the best solution nor the most desirable solution. On the other hand, policymakers, remote from operations, will choose from among alternatives in terms of desired goals rather than the feasibility of converting the alternatives into practical operations.

The dominance of the criterion of acceptability may lead to the rejection of alternatives without considering their worth or quality, because they are judged superficially as impractical by those closer to operations. They may arbitrarily reject high quality, long-term solutions for trivial reasons. Katz and Kahn (1966) argued that if the merits of a long-term plan are fully considered and found to be of high quality, means can usually be found to implement them.

Criteria depend on model. To the criteria of quality and acceptance, three others can be added: maximized outcome, displaced ideal, and objectives-oriented outcome. The five can be reviewed according to which model of the decision-making process we find appropriate: (1) anticipated utility; (2) satisficing; (3) displacement of the ideal; (4) political acceptance; and (5) incremental objectives.

Anticipated utility of outcome: The model of complete rationality

If we accept the model of complete rationality with its perfectly informed, perfectly sensitive, and perfectly rational, economic man, then his evaluations should maximize expected utility—or usefulness of the outcome to him.[1] To do so he must adopt a set of axioms. Objectives are fixed; there are no time and cost constraints; alternatives are quantitative and transitive; and the system is closed (Harrison, 1981). Circular judgments must be avoided along with wishful thinking in which the values of outcomes affect the judged probabilities. Only outcomes that help to discriminate among alternatives should be considered (Marschak, 1964). There must be a way of directly comparing the expected values of each alternative. MacCrimmon (1968) found that although executives violated one or more of these axioms in their actual choices, they believed they would accept them as norms of behavior and as guides to how they should make a decision. But as MacCrimmon (1974) notes, the main difficulty with expected utility is in trying to apply it. All possible alternatives to fully determine the decision-makers' differential preferences can never be completely generated; nevertheless, usually only the main alternatives need to be considered. But because the total number of possible relevant events is usually very large, the number of probability judgments is likely to make it impossible to do a thorough job of handling the

---

[1] An example of how this can be done provided one makes many simplifying assumptions is as follows:

Suppose a firm faces the choice of expanding its workforce to meet a possible increase in demand for its products. The subjective probability that demand will increase is estimated to be .4. Therefore, the probability that demand will not increase is .6. Then the values of four possibilities are estimated. Say, for instance, no increase in demand or workforce = 0; no increase in demand but the added expenses of an expanded workforce = −100; increase in demand but no increase in workforce = −50; and increase in both demand and workforce = 200.

	Increase in Demand		Expected Outcomes
	No (p = .6) Yes (p = .4)		
	Don't		
Work	Expand 0 −100		$(.6 \times 0) + (.4 \times -100) = -40$
Force	Expand −50 200		$(.6 \times 50) + (.4 \times 200) = 50$

The subjective estimated utility of expanding the workforce is 50 and of not expanding it is −40. Expansion of the work force is supported by the estimates.

uncertainty in the environment. Sensitivity analysis, which analyzes the movement toward or away from optimality with changes in the values of the parameters of the problem, can be employed to address this issue (Hillier & Lieberman, 1967).

The utility function can be obtained for well-structured problems where the outcomes can be located on a single dimension. But if many dimensions must be considered, no completely general techniques are available (MacCrimmon, 1974). The utilities of individual members of an organization may be combined to obtain a measure of a group's "social welfare function," but the calculation remains questionable (Radford, 1981).

Other problems with expected utility theory include the fact that a decision maker must know how much more he or she likes one thing over another. Indifference curves allow the scaling of utilities, but become very complex mathematically when going beyond several sets of alternatives. The utility scale of one person may not be comparable with that of another. Furthermore, utilities change over time (Rice & Bishoprick, 1971).

Nevertheless, for simple gambles, subjectively expected utility gives a good global fit to data about choice (Slovic, Fischhoff, & Lichtenstein, 1977). But even with well-structured bets, several paradoxes such as the greater preference for longshots can be cited to invalidate some of the required assumptions. Coombs (1975) sees risky choices as a compromise between trying to maximize expected value and trying to optimize risk. Risk preferences are particularly important in his portfolio theory.

Individuals differ widely in their utility functions, how much they are willing to risk for a given amount of gain or how much they value insurance against loss. Executives were found by Swalm (1966) to differ widely in their utility functions ranging from gamblers to extremely conservative risk takers. But they all were conservative about risking prospects of loss for their corporation perhaps because the penalty in organizational life for being responsible for one bad outcome is much greater than the rewards for selecting alternatives that do well.

Satisficing outcomes: The model of bounded rationality

What is rationality, anyway? It is selecting ends that meet needs and capabilities; it is finding means to achieve those ends. But note that needs and capabilities differ. It would be irrational to purchase one shoe unless one was one-legged. It would be rational for a one-legged man to purchase one shoe; it would be irrational for a normal person to purchase one shoe. Administrative rationality must take into account a mélange of facts about emotions, politics, power, group dynamics, and personalities

(Pfiffner, 1960). Diesing (1967) has identified five types of rationality involved in administrative decision making: technical, social, legal, political, and functional. Each type contains its own area of applicability. Quality of product and cost of production are goals of technical rationality. Substituting a new manufacturing process for an old one is rational if it results in a product of lower cost and higher quality. But the new process might achieve its lower costs mainly at the expense of social irrationality by eliminating craft positions which downgrade employment opportunities and the quality of community life. Introducing the new process might be rational in that it eliminates legal objections raised against the old process. It might be rational to introduce the new process because it was more politically acceptable to the community than the old one. Introducing the new process might be functionally rational. That is, it might work better, be more esthetically pleasing, and fit more smoothly with the overall production process. But whatever the basis of rationality, it is likely to be limited.

Simon (1959) argued that striving for an optimal choice to maximize outcomes is the exception. Given limited information, time and cost constraints, and imperfect sensitivity, the organizational decision maker (limited or bounded in rationality) tries to discover and select a satisfactory alternative rather than the optimal one. The satisfactory alternative is based on a set of criteria that describe the minimum satisfactory conditions which could be met by an alternative finally chosen to solve the problem. Alternatives are judged one at a time against these minimum standards of acceptability. The first alternative that minimally meets all of them is accepted.

This is satisficing. Satisficing eliminates the need to consistently rank all alternatives on a single dimension. Standards rise when satisfactory alternatives are easily found; standards fall when they are difficult to locate or invent. Furthermore, choices emerge from organizations conforming to the local rationality of the decision unit, constrained by the situation and the immediate uncertainties of the local decision units within an organization. And so the units ordinarily make decisions to satisfy criteria which are suboptimal when viewed in the larger totality (Sutherland, 1977). Unlike many religious leaders, managers, in general, are pragmatic rather than idealistic (Bass & Burger, 1979). They choose satisfactory solutions. What fits their scheme of values is to choose solutions that work, rather than to avoid choice until the ideal solution is found. So aspirations and objectives are adjusted if a reasonable solution is found. Less effective solutions than originally contemplated may be accepted as a trade-off for lower costs. In Cyert and March's (1963) four cases, two criteria, financial feasibility of a proposed solution, and improvement over current operations, were enough to lead to the choice of a solution.

The means-end chain. A choice is rational if appropriate means are chosen to reach desired ends. But the apparent end may be the means to some further end in a means-ends chain. This chain, in terms, is often obscure, and not completely connected. The ultimate ends are incompletely formulated. Conflict and contradiction in choice of means for ends and their linkages are common. To meet more rigorous antipollution standards, a firm reluctantly invests in special antipollution equipment. But the new, less toxic, waste produced prompts a search for using it. Ultimately the former pollutant is converted into a saleable product.

Rationality is not absolute but relative to the means and ends involved. A choice may be personally rational and organizationally irrational if it only meets personal goals. Or the choice may be personally irrational and organizationally rational if it only meets organizational goals (Simon, 1957). To be completely rational overall is clearly impossible under such circumstances.

Multiple objectives. Multiple objectives and multiple criteria are the rule rather than the exception. This makes judgments about antici pated outcomes difficult and further increase the likelihood of satisficing rather than optimizing.

As Kast and Rosensweig (1970) noted, different decision-making units in the same organization face a different mix of results for various alternatives. No single dimension can be used to appraise all relevant considerations. What's best depends on the locus and focus of the decision. For the organization, a compromise is needed involving trade-offs for cost, speed, accuracy, safety, quality, and many other factors pertinent to the problem. Organizational decision making thus usually involves a balancing among objectives to be satisfied. Also important may be the desire to avoid post decisional conflicts into which a policy may force a decision maker. Ideally, choices made today need to be evaluated in terms of the different objectives of relevant parties likely to be affected now and in the future: employees, managers, customers, clients, stockholders, financial lenders, community, etc. In addition, it must have some degree of "face" validity, look reasonable and be justifiable, to provide an excuse if things don't work out as well as expected (Pfiffner, 1960).

Information failure and policy. Satisficing rather than optimizing may also be likely because of the need to simplify available information, to meet schedules or stay within budgets. While reasonably complete information for solving a problem may be present in the organization, communication failures may cause its loss to the appropriate decision unit. Precedents and established policies may foreclose the deliberations and prohibit consideration of a whole range of alternatives. Selective discrimination may effectively limit decision making. "What decision makers 'see' is what they act upon" (Harrison, 1981). Staff groups may be directed to begin a search for desirable solutions but with the proviso that the search be fast and practical. Final answers are not expected. (Katz & Kahn, 1966)

Optimism. Optimizing requires that our predictions of outcomes not be influenced by our valuing of the outcomes. Yet, such is generally not the case. We believe that what we want to happen is more likely to happen. Individuals' expectations of the occurrence of an event were found by Morlock (1967) to vary positively with the desirability of the event's outcomes. Furthermore, less information was gathered before judging that a more favorable event would occur. Similarly, when possible outcomes had identical chances of occurring, Morlock and Hertz (1964) found that the likely occurrence of the more favorable alternative was predicted more frequently. We are more likely to be optimists than pessimists in the ordinary course of events.

Intuition, common sense and "gut" feelings. Managers, as pragmatists, tend to pride themselves on their intuition, or their ability to "fly by the seat of their pants." Yet, such intuitive judgments have been shown to be fraught with error and to result in outcomes far from optimum when completely depended upon.

Often, executives talk about the importance of common sense. It is common sense that "you can't teach an old dog new tricks" but also that "you are never too old to learn." Faced with the issue, executives make a judgment one way or the other about age, then use the appropriate aphorism as justification.

Evaluations can err immensely when information processing is severely constrained by time, cost, and incapacity so that decision makers are forced to fall back on "gut feelings." Zeleny (1981) noted, for example, that given five seconds in which to estimate the product of $1 \times 2 \times 3 \times 4 \times 5 \times 6 \times 7 \times 8$, the median estimate is 512 and for $8 \times 7 \times 6 \times 5 \times 4 \times 3 \times 2 \times 1$, the median estimate is 2,250. The true calculated answer, however, is 40,320.

Implicit favorite. Decision makers usually make choices early, before any lengthy search has been undertaken and completed (Webster, 1964). While the early choice is not explicit, it nevertheless remains the implicit favorite, and the comparison for alternatives subsequently found (Soelberg, 1967). Final choice is a matter of identifying an *implicit favorite*, then justifying it as the best possible choice from among the few fully considered. The implicit favorite may be established quite early in the overall decision process, making it easy for an observer to forecast the final outcome early even though the search for other alternatives will be continued. But these subsequent alternatives will be looked at with prejudice and compared to the implicit favorite, in such a manner as to increase justification of the latter. Thus, for instance, contracts may be "wired in" to a favorite contractor by a granting agency even though many other contractors' proposals will be considered for comparison before the final choice is made. Students were found to hold early career favorites by Soelberg (1967), who was able to predict 87 percent of the career jobs chosen two to eight weeks before M.I.T. graduate students even recognized that they had made their final choice.

Perrin and Goldman (1978) observed that some professionals, after listening to symptoms, make up their minds on the treatment quite early (i.e., "there's a lot of flu running around, therefore treat for flu"). First impressions exert a strong influence on the choice process. It may be that particularly potent is a favorable first impression about a person or project.

Promoting satisficing behavior is also the general approach for combining rapid with effective decision making. This approach appears particularly strong in Latin America where decisions made rapidly are automatically endowed with perceived effectiveness (Heller, 1969). Furthermore, there is resistance to changing prior choices and distortion or dismissal of information which is incongruent with the image of a good decision maker (Tosi & Carroll, 1976). Once a choice has been made, in the reluctance to change it, more effort sometimes may be expended in the renewed search supporting it than in the search upon which the initial choice was based (Pruit, 1961; Brody, 1965).

The ideal as anchor: The model of the displaced ideal

Zeleny (1981) sees satisficing as occurring for trivial, inconsequential decisions. Or, it occurs because decision makers lack competence and fail to search for or invent superior alternatives. There is no commitment to decision-making excellence. Zeleny conceives of a somewhat different evaluation and choice process unfolding for effective decision makers, neither satisficing nor optimizing. He sees the decision maker as initially searching for the ideal, the best solution. However, as discovering or inventing this ideal becomes infeasible, what is deemed achievable replaces it. Yet, the ideal alternative remains as a point of reference. With displacement, the choice continues to focus on the alternatives generated so far rather than evoking new alternatives. Displacement results in a reinterpretation and reassessment of earlier alternatives. More differentiation among them is sought to make the final choice easier.

This effort to differentiate among alternatives results in looking for additional new information. Measurements are retaken; subjective data is reexamined. New people are brought into the situation to reach agreement about the matter.

The process may begin with objective data, but if and when it becomes apparent that additional objective data will not change opinions and preferences, the process becomes more biased. Further additions of information may be ignored, reevaluated, or rejected as irrelevant. If it is difficult to choose among the alternatives, more information will be sought about them before a favorite emerges. But if the alternatives are clearly different in their attractiveness, and if they only differ along one dimension, little additional information will be sought. When matters begin to stabilize, a "partial" decision can be made.

In the case of personnel selection, this partial decision is the "short list." For example, a short list will be prepared of the final few candidates who will be invited to visit a firm to be considered for an open position. The long list will have contained several times as many applicants as the short list.

Removing many alternative possibilities and making a partial decision has many significant effects. The least popular alternatives are eliminated from further consideration. Modifications occur in the criteria for inclusion of alternatives in the final list. There is a strong likelihood that the ideal alternative will be displaced closer to the feasible set. In turn, what seems most important in the ordering of alternatives may change as a consequence. The remaining alternatives are now compared with a new, displaced ideal. For example, the ideal candidate originally may have been one who had international experience as well as specific experience in the firm's industry. However, the long list of candidates may have revealed none who combined both international and industry experience. Industry experience may be now judged as more important. The short list may contain candidates none of whom have international experience. International experience is no longer an aspect of the ideal candidate. The ideal candidate now has moved closer to what will be the final choice. An original objective—hiring an executive with international experience—has been displaced.

A common malfunction arising in organizations is due to a displacement in objectives that occurs at one decision unit, while alternatives still continue to be sought at another unit for the original objectives. Another malfunction occurs when the means to an end becomes an end in itself. Or, perceived side-payments may result in accepting a displacement which is further rather than closer to optimum.

Anchoring effects. The extent to which judgments are affected by an initial point of reference is well known (Tversky & Kahneman, 1975). Anchors for organizational decisions are precedents, constitutions, vested interests, known positions of vested interests, and perceived norms. People watch each other's choices if there exists a prominent option which can serve as an anchor for tacit agreement (Schelling, 1960).

Rationally, according to Arrow's (1967) axiom of Independence of Irrelevant Alternatives, a choice made from a given set of alternatives depends only on the ordering of those alternatives in that set. Only available or feasible alternatives have a bearing on the choice that is made. But Zeleny (1981) argues contrarily that, empirically, the attractiveness of available alternatives depends on where the ideal is anchored. The choice between 5 and 10 is trivial if the ideal is 500, but important if the ideal is 11.

With reference to foreign policies, both U.S. and Russian decision makers may have complete domination over each other as their unavailable, ideal option. Rather than making judgments on the costs and benefits of various military defense choices, they are likely to concentrate their decisions on defensive options towards making the chimera of hegemony a reality. For the individual decision maker operating in the context of an organizational setting, the choice to be made among explicit alternatives may be strongly affected by whether the decision maker views the organization as benign or malicious.

Satisficing is accepting a compromise choice which ignores the ideal. Such a choice does not eliminate the gap between the current and desired state of affairs. The extent and scope of the problem are not fully considered. To resolve or avoid conflict, decision makers may even settle for a relatively undesired solution, for satisficing can occur from finding a solution to achieve a desired state as well as adjusting the state downward to meet current solutions. We can satisfice by trying to change the world, or we can adapt to the world as it is.

Political solution: The model of accommodation and adaptation

Harrison (1981) summarized the political elements in organizational choice. Focus is on acceptance rather than quality in the abstract. Decision makers focus only on those policies that differ from existing policies rather than any comprehensive survey and evaluation of alternatives. Decision making is geared more toward alleviating current problems than toward the development and implementation of choices promising long-range benefits. As a consequence only a relatively small number of alternatives are considered. For each alternative, only a restricted number of important consequences are evaluated. Important outcomes, alternatives, and values are neglected.

The problem is continually redefined. An incremental approach is used. This allows for continuing ends-means and means-ends adjustments to make the decision more acceptable. Ends and means are not distinct.

A good decision is reached at this time when most of the decision makers agree on the likely outcome. By proceeding incrementally and comparing readily agreed-upon outcomes with established policies, uncertainty is kept low. The political approach is more sensitive to imple-mentation. The aim is to choose an alternative that will work and be used.

Expediency.   Instead of a diagnosis-induced search for suitable alter-natives, in the name of pragmatism, decision makers may choose to imitate what others have done, what has worked before or what has been traditional so as to have ready justifications for the choice (Pfiffner, 1960). Immediate pressures may force a hasty but not particularly desirable choice. (As Henry IV, Protestant, declared in ending civil strife in France by converting to Catholicism, "Paris is worth a Mass.") They may force the bypassing of a thorough analysis of the problem and a careful weighing of the consequences of the hasty choice. Momentary relief may be obtained from satisficing without really solving the problem (Katz & Kahn, 1966). Other inadequate responses to such threats may be inertia, panic reaction, or various pseudosolutions (Janis & Mann, 1977).

For Zeleny (1981), conflict management aims to move the political compromise toward the unattainable ideal, an overall near-optimization of multiple objectives. Rather than choosing from explicitly avoidable alternatives, sufficient search and invention is needed anchored by the unavailable ideal. But displacement is necessary. As Katz and Kahn (1966, p. 265) noted organizations "cannot maintain their goals in pristine priority without the risk of becoming ineffective or even ex-tinct." Survival, itself may become a salient goal, but if it becomes paramount at the expense of organizational flexibility, it can result in disaster.

Strategic striving: The model of objectives orientation

Managements may not be able to optimize. Nevertheless, they can try to come closer to an optimum solution to reaching a given set of multiple goals. While the process of strategic decision making tends to be disor-derly rather than systematic, it does not have to be.

Thus, Learned and Sproat (1966) rejected satisficing as the concep-tualization of consequence. They argued that firms vary in their decision-making practices from those that are dysfunctional to those that are consistent with normative standards. Some firms can establish overall superordinate strategic objectives which can guide decision units within the firm. Managers can see themselves as stewards needing to attend to such superordinate goals transcending self-interests. Company goals can be more than a bargain between members of a coalition. Firms can do more than follow the decision rule of choosing the first satisficing alterna-tive. Firms can be flexible, keeping their options open. Mandelbaum (1978) suggests that such flexibility may generate more effective choices than what might have even been, at first, considered optimum.

Although the individual decision maker's own level of aspirations leads to satisficing, such may not be in the best interests of the organization which (for the health of the firm, presumably) should take precedence over self-interests. Ordinarily, long-term considerations will be given more weight when one is oriented by the organization's objectives than by self-modified ones, shorter-term in character (Harrison, 1981). However, the reverse is also possible. Long-term, self-interested, career considerations may outweigh immediate needs of the organization. Engineers have been seen to design new equipment rather than use available items "off-the-shelf." This provides a bigger job, a learning experience, and a better resume for the engineer but an increased cost for the organization.

Linked choices.   Choices oriented by objectives are likely to be interconnected because objectives tend to intertwine. One choice may be embedded in another. A tactical choice may be part of a larger strategic choice. One may facilitate or constrain the other. A constraining linkage may prohibit making a particular choice. A facilitating linkage may provide the opportunity to choose which was otherwise not possible. Linkages may affect preferences of the participants for outcomes. An undesired outcome (low pay) may be acceptable in conjunction with an outcome (challenging work) in a linked choice.

Strategy relates to the final outcome that one wishes to bring about. Tactics are chosen to progress towards the desired outcome. Tactical decisions thus are likely to be nested among strategic decisions. A choice among tactics may be dominated by a previously chosen strategy. A choice among strategies may emerge because of the tactics that already have been chosen. A firm may decide to take a strike after weighing clearly defined short-run disadvantages in the short run with less clearly-defined benefits of a longer-term strategy. Thus tactical analysis is partitioned into two components. One is concerned with the immediate consequences of a choice of tactics. The second is concerned with the longer-term effects, assessing the linkages with a desired strategic outcome (Radford, 1981).

To sum up, we see five alternative models of the choice process to which many others such as the garbage can model (Cohen, March, & Olsen, 1972) could be added. The different models may each fit particular limited situations. Near-complete rationality may work reasonably well for particularly well-structured problems; politics and satisficing, for particularly ill-structured ones; and ideal displacement and objectives orientation for trained planners. The constraints may make a big difference in which model best mirrors reality. Cutting across all these models is the question of how decision makers deal with the uncertainty they face and the ways efforts are made to reduce such uncertainty to increase the decision makers' confidence that they are making the right choices.

DEALING WITH UNCERTAINTY

Risk and uncertainty

For over half-a-century, economists have distinguished between risk and uncertainty (Knight, 1920). We take risks knowing the probabilities of success or failure. We face uncertainty because we lack the information about the probabilities. But MacCrimmon (1968) concluded that experiments with business executives showed few making the distinction between risk and uncertainty in their choice behavior and few thought it was reasonable. Whether the missing information is about probabilities of success or about other matters seems of little consequence to the choice process.

Avoiding uncertainty. Decision units are usually faced with uncertainties about the problem, whether to become involved, the resources available to deal with it, external events affecting the outcome that are pending, and so on. Such uncertainty can be equated with lack of relevant information. Uncertainty may be ignored or avoided, without further intervention or negotiation with the environment, or adaptation to it. On the other hand, efforts may be made to reduce uncertainty. Available information may be processed to better describe the situation. Efforts to model and explain the situation may be attempted. Or, more information can be gathered from the environment (MacCrimmon, 1974).

Uncertainty may be avoided by ignoring its sources or crediting the sources of information with greater reliability than warranted (to the detriment of ensuing decisions). But a wait-and-see policy of coping with uncertainty can pay off in building up a more adaptive capability to respond quickly as more situational clarity finally emerges (Weick, 1969). Uncertainty may be erroneously avoided by assuming that the future will be a linear extrapolation of the past or that the future will take place as imagined to justify present choices (Cyert & March, 1963). To avoid uncertainty, organizations often adopt strategies stressing solutions to short-term problems rather than emphasizing long-term plans. Avoided are the difficulties of anticipating future events and conditions, anticipations fraught with greater uncertainty. Again, to avoid uncertainty, an alternative may be chosen because it is assumed that the organization has control over the implementation of the particular alternative.

Reducing uncertainty

While search efforts are directed toward relevant alternatives, the rules and strategies employed in the search are unusually constrained by the desire to reduce uncertainties (Harrison, 1981). Organizations try to realistically reduce externally-caused uncertainty by interacting with their environment and by attempting to control perturbations in numerous ways. They diversify to spread risks, to diffuse responsibilities, or to level variations in income or use of labor and capital. They hedge to transfer uncertainty. They take out insurance, make only short-run investments, accept choices with short-term payoffs, negotiate long-term contracts, collude with competition, form cartels, and administer prices (the industry price leaders are followed by the other firms in the industry when setting prices).

Uncertainty of operations internally is reduced by standard operating procedures and programming.

Instrumental and value uncertainty. Thompson (1967) distinguished between *instrumental uncertainty,* uncertainty concerning causal relationships, and *value uncertainty,* uncertainty about preferred outcomes. One can be uncertain about what is wanted and/or how to attain what is wanted. In a turbulent social environment, both uncertainties are high. Both causal relationships and values are in rapid transition and renegotiable between organizations and institutions. But, increasingly, with the continually political and economic shocks of the 1970s and 80s, organizational decision makers are learning to deal with what Thompson (1967) saw as an untenable situation over a lengthy time period (Alexander, 1972). The result has been that organizations have become increasingly adaptable, structured for quick reaction to unforeseen contingencies. They keep their options open and avoid implementing policies effective beyond the time horizon of known value certainty. Planning horizons are contracted. Long-term bond markets suffer. Long-term investments in research and productivity with delayed payoffs are avoided. This makes difficult scientifically and technologically-driven innovations in contrast to more minor innovations to meet changeable market demands.

Response to uncertainty

With increasing uncertainty, acceptable levels of risk may be increased, but limits will be reached on how much uncertainty can be tolerated (Alexander, 1975). With increasing uncertainty, vision narrows (Feldman, 1981). Perceived vulnerability makes a difference.

In a laboratory experiment Thompson and Carsrud (1976) found support for the proposition that the extent to which risk is avoided depends on the participants' sense of organizational vulnerability. Higher risks will be accepted if it is believed that one is less vulnerable rather than more vulnerable to the vicissitudes of environmental uncertainties.

During the length of time that a decision is to remain effective, the decision maker must assume that the values involved will remain stable. The decision maker must feel that the decision making is based on a stable set of values. The length of time for a planned policy, or the planning horizon depends on premises about the extent the values involved will persist. This is one reason that organizations seek to control their environments, or if not possible to do so, to adapt to them. This was seen by Simpson and Gulley (1962). In comparison to organizations facing little environmental variation in pressures, they found that organizations facing a wide range of pressures were less centralized in authority, emphasized attention to internal communication, and member involvement in organizational activities. But the reverse occurred when environmental pressures were restricted. Again, in a study of 16 social welfare organizations, Aiken and Hage (1968) found that organizations with many joint programs with other organizations were more likely to be decentralized and had more active internal communication channels. They were also more innovative and differentiated, that is, there were a greater variety of occupations in the interdependent agencies.

Lawrence and Lorsch (1969) studied firms in industries such as plastics with much environmental uncertainty in contrast to firms in the container industry which were in a more stable environment. Again, differentiation in internal structure, goals, and interpersonal relations were greatest in the plastics firms, and least in the container firms. Formal integration of efforts to achieve adequate coordination was seen in the plastics industry. But, in the container industry facing a more certain environment, such coordination could remain informal.

Pfeffer (1972a, 1972b, 1972c) found that the more an organization depends on its environment for critical resources, the more likely that its managers are to spend time with outside organizations. Similarly, organizations that depend on outside financing select more outside members for their boards of directors. When firms are more subject to influence by legal regulations they hire more attorneys. As with the social agencies, firms interdependent with other firms are more likely to merge and exchange executives.

Again, as had Lawrence and Lorsch, Khandwalla (1974) found that high-performing companies, faced with the uncertainties of competition, were more likely to differentiate and integrate internally to reduce uncertainty while low performing firms facing the same uncertainties were less likely to do so.

Isolation. Following Thompson's (1967) lead, Bobbit, Breinholt, Doktor, and McNaul (1974) see a variety of ways organizations deal with environmental uncertainties. The organization buffers or shields the technical core from the uncertain vagaries of its environment. It reduces the immediate effect the environment has on the technical operations of the organization. A number of mechanisms are used. One is isolation. Prisons isolate inmates; cult groups isolate trainees. A company moves a manufacturing operation from a strong union area to a nonunion area. A country (e.g., Japan from 1600 to 1853) closes it borders to foreigners and foreign influences.

Buffering. A second mechanism is the buffer to absorb variations created by environmental factors beyond the organization's control. The buffer may be established inside or outside the organization. Organizations can smooth or level variations before they penetrate the boundaries of the organization. Sales promotions to stimulate purchases during off-seasons are illustrations often used to stimulate buying. Utilities provide special nighttime rates to level day-and-night usage. Firms will contract for limited amounts of investment, personnel, time, and effort with satellite companies. The firm itself will not have to expand or contract in investment and personnel as market conditions change. The satellites must do the expanding and contracting.

The buffer can be internal. Inventories of supplies and finished products are established to enable the organization to maintain steady production in the face of uncertain supply and market conditions. The inventory acts as a permeable buffer. Cadres of personnel may be inventoried based on anticipated organization needs.

Cost of buffering. As Bobbit et al. (1967) note, dealing with environmental uncertainties by buffering is often expensive. Monitoring and control activities must be introduced into the flow of inputs and outputs. Special staff departments are required to service the process. Sometimes, the cost of buffering becomes greater than the gains from offsetting of environmental uncertainties. For example, the military services can compete with each other by hoarding in inventories scarce, qualified manpower sources. Too many personnel may be kept in training pools in each service in the desire to avoid possible operational shortages.

Deterministic, routine buffers such as inventories are likely to be preferred over more creative ways of absorbing uncertainties. But high interest rates may demand greater organizational sensitivity to the environment and alternative buffering solutions. For example, it may be less expensive to airfreight machine parts from a geographical inventory center than require scattered inventories closer to the production facilities. Such a central inventory can be much smaller than the combined stock required in all the scattered inventories.

Uncertainty absorption.   March and Simon (1958) noted that as information flows through an organization, it is subject to systematic uncertainty absorption. "The successive editing steps that transform data obtained from a set of questionnaires into printed statistical tables provide a simple example of uncertainty absorption" (p. 165). Uncertainty absorption limits each receiver's ability to judge the correctness of information flowing through the organization. The receiver must remain confident about the editing process since he or she is unable to directly examine the evidence. Direct examination of information is limited to the specialists who gather the original raw data. Direct perception of customer attitudes is limited mainly to the salesmen. The editors who summarize information have a great deal of discretion and can exert influence and power as a consequence.

Uncertainty absorption occurs closer to the source of information when data is more complex and when the organization's language is less adequate. On the other hand, when each unit is likely to develop interpretations, estimates, and premises of its own; central, official editing is needed to assure organizational coordination.

Adaptation and restructuring.   If a more permanent environmental change is anticipated by the organization, variance absorption and variance leveling gives way to planned adaptation. Long-term plans may be developed to transfer seasonally-required employees instead of hiring them at the beginning of each season and laying them off at the end. With anticipated permanently higher or lower environmental demands for its goods and services, preparations will be made by the organization to meet the change in demands. Or, if it does not see itself able to do so, the organization may need to engage in rationing its resources by a reallocation process. High interest rates may make it impossible to borrow funds for the needed expansion. Instead, funds will be obtained by selling some less desired units of the organization or reducing budgets of some of the units to favor the expansion of others (MacCrimmon & Taylor, 1976).

As Duncan (1973) found, decision units in more effective organizations were structured differently under differing conditions of perceived uncertainty and perceived environmental influence. Specifically altered in their design were the hierarchy of authority, degree of impersonality in decision making, degree of participation in decision making, degree of specific rules and procedures, and degree of division of labor.

Organizations can be structured to reduce uncertainty by providing continuing search and scanning mechanisms. More information usually has costs but its acquisition reduces uncertainty. Such mechanisms include market and environmental research departments, subscription to information services, espionage, and so on.

Planning may take the form of preparing alternative scenarios. For ill-structured and complex circumstances, multiple contingent possibilities are handled by decision makers sketching out alternative scenarios based on estimates of the probable joint occurrences of events. The probable need for U.S. military intervention in simultaneous Middle Eastern and Latin American flare-ups can be estimated (MacCrimmon, 1974).

Risk, uncertainty, and subjective probability

Much has been made of the distinction between risk (probabilities are known) and uncertainty (probabilities are not known). In either case, it is subjective probabilities that are important to decision-making, not whether they are known objectively. Executives may base a decision on some probability estimates, implicit or explicit, derived from available data, experience, beliefs and needs. In the absence of information, they fill in some of the gaps with hope and expectations. Thus, they can seldom subjectively remain in a completely uncertain situation. Complete uncertainty is an academic chimera. Subjectively, we always have some sense of information about risk possibilities. As noted earlier, MacCrimmon (1974) found that few executives make the risk-uncertainty distinction at any time and few have found the distinction to be reasonable (MacCrimmon, 1968). Complete uncertainty is the complete absence of information. Yet we know that there is a strong cognitive tendency to fill in for missing information, to project information from one's own experience and needs into what may be an objectively random situation. Cause-and-effect hypotheses will be formed about random events. Witness the argument that the stock market, as a whole, is a random walk and that one can select a broad base of stocks as well by throwing darts at a board as by following the myriad of hypotheses advanced by newsletter and institutional analysts about why some stocks will rise in price and others will fall. In fact, one seems to do better than the market averages by buying stocks neglected by the analysts (Arbel & Strebel, 1982).

Most empirical studies support the conclusion that individuals are not consistent in generating their subjective probabilities, nor as we note elsewhere are they particularly accurate in matching the objective probabilities in a situation with their subjective estimates. Subjective probabilities, for example, may be greater than 1.0 for a set of mutually exhaustive and exclusive alternatives which objectively must sum to 1.0. Some experiments show systematic error in findings. The average subjective probabilities for objectively lower probability events are larger than the objective probabilities; the average subjective probabilities for higher probability events are smaller than the objective probabilities involved (Radford, 1981). In the same way, objective losses seem more likely to have subsequent subjective effects than objectively comparable gains (Slovic & Lichtenstein, 1968).

Probability estimates are further biased by an "availability heuristic." According to Tversky and Kahneman (1973), events are judged as more likely to occur if they are easy to imagine or recall. Likely occurrences are easier to imagine than unlikely ones. Instances of frequent events are ordinarily easier to recall than instances of infrequent events. Availability is also affected by familiarity, similarity, recency, and emotional saliency. All things being equal, we tend to be overconfident in our judgments of probabilities (Slovic, Fischhoff, & Lichtenstein, 1977). However, many such biases are task specific.

The costs of additional information affect how much uncertainty individual decision makers are willing to accept. It may be seen as better to live with uncertainty than to pay the price for added information which would increase confidence that the decision-making choice was the right one to make (Streufert & Taylor, 1971).

Studies suggest that in simple betting situations people may be more comfortable about taking greater risks when they feel that they have the skill to control the outcomes of their decisions than when they feel that the outcomes of their decisions are due to chance forces beyond their control (Cohen, 1960). Nevertheless, in complex decision making in a simulation of international negotiations, the reverse appears true: those participants who perceived that their situation was due to their own decisions tended to take fewer risks than participants who perceived that their situation was due to forces beyond their control (Higbee & Streufert, 1969).

CHOICE AND COMMITMENT

The third constituent of the choice process is the final choice of one particular solution and commitment to it. We have been unable to establish mathematical laws of preferential choice despite considerable effort. Choice behavior cannot be expressed as a simple monotonic function of abilities or scaled values. The task and situation often affect how information is processed into a choice (Slovic, Fischhoff, & Lichtenstein, 1977). The importance of a situation is seen to affect willingness to take chances with it. In Exercise Kolomon—a risk preference exercise—participants accept the riskier but higher payoffs (i. e., exploration for new oil rather than exploitation of known reserves) when the issue is of less importance to the decision makers. Indian policy makers can take less chances with agricultural production because of its importance to immediate national welfare (Tullar & Johnson, 1972).

Our inability to establish laws of choice may be due to the fact that participants use different kinds of rules and strategies as they make a choice. Choices may use different rules at different stages. Early on, participants compare a number of alternatives on the same attribute and use conjunctive rules to reject some alternatives from further consideration. Later on, they employ compensatory weighting of advantages and disadvantages on the smaller set of alternatives. As the decision becomes more complicated because of incomplete data, information overload, and time pressures, noncompensatory strategies will be used (Slovic, Fischhoff, & Lichtenstein, 1977).

Conservatism: The rule or the exception? Slovic, Fischhoff, and Lichtenstein (1977) observed that a complete reversal has taken place in one decade of research about *conservatism*—when integrating probabilistic information to make a final choice. With conservatism, posterior probabilities are produced which are nearer the prior probabilities than those specified by the Bayes' theorem.[2] Conservatism was seen as the common finding of Bayesian information integration research (Slovic & Lichtenstein, 1971). But subsequent research found that conservatism was limited to only certain kinds of inferential tasks. When cascaded inferences are required, as when a physician builds up a diagnosis starting with unreliable cues, posterior probabilities are more extreme rather than those prescribed by the Bayes' theorem. Humans are not good intuitive statisticians according to Peterson and Beach (1967). In evaluating evidence, we are not conservative Bayesians. We are not Bayesian at all. We systematically violate the principles of rational decision making when judging probabilities, when making predictions, or otherwise dealing with probabilistic tasks (Abelson, 1976).

Escalation or curtailment? Within investment decision contexts, negative consequences may actually cause decision makers to increase the commitment of resources and undergo the risk of further negative consequences. After a loss, we may double our next bet.

Levi (1981) completed a simulated military decision-making experiment on escalation or curtailment of commitment of resources as a function of the accountability of the decision maker, the way territorial gains

---

[2] Bayes theorem is a centuries-old mathematical formula for rationally revising one's prior probabilities about an outcome, say, the likelihood of meeting an objective. The equation combines new information with the old to obtain the posterior subjective probability, in this case, the likelihood of meeting an objective in the light of the added new information.

and losses were evaluated, and the perceived stability of the causes of military setbacks. Participants chose to escalate significantly more often when the territorial reference point led them to perceive large rather than small losses of territory and when setbacks were attributed to unstable rather than stable causes. Although accountability for the decisions did not affect the choice to curtail or escalate commitment, it did lead accountable participants to commit more resources if they chose to escalate.

Commitment escalated in a simulation of a business investment decision. When 240 business school students participated in a role-playing exercise, they committed the greatest amount of resources to a previously chosen course of action when they were personally responsible for negative consequences (Staw, 1976). From these results, Staw (1981) constructed a model of the antecedents of commitment to a course of action. First, there was commitment due to the prospective rationality of the perceived probability and value of future outcomes. Second, as a consequence of socialization, commitment became an effort to be consistent with cultural and organizational norms. Third, commitment justified previous actions.

Policy capturing with linear regression models[3]

Hammond (1966) assumed that most judgments depend upon a mode of thought that is a synthesis of analytic and intuitive processes. The elements involved are cues or attributes, their weights, and their linear and nonlinear relationships to both the environment and the judge's responses. The Brunswik's lens model and multiple regression make it possible to derive equations representing the judge's cue utilization policy.[4] Despite what was said earlier about the potential for some degree of accident and randomness in organizational decision making, numerous empirical studies attest to the ability of linear regression models to capture the policies that lie behind people's complex judgments. We

---

[3] Linear regression refers to the straight line that best fits the data from one variable plotted against another. The data points plotted on a coordinate chart of the two variables lie at the minimum squared distance from this line. The slope of this line of best fit yields the product-moment correlation between the two variables when their values are standardized with means equal to zero and variances equal to 1.

[4] Suppose we ask five interviewers to each decide on whether they would or would not hire each of 20 sales job applicants. We also ask them to rate each applicant from 1 to 10 on each of four scales which assess motivation, educational achievement, intelligence, and sociability. We correlate their ratings with their hiring decisions (and the ratings with each other) to determine how much weight we need to give each of the four ratings so that when combined, we get the most accurate prediction of their hiring decisions. These weights tell us how much importance the interviewers attached to each scale when deciding whether or not to hire applicants.

capture the policies of a group of decision makers by calculating the differential regression weights of the different components of their judgments when combined in a multiple regression to predict their final choice. The relative importance they actually attached to each component is obtained as a regression weight (Hammond, 1974).

Linear equations can account for much of the predictable variance in these complex judgments. The coefficients of these equations provide useful descriptions of the judge's weighting policies. They also describe the sources of interjudge disagreement and nonoptimal cue use. The judges studied have included managers, auditors, accountants, loan officers, military officers, trout hatchery employees, and United States senators (Slovic, Fischhoff, & Lichtenstein, 1977).

To some degree, the relative importance of different components of judgment or the cues affecting policymaking is a matter of learning.

Multiple cue probability learning. According to reviews of Slovic and Lichtenstein (1971) and Slovic, Fischhoff, and Lichtenstein (1977), empirical research has established that:

1. People can learn to use linear cues appropriately.[5]
2. Learning of nonlinear functions is slow, particularly when nonlinearity is unexpected.
3. People are inconsistent, particularly when task predictability is low.
4. People fail to consider cue intercorrelations.
5. Feedback is not very helpful.
6. Improper cue labels mislead judges despite adequate statistical validities of the cues.

The superiority of linear over nonlinear models may be an artifact of the tendency to use predictors monotonically related to the criterion rather than a truer description of the complex policy capturing process.

Wright (1974) questioned the expectation that weighting is likely to be stable across different conditions. For example, he found that when less time to ponder is available and distractions are greater, subjects tend to place more weight on negative evidence and use fewer attributes. The harassed decision maker is extremely alert to discrediting evidence on a few salient dimensions. However, if all alternatives contain the same level of an important attribute, then that attribute is of no further significance in the choice process (Zeleny, 1981).

---

[5] A linear cue maintains a simple, constant relationship of increase or decrease with the variable it is signalling. A nonlinear cue bears a curvilinear relationship with the effect it is cuing. For instance, a reward cue seems to bear a hyperbolic relation to its reinforcement of the behavior cued by the reward. At low amounts, small changes in cue have large reinforcing effects. At higher amounts, it takes much larger increases in cue to further strengthen the behavior cued.

Making inferences and applying rules to make choices

In complex decision making, given a multiplicity of cues contributing to predictions of the criterion solution, judges search for rules that will produce satisfactory inferences. The hypotheses they develop about the rule relating cues to criterion is sampled from a hierarchical set based on previous experience. But in using previous experience, judges seem to pay attention mainly to the implications of the most probable events in each earlier stage. They ignore less likely events that could have occurred earlier (Gettys, Kelly, & Peterson, 1973).

Judges underestimate the probabilistic nature of the task and keep searching for deterministic rules that will account for the random elements in a task but since there are none, they change rules frequently and may return to previously discarded rules. Even when informed of the correct rules, judges have trouble applying them consistently, particularly if the rules are nonlinear (Brehmer, 1974; Brehmer, Kuyenstierna, & Liljergren, 1974). Anyone who has played with Rubik's Cube knows that the task remains difficult for the novice to complete even after having been informed about appropriate rules for successful rearrangement of the cube.

Actual choice ordinarily involves a great number of nonquantitative factors. The process is crude. Values and facts involving politics, power, emotions, and personality must be considered along with continuing change and various uncertainties. "The evaluation-choice routine gets distorted by the stresses from information overloads, intentional and unintentional biases" (Mintzberg et al., 1976). Soelberg (1967) sees that with multiple goals, the same one decision maker may accept a marginly satisfactory achievement about some goals and try to come closer to optimum on others. Each alternative is evaluated independently although a fully rational approach would dictate otherwise. A screening process is observed in which secondary constraints are used to reject alternatives, i. e., "that plan requires too many rule-changes." A primary goal may determine the acceptability of remaining alternatives which are then compared, unless an "implicit favorite" has emerged. Remaining alternatives will then just be compared with the favorite and probably rejected.

Authorization

In 33 instances of observed organizational decision processes, Mintzberg et al. (1976) found that decisions had to be approved by higher authority. The unit originally reaching its final evaluation and choice moves the process to higher authority or outside the organization for authorization. Sometimes, higher authority would be asked to endorse initiation or search activities by the originating unit.

The larger the organization, or the environment in which the decision units must operate, the more likely it is to suffer from uncertainty and lack of information about the significant sources of authorization for a sequential decision process originating in a remote decision unit. Or, remote constraints may not be taken into account during lengthy deliberations. Literally, years may be spent trying to find the solution to a problem by those units close to it. When agreement on a choice has finally been reached, only then they may discover some remote authority in the organization or some remote legality which may completely invalidate the final choice.

It would seem useful early on, as a problem is outlined, for a careful search to be made about such remote elements and how to take account of them. Several years of academic deliberation by a committee composed of faculty from psychology and from management, were required to design and receive authorization for a Ph.D. program in organizational psychology by appropriate university councils. Subsequently, one state licensing officer blocked its implementation for another several years by introducing an unexpected interpretation of relevent rules for Ph.D. programs in psychology. The effect, in fact, was to destroy the program before it could be started. In large hierarchies, it is not unusual to find that it takes a decade for an innovative program to be conceived in response to a problem at a local decision unit and for final authorization to be received from a remote authority. Various committees which meet infrequently must be convened. Various bureaucracies must move mountains of paper from inbasket to outbasket. Innovation in such circumstances is a heroic effort.

JUSTIFYING THE CHOSEN ALTERNATIVE

Francis Bacon observed 350 years ago that "the human understanding when it has once adopted an opinion . . . draws all things else to support and agree with it." For Katz and Kahn (1966, p. 261), "Men act first and then rationalize their actions. . . ." Considerable after-the-fact energy is expended justifying the commitment just made. Following Festinger's (1964) cognitive dissonance conceptualization, Zeleny (1981) sees that a process of subjective reevaluation of attributes is initiated. The attractiveness of discarded alternatives is reduced and that of the chosen alternative is amplified. If the decision-making process is dynamic and the components are interactive, then preliminary commitments occur. The ideal, but infeasible alternative, is displaced closer to the set of available alternatives. This is coupled with justifications resulting in a "spreading apart in attractiveness" of the preliminary commitment from the other alternatives. Such justifications increase as the final choice is approached supporting commitment to it. As the final choice is approached, options have become highly restricted. Subjective biases have become dominant. It is difficult to return to earlier rejected alternatives. The usual dominance of rationalization over rationality at this time may be one reason that Maier and Hoffman (1960) found that going back to the same problem after it had been solved the first time resulted in a better solution to it.

If cognitive dissonance is present, there is a selective exposure to information favoring the consonant over dissonant information. Dissonant information is not avoided or ignored, but reinterpreted in the direction of the chosen alternative. New information may be sought, but it is primarily to increase confidence in the choice already made and to reduce regret about lost opportunities. The implicit favorite model of Soelberg (1967) suggests that an implicit favorite among alternatives is found early, but search continues. Other alternatives are evaluated against it and rejected. Commitment to one alternative occurs after other rejected alternatives already have been overtly reviewed and rejected. A confirmation process is completed. Often, participants in a decision process do not realize it has already occurred. The announced agenda for a meeting may be to search for, and to choose, a solution to a problem. The hidden agenda may be to explain a solution already chosen by the executive calling the meeting.

EVALUATION OF OBTAINED OUTCOMES

Open systems models of organizations see the organizations as learning and adapting. Choices are evaluated and the feedback is stored in the organization's memory of information, policies, procedures, and decision rules to provide the basis for subsequent problem identification and diagnosis (Alexis & Wilson, 1967). Over time, members learn why certain behavior has been successful. This is then exploited through deliberate and conscious planning (Katz & Kahn, 1966).

Implementation

To fully evaluate the adequacy of a decision requires that it be implemented. Too often, this does not happen. Yet, without implementation, decision making is an academic exercise. The implementation process is such a vast topic in itself that it can only be touched on here. An important line of investigation by Van de Vall, Bolas, and Tang (1976) points to the importance of coupling the concepts and methods in diagnosis and search to the language of those who will be expected to implement the decisions deriving from the search.

Successful implementation of a decision requires avoidance of conflicts of interest, positive rewards for risk taken, as well as understanding of the decision by those who must carry it out. Trull (1966) studied decision-making processes in 100 organizations. Not unexpectedly, he found that the greater the authority of the decision maker, the greater was the effort made by the organization to ensure the decision's success. Unexpected was the less than rational tendency for managers to accept more uncertainty in the outcomes of their decisions without demanding commensurate rewards. This may have been due to their inability to assess the uncertainties in their decisions. As expected, understanding of what was needed in implementation was greater with participation and open communication.

Participation of the executors of the decisions in diagnosis, search, and choice are also seen as particularly important to implementation. Presumably, learning and adaptability are enhanced by participative decision making. As might have been expected, Cohen and Collins (1974) found that the more effective units in a government agency tended to use participative decision-making processes. (For discussion about the utility of industrial democracy and participative decision making, see Bass (1981; 203–206, 309–330). Particularly, if one is concerned about implementing a decision, participative approaches enhance understanding of the decision reached by those who must carry it out.

An empirical study by Bass (1977) with managers in 12 countries using a simulation of planning and production demonstrated the utility of participation in planning. The reasons included better understanding of the plans by those who executed them, more satisfaction and commitment to them, less conflict between planners and doers, fewer communication errors, validating behavior by participating planners, and less competition between the decision makers and those who had to carry out the decision.

Criteria for evaluating obtained outcomes

Evaluations following implementation may be realistic comparisons to the extent to which the alternative chosen and implemented, in fact, did solve the problem. Or, these evaluations can be used to justify or rationalize the choice made. The evaluation can be distorted by what outcome was anticipated or desired. The biases in the original estimated effects find their way into the perceived outcomes. Rational or rationalizing reevaluations may result in adjusting aspiration levels. Felt success may raise levels; felt failure, lower them.

Kilmann (1976) argued that most critical for the entire decision process is properly conceptualizing how to evaluate its outcomes. Attention must be given to the effects of the chosen solutions on improving the firm's internal efficiency, external efficiency, external effectiveness, and internal effectiveness. Effects on personnel, structure, technologies, environment, and objectives, and objectives of the firm need to be considered.

With more emphasis on the effects on organizational processes, Shull, Delbecq, and Cummings (1970) offered three bases for evaluating the goodness of a decision: (1) the subsequent viability of the decision; (2) the degree of congruency between the anticipated and obtained results with the chosen solution; and (3) the enthusiasm and skill with which the proposal has been carried out. Another set of criteria for evaluating a decision was proposed by Trull (1966): the decision's timeliness, its use of information, and its compatability with existing organizational constraints.

Postdecision cost-benefits analysis

Also required are ways to judge the value of the resulting improvements against their costs. Cost accounting is commonly employed. Expenditures often can be related to organizational goals through suitable cost accounting (Peters, 1973). Even when such is not feasible, proxy measures may be used. The response time of an ambulance service may be seen as a proxy measure of the benefits. But proxy measures may be unreliable or invalid and have to be chosen with care (Radford, 1981).

The practical difficulties of accurate, reliable, and adequate cost accounting make it necessary to combine it with other evaluations. Profitability and growth are additional indicators of the overall evaluation of organizational effectiveness, however, "the feedback loop is so long and the information reflects so many causes that the criterion is less than satisfactory. Rate of growth is even more complicated and ambiguous" (Katz & Kahn, 1966).

Cost-benefit analysis requires measuring both the costs and the benefits of outcomes. It focuses attention on the need to specify the outcomes of decisions in terms, for instance, of marginal costs, sunk costs, and opportunity costs (MacCrimmon, 1974). The private sector usually can rely on sales figures, costs of production, revenues, profits, return on investment, and so on, as objective measures for evaluating organizational performance. It shares with public sector organizations the availability of such measures as training times, employee replacement costs, overhead costs, accident rates, and inventory storage costs. But in the public sector, objectives may not be compatible with economic rationality. The result often is an unrealistic analysis (Treddenick, 1979). As a consequence, various substitutes to cost-benefit analyses have been proposed to evaluate public resource projects including the efficiency method, environmental evaluation systems, value information, and economic uncertainty analysis (Taylor & Davis, 1975).

Estimates of certainty and optimism about outcomes are particularly sensitive to the mutual reinforcement and support that collectivities of decision makers give each other. Whether they are in conflict or in agreement in perception of the problem, possible solutions and outcomes are obviously of particular importance to the organizational decision process.

6

Dealing with conflict

As decision makers strive for a mutually acceptable choice, differences among them in perceptions, cognitions, values, interests, needs, and preferred alternatives give rise to conflicts. This is most apparent in complex organizations with highly differentiated structures, and complex tasks operating in an uncertain environment (Pettigrew, 1973). Conflict is also generated by the differences in the needs and interests of each individual member and the organization as a whole. It is also generated by differences between organizational entities such as departments. Higher authority and greater power may be the basis for resolving a conflict. Or the conflict may be settled adaptively by joint problem solving or by negotiation and bargaining. For example, bargaining will occur among units of equal power competing for scarce resources. Coordinators and arbitrators may be employed. Optimality can be approached through integration of the conflicting interests to yield mutually advantageous solutions rather than merely trying to compromise the conflicting interests.

Narayanan and Fahey (1982) provided a summary conceptualization of organizational decision outcomes as the consequence primarily of a political, power, and coalition-determined process. Cognizance of problems of concern to individual organization members or units *activates* them. They are aroused to the degree that the problems are salient, and they have confidence in their ability to do something about the problem without fear of failure or punishment. Competing claims on time and energy are low. The initially fuzzy problem is satisfactorily articulated so that it can be shared with others who are now mobilized to help. As awareness of the issue spreads, a transitory coalition emerges to pool resources to generate alternatives, select, and agree on a solution to the problem. Divergent preferences are negotiated within the coalition. Differences in power and persuasiveness among coalition members as well as side payments result in a program or plan which the coalition will support in encounter with other parts of the organization whose agreement must be obtained. Here various gambits may be employed, timing or withholding the release of relevant information which will make the favored solution appear a rational choice for the organization. Compromise, accommodation, or better yet, consensus are ways to reach organizational conflict resolution. Real resolution of the problem as originally seen may or may not occur. The problem may be changed, the issue dropped, or action postponed. Often symbolic actions will take place such as a show of solidarity among the coalitions or a rationalizing away of the problem.

One can thus look at the decision process not in terms of problem, search, and choice, but rather in terms of activation of individuals and units, mobilization of others into a coalition, negotiation with other units and coalitions, and compromise, accommodation, or consensus to reach final choice.

But instead of being resolved or reduced through compromise, conflict also can be avoided by inertia, by hasty superficial agreements, or by directing attention elsewhere. Other defensive, maladaptive reactions that may be employed include procrastination, buck passing, or individuals providing uncritical support to each other (Janis & Mann, 1977).

Sources of conflict

One source of conflict is inherent in the organizational decision process. It must meet what may be incompatible multiple criteria of acceptance. The personal interests of the decision makers usually need to be satisfied. Next, the decision needs to be accepted by those responsible for authorizing and implementing it. Furthermore, the decision needs to look reasonable, to have face validity. Finally, it needs to contain built-in justifications and excuses if it results in unexpected outcomes.

A second source of conflict is due to the way information flows in the organization. Instead of an orderly, upward or downward flow through the hierarchy, it follows a grid of communications made up of overlapping, often contradictory and elusive channels (Nicolaidis, 1960).

Disagreements about means or ends can lie between individuals, between groups or between organizations as well as between the individual and group, individual and organization, and group and organization. Thomas, Walton, and Dutton (1972) studied the sources of friction and frustration in departments of a telephone company. They revealed the salience of competitive incentives, jurisdictional ambiguities, scarcities of resources within each department, opposing expectations, and inhibited communications due to obstacles in physical communication as well as to verbal and interpersonal difficulties.

An important source of conflict arises in the allocation of resources which price theory suggests can be done optimally but, in fact, can only approach optimality. What corporate headquarters sees as organizational slack may be regarded by individual divisions as necessary buffers for uncertain schedules. A compromise must be worked out.

The incompatibility of unit and organizational goals may be seen, when, as a move toward optimality, unit profit centers are permitted to purchase supplies on the open market rather than by transfer purchases from a central store inside the organization. Where they buy depends on where the price is lowest. Unit profitability is enhanced, but the possible economies of scale envisaged in one large central purchasing agency may be lost.

For Thompson and Tuden (1959), negotiated compromises are most likely to be seen if the disagreements center about ends but not means. Settlement by inspiring authority is likely if disagreement exists about both ends and means. If disagreement is over only the means, not the ends, then settlement will be a matter of judgment.

The individual versus the organization. A continuing conflict over means and ends is seen in the differences in approach to innovation of the enterprising, compared to the conforming, manager in the large organization. Organizations find it hard to tolerate the entrepreneurial manager. They expect orderly advances. They impose controls too soon on the budding innovations of the entrepreneur who may have to bootleg activities outside the approved budget in order to continue with the innovations. Intolerant of surprises, organizations fail to reward such risk taking. They overemphasize short-term results and fail to look ahead (Quinn, 1979).

Many other conflicts of interest lie between the individual and the organization. The R&D organization, working within cost limitations imposed by a contract, may be striving for a satisfactory product at the lowest possible cost, making use, whenever possible, of available off-the-shelf components. However, the individual engineer may find it more important to design all the components of the new product, forcing up the development costs. The engineer develops himself or herself and gains needed experience in preparation for when the development project is completed and he or she will need to seek new employment.

Managers can face conflict between their personal moral standards and organizational expectations (Carroll, 1975). Available evidence suggests that most often they seem to compromise themselves (Newstrom & Ruch, 1975). Managers in the public sector see those in the private sector as less ethical (Bowman, 1976) but lack of generally accepted ethical standards for management makes it likely that managerial decision makers "will continue to respond to organizational pressures within their own definitions of ethical behavior" (Harrison, 1981, p. 171).

Change, assumptions and conflict. Change, in itself, is a source of conflict in organizations. When efforts are involved to change traditional organizational policies, Mitroff and Emshoff (1979) see win-lose negotiations occurring that maintain conflict rather than integrated problem solving. Organizations seem unable to consider new but radically different alternatives to current policies in a systematic and explicit way. Organizations seem to be impervious and self-sealing when it comes to sharp changes with the past. Policy conflicts seldom challenge the basic underlying assumptions supporting the new and old ways. Rather, contention remains superficial and the real conflicts in assumptions remain unresolved. Data alone are insufficient to convince the opponents of change. Both opponents and proponents can selectively muster the data to provide convincing support for their own positions based on different assumptions. Ego involvement, polarization, and hardening of positions makes any synthesis impossible. A usual outcome is to delay decision until the original problem mounts into a crisis, responded to hastily and inadequately. New policies challenging the assumptions underlying the old policies are what are needed.

The failure to examine underlying assumptions not only reinforces continuing worn-out policies, but it may also make it impossible to even formulate a better strategy, much less get it accepted. Katz and Kahn (1966) see conditions where organizations

> suffer from the failure to recognize the dilemma character of a situation and from blind persistence in sticking to terms of reference on the basis of

which the problem is insoluble. . . . management (may) try a series of related efforts which are doomed to failure because the problem as conceived is insoluble (p. 277).

Mitroff and Emshoff (1979) offer an approach to deal with proposed policy changes systematically involving specifying assumptions, engaging in a dialectic analysis, integrating what emerges from the dialectics to create acceptable assumptions for which data will point to the best strategy.

RESOLVING CONFLICTS IN DECISION MAKING

Conflicts may be reduced or eliminated by the toss of a coin. More often, conflict about the nature and importance of a problem and its solutions may be resolved by the dictation of the more powerful interests in the organization to the less powerful. Or it may be resolved by persuasion. When several decision-making units of an organization deal with a conflicting issue, we are most likely to see the formation of coalitions, negotiation, and joint problem solving.

Authority and power

Problem discovery, search, and choice, as we have noted earlier, can be accidental or random. Organizations can stumble into problems without much awareness; search can be by blind trial-and-error, and choices made by tossing a coin. But much more often, power affects where search will be directed and what choice will be made. The most powerful person may make the choice, ignoring the beliefs, values, and opinions of the others.

Power is used to generate support for one's demands for scarce resources, promotions and positions, when clear priorities have not been established by the organization. The final decisions that emerge reflect the different amounts of power mobilized by the parties in competition (Pettigrew, 1973). The marketing department may have a strong case for increasing the advertising budget which will fall on deaf ears if the president decides to decrease, rather than increase, it because of a personal dislike of individuals in the advertising agency involved.

Individuals may not be able to influence an organizational decision because they lack access to the locus of decision making. Power may be a matter of location or the openness of communication flow in an organization. Whether superior or subordinate, whoever controls the communication channels has the power to decide. This was seen by McCleary (1960) in a prison. The way power is distributed in an organization strongly determines who decides for whom. Classical management calls for specifying where authority is to reside so that someone is responsible for supervising all essential activities of the organization. The industrial pyramid of superior-subordinate relationships and chains of command are mandated. Decision making below is minimized by official structuring of positions with clear, written job specifications and role assignments (Bass, 1981).

Superiors and higher management lose power over decisions if they are seen as illegitimate or incompetent. They lose power if they are rejected as representatives of the unit they supervise and cannot control the distribution of rewards and penalties supposedly available. Subordinates and subordinate units gain power in the decision-process norms by legislation (such as with industrial democracy), by collective action, or by possessing exclusive knowledge and competence. Subordinates most often gain power over decisions when superiors become dependent upon them (Mechanic, 1962). Scheff (1961) described this as occurring between nominally superior physicians and nominally subordinate hospital attendants.

Patchen (1973) conceptualized the interplay among the more and less powerful organizational members in terms of the role and resources of the more powerful, interacting with the role and needs of the less powerful. Table 1 displays the suggested kinds of interactions and their effects.

For Hinings, Hickson, Pennings and Schneck (1974) decision-making power of units within an organization results from their contingent dependency on one another. This is created by their respective needs to cope with uncertainty. A unit is more powerful if it is more central to the workflow, if its operations are immediate and pervasive, and if no substitutes can be found for its contribution to the organization. Coping with uncertainty is most important to a unit's power, followed by its immediacy, nonsubstitutability, and pervasiveness. The public relations department has less power within the firm than the production department.

Based on a study in four hospitals, Jackson (1966) proposed a simpler scheme. Units within the hospitals derive their power and authority to make decisions from emerging approval-disapproval norms and expectations which crystalize the norms. Units are also seen to have different conflict potentials. These interact with their normative power to determine their decision-making behavior. When there is a lot of technical uncertainty, experts can be most influential by serving to reduce the uncertainty. Unfortunately in complex organizations such as large hospitals, the organizational politicians and the experts come into conflict and work to undermine each other's influence.

Persuasion

Decision units are more likely to be persuaded by credible sources. This initially includes implicit acceptance of some of the unit's views. The source as well as the message needs to be acceptable. Persuasion will be easier to accomplish in more ambiguous situations and with decision units lower in confidence and competence. The persuasion will be more effective if it comes from multiple independence sources (Zimbardo & Ebbeson, 1969).

Beliefs about causation may underlie how decisions are reached. If individuals or units in an organization share goals and beliefs in how to reach them (means and ends agreement), the decision will be a matter of calculation. But, if they are in disagreement only about goals, then compromise will be necessary. If they are only different in beliefs about cause-effect relations, the means to reach the shared goals, then persuasive judgments will be the basis of decision (Thompson & Tuden, 1959).

To what extent subordinates in a large Spanish bank will attempt to persuade superiors was studied by Filella (undated). He found that superiors and subordinates at higher levels tended to exhibit about the same patterns in attempting to influence each other. However, at lower levels, although superiors and subordinates did about the same amount of persuasion and reasoning with each other, subordinates were much less likely to bargain, use coalitions, friendliness, or assertiveness, in trying to influence their superiors.

Nevertheless, in large complex organizations, faced with the uncertainties of internal technologies and external environments, authority and persuasion alone cannot make a central individual sufficiently influential as a decision maker. He must be a power broker as was Robert Moses, the master builder, who dominated and shaped the construction of New York State's roads, bridges, tunnels, dams, and parks for over half a century (Caro, 1974). The power broker combines his or her own power and persuasive ability with the ability to form alliances, as needed, with additional sources of power inside and outside the organization. The power broker shapes and controls the formation of coalitions.

Coalition formation

Coalitions are alliances of organization members combining their individual powers, resources, and persuasive efforts to achieve greater influence on decision processes than the members could accomplish alone. Coalitions are commonly observed when conflicting interests are present in an organization.

To increase one's negotiating power, one may join forces with others in the larger organization in cliques, cabals, and coalitions that will

TABLE 1 A framework for analyzing social influence with some examples (from Patchen, 1973, p. 197)

Person exerting influence			Target(s) of influence			
Characteristics	*Resources*	*Decision role with respect to target*	*Characteristics*	*Needs*	*Decision role with respect to influencer*	*Effect of influencer on target*
Expertise; special training, special experience, etc.	Knowledge about how to reach certain goals	Investigates, makes tests, gives information to others	Unexpert	Wants to find best ways to reach goals	Reviews information presented by experts	Sees new options; sees new favorable or unfavorable consequences following various actions
Occupies important position in hierarchy	Control over material rewards (money, promotion, etc.)	Makes request, coupled with promise of reward for compliance	Occupies less important position in hierarchy	Wants rewards controlled by influencer	Decides whether to accede to request of others	Compliance seen as means to rewards
Occupies important position in hierarchy	Control over material penalties (fines, demotions, etc.)	Gives order, coupled with threat of punishment for noncompliance	Occupies less important position in hierarchy	Wants to avoid punishment but maintain self-esteem	Decides whether to accede to order	Compliance seen as way of avoiding penalty but may be seen as blow to self-esteem

Strong; successful; has attractive qualities	Approval	States own opinions, preferences	Less strong, less successful	Wishes to be similar to, approved by, influencer	Hears opinions, preferences of influencer	Sees compliance as way of being similar to, approved by, influencer
Occupies legitimate position of authority; secured position by legitimate methods	Symbols of legitimacy; label of other's action as right or wrong	Announces decision; asks for support	Occupies position of subordination; accepts legitimacy of other's position	Wishes to fulfill moral obligations	Gets request from authority	Sees conformity to requested action as morally correct
Is affected by certain decisions (by virtue of work needs, responsibilities, etc.)	Own cooperation; (may also have some resources listed in other rows)	Vigorously makes preference known to others	Peers or final decision-making authority	Want high level of cooperation from influencer	Decide whether to accept recommendation	Sees accepting recommendation as leading to future cooperation by influencer

Source: M. Patchen. The locus and basis of influence on organizational decisions. *Organizational Behavior and Human Performance*, 1974, p. 197.

exercise influence over promotions and appointments in the firm and give better access to the organization's uncommitted resources (Burns, 1965). The political struggles for scarce resources within the firm are a major source of continuing conflict and bargaining. But despite the "wheeling and dealing," continuing working relations between competing units are maintained by common interests in unit privileges and consensus about minimum standards of efficiency. Conflicts may simply be avoided or reduced, and accommodations shaped in coalitions based on the mutual needs of the conflicting units to continue to live and work together (Crozier, 1964).

Cyert and March (1963) built much of their behavioral theory of the firm around coalition formation. Coleman (1975) described such coalitions forming in educational administrations because of value differences among the groups involved. Stable patterns of interactions between coalitions of groups can be observed. The groups have a collective identity, pursuing interests and accomplishing tasks, coordinated through a system of authority.

Coalitions are particularly important in their effects on how resources are allocated in the organization. Although the organization may strive for optimal distribution as suggested by traditional price theory, it will have to settle for less (Alexis & Wilson, 1967). Corporate staff planners may determine a seemingly, optimally profitable advertising and marketing strategy for introducing a new product. But the manufacturing department concerned with production costs, and the R&D department concerned with product quality may force a compromise. They may demand a shift of some resources from the advertising budget, and a delay in launching a major campaign for the new product, to meet the multiple goals of sales, cost containment, and product quality. Success in modifying the corporate level decisions will depend partly upon the strength of the manufacturing R&D coalition. Conversely, if manufacturing and R&D are already in deep conflict, if the goal of cost containment is completely incompatible with the goal of product quality, the coalition of manufacturing and R&D is unlikely to form. The corporate marketing decision is less likely to be modified.

Cyert and March (1963) saw coalition formation as fundamental to organizational functioning. Individuals contract to work for the firm and to participate in its decision processes. But they differ in interests. Their subsequent goals and commitments are a consequence of negotiation which resolve the conflicts in their differing interests. Such resolution occurs when one coalition becomes dominant. Or it can occur through compromise among equally powerful coalitions. But because of precedents and norms, not everything needs to be continually a subject of negotiation. Past bargains tend to be perpetuated.

Coalitions are less likely to form when rules, objectives, and constraints are clear. However, if the management task is more complex and
unstructured, if the required technologies and environmental situation
are uncertain and unstable, coalitions are more likely to arise to influence
the means-ends decision processes (Thompson, 1967). The traditional
top-down hierarchical flow of decisions free of the influence of coalitions
can only take place effectively where technology has been standardized
and the environment is stable. Within the organization facing many
uncertainties, it is the dominant coalition which usually provides stability. For an individual to become the central power figure, the power
broker in the organization, he or she must learn how to work with the
coalitions. Without these "superb politicians" who can work with coalitions, most large complex organizations become immobilized.

Coalition experiments. Experimental findings are sparse. They
usually employ a triad of participants in which resources are distributed
4-3-2. Most studies support Gameson's Minimum Resource Theory
(1961) that the cheapest winning combination, 3-2, is the combination
that carries the day. The division of rewards within the winning team
(3-2) is consistently between parity (60-40 split of rewards) and equality
(50-50) (Davis, Laughlin, & Komorita, 1976).

Gambits. To achieve their goals, coalitions engage in substantive
and temporal gambits. These are the articulation and rationalization of
their position on an issue. The substantive gambits deal with the advo-
cacy of the desired changes in goals and the means to achieve them. The
temporal gambits are diversionary tactics, "red herrings" to support the
main thrust by focusing attention selectively. The appearance of rationality is maintained (Narayanan & Fahey, 1982). But coalitions and decision
units can move on collectively to a higher form of conflict resolution as
far as the total organization is concerned—joint problem solving.

Joint problem solving versus negotiating

Walton (1972) outlined the conditions under which decision units can
work together to solve a problem, or when they must negotiate an
acceptable joint decision. Problem solving occurs when the joint gain
available to both parties is variable. It is a nonzero sum game from which
both parties can emerge as winners. The earlier processes of decision
making we have presented will be seen. The total payoffs to both parties
will depend on the parties' abilities to discover the compatability of their
interests and to discover or invent ways to work together for their mutual
profit.

On the other hand, bargaining to reach a decision occurs when the joint profit available to the parties is fixed, and as yet, their relative shares have not been determined. Whatever one side gains is at the expense of the other. It is a zero-sum game. One party is likely to attempt to modify the other party's perceptions of the benefits of various courses of action so that the other party will be less resistant to a decision favored by the first party. The first party is likely to attempt to structure the other party's expectations about what outcomes would be minimally acceptable to the first party. The negotiators will take seemingly immovable positions and make threats to prevent the opposition from implementing the same operations. They will rationalize away earlier commitments which become untenable.

> In taking a bargaining position, the verbal or tacit communication is important: How much finality is implied? How specifically is the position indicated? And what consequences seem to be associated with a failure to reach agreement? Each of these considerations requires deliberateness in communicating with the other. However, equally important are the tactics which lend credibility to these communications: presenting one's proposal first, reducing it to writing, and persistence in discussing it; arousing one's organization in support of a position; taking a stand publicly; behaving belligerently . . . (Walton, 1972, p. 97)

Bargaining also usually entails the negotiation of side payments to facilitate agreement and overcome conflicts between opposing parties and coalitions (Cyert & March, 1963). Bargaining thus makes use of a variety of gambits: bluff, persuasion, promises, threats, and mutual adjustments. Or, it may require arbitration by third parties (MacCrimmon & Taylor, 1976). Whether the outcome will be constructive requires further understanding of what is in dispute.

Instrumental versus expressive stakes. What takes place depends upon whether the conflict or lack of compatibility is over instrumental or expressive stakes. Instrumental stakes are outcomes affecting the goal achievement of the conflicting parties. Expressive stakes are the identity sought and the identity accorded opponents by the participating disputants (Walton, 1972).

Examples of instrumental stakes in interagency planning include how much emphasis will be given each party's programs and philosophies, how much of each party's scarce resources will need to be committed to the joint effort, how much control each party will be able to maintain over the joint venture, which party's bureaucratic procedures will be paramount, and how credit for success, or blame for failure, will be shared.

Examples of expressive stakes include being seen as superior (or equal); as similar (or different); as aloof (or committed); or as confident (or tentative) as the opposing party. If both parties identify needs that are compatible, then they can reinforce each other. But when needs are incompatible, assertions of identity by one party will be frustrated by identity-denying actions by the other.

> Initiatives to assert one's identity include self-reference posturing, and telling anecdotes about past experiences that lay claim to the preferred attributes. Identity initiatives also include manipulating the agenda or discussion format in order to facilitate a participant's efforts to do any of the above, as well as choosing physical aspects of the setting for the meeting; for example, the location, the type of conveniences available, etc., which tend to create the appropriate identity. (p. 98)

Identity-denying responses may involve passively ignoring the other party's identity bids, continuing to treat the other party as initially perceived and perhaps deliberately undermining its efforts to establish its preferred identity. Management negotiators escalate conflict with union negotiators by accusing them of failing to represent the true interests of the rank-and-file employees. While continuing identity conflicts will inhibit problem solving, identity reinforcement will facilitate problem solving. Accepting union negotiators as concerned about the health, safety and welfare of the rank-and-file employees can produce agreement on ways to improve both productivity and working conditions. In turn, such problem solving will promote identity reinforcement and reduce identity conflict. On the other hand, bargaining will continue to promote identity competition and to reduce identity reinforcement.

Walton goes on to suggest that problem solving will interfere with bargaining just as bargaining will interfere with problem solving. If one party is pushing for the best quality solution to a problem, its position is likely to be incompatible with one that suggests a compromise around a lower quality solution in order to gain its acceptance by the other party. In the same way, if each party is mainly concerned about winning points in a controversy, the situation is not conducive to a joint search for the best solution to the problem.

Negotiation, of course, is not limited to intergroup relations. For example, in the absence of clear, mandated job descriptions, particularly in technically advanced and dynamic organizations, individuals negotiate over a considerable period of time with other individuals and departments about their job responsibilities (Pettigrew, 1973). Joint problem solving can take place between individuals, between individuals and groups, between groups, between individuals and organizations, between organizations, and between groups and organizations.

Improving joint problem solving. Walton's analysis leads to suggestions on how to move toward optimization of joint problem solving. Since one's bargaining effectiveness is reduced by joint problem solving (for instance, one has to be completely open about one's needs when problem solving), one should try to minimize the mixing of the two approaches. This can be done by agenda, by ground rules, and by norms. Or, it can be done by using different people or different locations to settle different conflicts. Settlement by bargaining over respective shares can be first achieved before proceeding to problem solving.

Problem solving can be improved by developing mutually acceptable and acknowledged identities. This promotes trust, which enhances the accuracy of interpersonal communication and the willingness of one party to expose tentative ideas and judgments to others. By reducing identity conflicts, judgmental "we-they" distortions can be reduced, reducing potential bargaining deadlocks, and improving problem solving. Identity conflicts can be reduced by selecting mutually acceptable negotiating representatives, by clarifying the scope of the required decision making and the extent identities are at risk, by off-the-record discussions where identities are deemphasized, and by confronting the identity issue as an agenda item separated from the rest of the decision process.

It is common for joint discussions to terminate with innocuous or ambiguous outcomes. This is a way of avoiding solutions. Such avoidance occurs readily when the problems involved are long term. Opportunities may be lost by such avoidance, but little is risked and no costs are added to each party's operations. Governmental agencies are inclined to avoid collaboration and to proceed on their own because the combined constraints laid upon both agencies are avoided if each continues to proceed on its own. Interdependent ventures of governmental agencies increase the visibility of each agency to the others, opening it to criticism and attack. Identity may be lost in the combined efforts. Once jurisdictional boundaries are created after forming distinct decision-making units of equal authority and power, it is clear that then trying to coordinate the decision-making units becomes a difficult process. An intervening third party may help two deadlocked units in conflict.

> If the immediate need is to break an impasse allowing a particular interunit decision to be made, then third party interventions can focus exclusively on interunit processes. To break a strictly bargaining impasse involves mediation; to break an impasse based on identity conflict involves conciliation. (Walton, 1972, p. 110)

In his chambers, a court judge can appeal to disputing lawyers who respect each other's identities but who in public must advocate immobile opposing positions. Before trial, the judge will consult privately in his chambers, in turn, with each lawyer in a case to determine each party's level of aspiration. If the plaintiff and the defendant are actually not far apart privately, the judge can mediate the dispute. A lengthy trial may be avoided. Publicly, the plaintiff may be suing for $100,000 in damages but privately expects and hopes to settle for no less than $30,000. The defending attorney publicly has declared complete lack of responsibility for damages but privately expects and hopes to pay no more than $20,000 to settle the matter. An out-of-court settlement may be quickly achieved when the judge proposes to split the difference with a $25,000 payment.

If more general improvement is sought in the interindividual or interunit working relationship, then changes can be made through recourse to superordinate goals to provide better joint payoffs for collaboration. Or, sanctions can be imposed on conflicting units for failure to cooperate. To promote the compatibility of identity needs of the units in conflict, changes in attitude and education would be required.

Integrating the individual and the organization. Argyris (1964) argued that the needs of a mature personality and the demands of a formal organization are incongruent. Individuals seek a variety of tasks, a long time horizon, the use of their numerous skills, and psychological independence. Ordinarily, organizations require limited tasks, limited use of one's skills, a short time horizon, and psychological dependency. The incongruity of person and organization can be alleviated. Decision making can be improved through improving the quality of interpersonal relationships. According to Argyris, openness, trust, and owning up to one's feelings can lead to improved decision making. Culbert and McDonough (1980) started with the same premise as Argyris and emphasized the need to be aware of one's own and others' self-interests. They saw people aligning their self-interests with the task requirements of their jobs. Such tasks can be completed satisfactorily in different ways to meet self-needs as well as organizational needs; for example, by using flextime.

The rapid growth of many advanced-technology firms illustrates how the interests of the organization can be integrated with those of its innovating, enterprising individuals. During their expansion, these firms placed a premium on their own technical and economic development. Needs rather than solutions were defined. Multiple competing approaches within the organization were encouraged. Those ultimately responsible for production and service were involved in the developmental phases. Longer-than-usual time horizons were accepted. Support for risk-taking projects came from top management. Commitment for them was obtained by making clear their objectives and identifying their high value. The organizations were opportunity-driven rather than focused on rationing scarce resources.

Merging individual entrepreneurial and organizational needs for innovation requires opportunity planning. This is portfolio planning which supports long-term, developmental activities. It requires toleration of failure; usually, only a few of the innovative efforts eventually pay off (Quinn, 1979). It requires domination of the control system by the growth strategy. Innovative teams are protected by setting them off by themselves in an autonomous "skunkworks" unconstrained by larger formal units. Such constraints are among the most salient features of organizational life.

7

Constraints on organizational
decision process

To come to grips with organizational decision making, for the purpose
of exposition, we need to take a moving picture of the decision makers,
immersed in the organization, moving through the decision process, as
such, surrounded by numerous constraints. The decision makers may
affect the constraints, but more often the constraints affect the decision
makers in what they do as the process unfolds.

ENVIRONMENT, GOALS, AND TASKS AS CONSTRAINTS

Definition of constraint

By constraint, we mean a driving force or a restraining force, ex-
ogenous to the decision process, which modifies the process. Constraints
can curb, check, hold back and narrow the process, but they can also
push, facilitate, stimulate, and expand it. Although the absence or presence of these constraints makes a difference in the process, they are

ordinarily beyond the immediate, complete control of the decision makers. Constraints limit the available alternatives. But since decisions are future directed, the decision maker usually must estimate the future behavior of the constraints and boundary conditions involved. If decision makers do have control over these constraining forces, the control is, at best, limited.

Sources of constraint

What variables and fixed entities constrain the decision process? Glueck (1976) suggested that strategic decision makers heading business firms are affected by the geography, extensivity, age, size, and power of their enterprise; the technology and volatility of the enterprise's environment; the businesses the firm is in or could be in; and the attitudes and experiences of the strategic decision makers themselves. Tannenbaum (1950) added as constraints in the typical organization decision situation: organizational policies and rules; limitations of individuals involved; climate and physical resources; and money available. Feldman and Kanter (1965) summarily noted:

> Organizational decisions are constrained by the actions of the organization itself, by the physical and mental characteristics and previous experience of its members, and by the social, political, and economic environment of the organization and its members (p. 619).

But the same constraints can have opposite effects on organizations with different tasks and goals. Generally, the small business firm is seen as the site of more rapid decision making, innovation, and change, but fundamental development of such scientific breakthroughs as the transistor or the laser may take the large, sheltered resources of Bell Laboratories. The impact of size on innovations in hospitals, for example, also seems quite the opposite from what is expected in business innovation. Interesting regularities in the tendency of hospitals to be innovative were seen as a consequence of various constraints (Kimberly & Evanisko, 1981). First, in the data from 210 hospitals, the differences in adoption were highly reliable. Second, a correlation of .42 was found between the tendencies of hospitals to adopt technological innovations and to make administrative innovations. According to multiple regression analyses, hospital size (log of beds) made the greatest contribution to both kinds of innovation. Technological innovation was also influenced by the age of the hospital, its specialization and degree of decentralization. But the only other significant factor—apart from size—contributing to the tendency for administrative innovation was the cosmopolitanism of the hospital administrator.

Environmental constraints

A variety of institutions and forces external to the organization limit organizational actions and control the outcomes of its decisions. These include customers and competitors, governmental agencies, parties to contracts, trade associations, and general social customs of the society (Ebert & Mitchell, 1975).

For McWhinney (1968), these differing environments determine *what* aspects of the environment are to be of *concern*, what phenomena should be *noticed*, and what variables should be introduced into the criterion function for the organization's performance. The environment also affects the sense of certainty in decision making and the need for dealing effectively with risk.

A current example of how organizational decision making is shaped by extraorganizational constraints imposed by national and cultural factors is seen in the evidently greater long-range, broader, strategic focus of Japanese firms in contrast to more often observed tactical single-option planning by firms in the United States. The Japanese, for instance, use multiyear market penetration plans. Financing is through massive debt/equity arrangements operating with only "understandings" as to timing and regularity of interest payments. In the United States, subordinated income debentures with income contingency provisions are required (Stanley, 1981) clearly setting out the schedule of fixed payments of principle and interest unrelated to the firm's performance.

Organization needs to match environment. According to Ashby (1964), the decision-making structure of any system needs to match its environment. A variable environment requires a varied structure. Faced with a more complex environment, an organization becomes more complex to deal with it. His concept of *requisite variety* proposes that by adding variety of its own, a system can reduce the effect of the variety being faced. Bobbitt, Breinholt et al. (1974) add that if faced with both a varied and a dynamic environment, the organization needs to respond with adaptive and decentralized decision making.

Since how adaptive an organization must be depends on the complexity and rate of change in its environment, it becomes useful to describe organizational environments in terms of whether, in combination, they are high or low in complexity and rate of change. A complex environment contains varied and interactive institutions, customers, technologies, and so on. A simple environment is one of uniformity. Although both complexity and change add uncertainty to the decision process, rapid rate of change probably generates more uncertainty than does environmental complexity (Harrison, 1981). But complexity is still an important consideration.

Altogether, Emery and Trist (1963) identified four ideal types of environments: (1) placid, randomized (simple, stable); (2) placid, clustered (complex, stable); (3) disturbed, reactive (simple, unstable) and (4) turbulent (complex, unstable). There are only a few small organizations coexisting in an unchanging placid, random environment. There is little difference between tactical and strategic decisions in these small organizations. In the placid, clustered environment, organizations grow, differentiate, and tend toward centralized control and coordination. Causes of events can be identified and best actions selected based on probabilities. At the other extreme, in disturbed, reactive environments, organizations are more competitive. Operational decisions are separated from strategies. Controls are decentralized. In turbulent fields, the environment as well as other organizations within it are sources of uncertainty. Buffering is difficult. The turbulent environment requires internal mechanisms for keeping up both technological change and the ability to make both short- and long-term decisions. Organizations in the simple, stable, placid environment require no such mechanisms, but, mainly, the ability to make short-term, tactical, decisions.

Impact of environmental complexity. The complexity of the environment of the decision has been found to play an important role in determining the match in decision-making complexity which accompanies it. It increases up to a certain point with increasing environmental complexity, then it falls off (Schroder, Driver, & Streufert, 1967). (A more complex decision contains more differentiation as well as more integration of decision elements. Decision integration is defined as a conceptual relationship between different kinds of decisions made at different points in time. Differentiation is defined in terms of the number of independent concepts or categories used by a decision maker. Integration refers to the relationships among these differentiated categories. The number of independent decision categories used is an index of differentiation.) How much complexity in decision making occurs will depend on the experience of the decision makers. For some, the environment may be too simple or too complex.

> . . . the systems differ not only in information-processing capacities, but also in motivation for a particular amount of input complexity. (Driver & Streufert, 1969, p. 277)

But while experimental evidence was found by Streufert (1970) that increases in environmental complexity produce increasing and then decreasing integration, as environmental complexity increased, differentiation increased and then remained constant.

Consequences of failure to adapt. A basic tenet of behavioral analyses is that organizations adapt to their environments. Central to this is the ability to cope with environmental uncertainty and instability (Crozier, 1964). Duncan (1972) studied 22 decision groups in three manufacturing and three research and development organizations and showed that the groups modified their approach to routine and nonroutine decision making depending on how much influence they perceived they had over their environment and how much uncertainty they perceived in the environment. However, in a laboratory study by Leblebici (1975) simulating bank loan decisions, although the external environment affected perceived uncertainty levels, the latter had little influence on decision-making strategies.

Firms ignore their environments at their own peril. The effects can be serious, sometimes fatal. Dunbar and Goldberg (1978) examined 20 European mismanagement cases revealing that external market factors contributed to crises in many of the firms. But even more important was management's lack of appreciation of the changing market conditions. Centralized decision making, unwarranted expansion of production facilities, marketing strategies aimed at achieving sales at any cost, and the rejection of feedback all contributed to the firm's difficulties. In addition, headquarter staffs, who relied on budget comparisons rather than local knowledge, most often halted promising efforts by local managers to turn around subsidiaries in trouble.

By examining decisions of the U.S. Supreme Court and lower courts, Allen (1966) demonstrated that current standard organizational decision rules impose constraints on organization decision makers, even when relevant environmental conditions have changed so much that the expectations of use of a standard decision rule no longer exists. Support was found for Cyert and March's (1963) explanation of this phenomenon. The organizational decision maker avoids uncertainty by using standard decision rules whenever possible. The rules are maintained. Only under duress would they be redesigned. Even when the environment changes suddenly, the firm is likely to be relatively slow in adjusting. It will still usually attempt to use its existing model of the world to deal with the changed conditions.

Boundary spanners. The extraorganizational environment outside the control of the organization becomes a crucial problem for those organizational decision makers at the edges of the organization— boundary spanners. Their jobs can be standardized to the extent the environment is stable and homogeneous. Or their decision making can be routinized in more unstable conditions by special structuring of how to deal with various contingencies. Faced with a heterogeneous, shifting task environment at its periphery, an organization may create specialized structures to deal with its environmental contingencies. In doing so, it removes the need for much decision-making discretion by its individual boundary-spanning job occupants. Contingencies, thus, are dealt with by specialized units or by giving individual decision makers discretion to do so (Thompson, 1967).

Organizational goals as constraints

As noted earlier, Simon (1964) argued that many, if not most, constraints on organizational decisions that define what actions will be satisfactory are associated with an organizational goal. These goal requirements relate only indirectly to the personal motives of the individual who assumes that role. Organization goals refer to constraints imposed by the organizational role, not to the personal motives of the decision makers.

The organizational decision-making system, is likely to contain constraints that

> reflect virtually all the inducements and contributions important to various classes of participants. These constraints tend to remove from consideration possible courses of action that are inimical to survival. They do not, of course, by themselves, often fully determine the course of action. (Simon, 1964, p. 21.)

Assuming the organization is a hierarchy, organizational goals refer particularly to the constraints sets and criteria of search that define roles at the upper levels.

> Thus it is reasonable to speak of conservation of forests resources as a principal goal of the U.S. Forest Service, or reducing fire losses as a principal goal of a city fire department. For high-level executives in these organizations will seek out and support actions that advance these goals, and subordinate employees will do the same or will at least tailor their choices to constraints established by the higher echelons with this end in view. (Simon, 1964, p. 21.)

Given the decentralization of decision making typical of the large modern organization, constraints are likely to differ for different positions and specializations. While profit would enter directly as a goal or constraint for the corporate head, at lower levels, it might be meaningless for understanding the local decision process. Profit will also be a distant or indirect constraint. Thus,

> the decision-making mechanism is a loosely coupled system in which the profit constraint is only one among a number of constraints and enters into most subsystems only in indirect ways. . . . most business firms (are) directed toward profit making . . . operating through a network of decision-making processes that introduces many gross approximations into the

search for profitable courses of action. . . . (This) goal ascription does not imply that any employee is motivated by the firm's profit goal, although some may be.

. . . In actual organizational practice, no one attempts to find an optimal solution for the whole problem (such as a system for controlling inventory and production). Instead, various particular decisions, . . . are made by specialized members or units of the organization. In making these particular decisions, . . . (they) find a "satisfactory" solution for one or more subproblems, where some of the effects of the solution on other parts of the system are incorporated in the definition of "satisfactory." (Simon, 1964, pp. 21–22)

For example, a production head may face cost overruns when operations fail to meet standard costs constraints. In the search for lower costs, it is discovered that longer production runs will solve the problem. But this will reduce the ability of the sales department to meet special customer requirements, constraints introduced by the sales department's goals. Attachment to designated objectives is strongly associated with one's unit identification and one's consequent definition of one's task environment (Alexis & Wilson, 1967).

For the better structured problems, Benson, Coe, and Klasson (1975) proposed an algorithm to take advantage of the symmetry between constraints and goal criteria. They use satisfactory goals to form constraints from criteria, confining solutions to those that can be exercised through constraints. In this algorithm, decision makers react to trade-off information either by specifying altered goals or selecting different criteria as an objective function.

Tasks and technology as constraints

The organization is not merely a passive reactor to its environment. It determines what goods and services it will offer to what part of a larger segment of the total environment. A university's domain, for example, is the role the university claims as its unique task, the kind of student it tries to serve, the particular curricula and community services it designs, and how it differs from competitors in its offerings (Baldridge, 1971). Convenience food establishments define their own domains in terms of the market segment to which they appeal and the quality of service they try to offer. Some emphasize speed, self-service, and simplicity for families in a hurry; others stress table service, larger menus, and quality for adults. The former can organize assembly-line service with employees requiring minimum training assigned to highly specified jobs. Rapid turnover is the rule. The latter need to pay more attention to employee training and attitudes.

The decision process clearly depends on the task it is intended to perform; the purpose it is to serve. Likewise, decision processes may be affected by or may be about the technology employed by the organization. The organization houses the technology which poses contingencies and constraints on organizational actions. The organization's available technology can determine what is possible in problem delineation, search, and choice (Ebert & Mitchell, 1975). ". . . organizations seek to adjust to the demands of their technological core to permit economic and efficient coordination and scheduling of interdependent parts" (Filley, House, & Kerr, 1976, p. 293).

Thompson (1967) conceptualized technologies as long-linked, mediating, or intensive. Mass production operations are *long linked*. The subunits are severally interdependent. The *mediating* technology is one which links, for example, buyers and sellers, as does a securities exchange or real estate broker. The operations of the mediating technology are standardized to facilitate the matching of multiple clients distributed in time and space. The *intensive* technology is seen in customized techniques and services applied in varying combinations depending upon the state of the client. One hospital patient may require an X ray, then surgery; another may require laboratory tests and medicinal prescriptions.

Long-linked technology can remain more closed to the outside environment for longer periods of time through the use of inventories, for example, as buffers. But mediating and intensive technologies, more often dealing with services, have less control over intrusions. Different types of uncertainty are faced as a consequence of the different technologies. Single decisions can be more of a disaster in long-linked technology and more flexible decision making is required in mediating and intensive technologies.

Evidence. Woodward's (1965) study of 100 English manufacturing establishments concluded that the differences in technology—continuous, mass, batch, or continuous production—strongly affected decision processes within the firm. In continuous processing—say in a petrochemical refinery—decisions were usually to introduce or change policies of lengthy consequence. They were made in consultation with committees of specialists. At the other extreme, decisions in custom production had no policy implications and set no precedents and were usually directed from the top.

Khandwalla (1974) used a continuum from long-linked to intensive technology for manufacturing firms, from mass-output orientation (continuous or mass production) to batch and custom processes to study 79 manufacturing firms. With more mass output, more buffering and insulation from the environment was seen needed and provided.

Vertical integration is one way of achieving such security; the firm gains control over its sources of supply, for example. In turn, this leads to more need for decentralized top level decision making as more diverse units must be managed along with more sophisticated controls and coordination efforts.

In several laboratory experiments, Mackenzie (1975) illustrated the importance of the technological imperative. Five-person groups each carried out one of two types of tasks. One task required only the strict application of a set of rules for deductions in proper sequence. The other task required the generation of all combinations of a set of elements. These combinations could not be deduced but had to be inferred. Groups performing the deductive task were much more likely to develop a centralized communication pattern than groups performing the inferential task. That is, with the deductive tasks a single member could serve as the center of communications for exchange of all messages. But to generate all possible solutions, the inferential tasks required more participation of all members, and therefore less centralization of decision making.

More will be said later about how centralized structures as such in contrast to decentralized organizational structures affect organizational decision making.

Combination and change in technology. The mix of technologies found within an organization will be important to consider. Most will involve a combination of long-linked mediating and intensive technologies. As these combinations of technologies increase, the organization must balance capacities among them. In addition, organizations facing dynamic technologies are likely to experience more frequent changes in organizational goals (Thompson, 1967).

The degree of mix and stability of the technologies suggest that different skills and orientations are needed by decision makers responsible for the organization's technology. "The individual characteristics required to cope with the shifts in organizational goals that accompany dynamic technologies seem to differ from those necessary for stable technologies." (Ebert & Mitchell, 1975, p. 43)

Management's role. Thompson (1967) further argued that management facilitates technological performance by buffering unpredictable disturbances to the technological core, or by providing a structure that can react to demands from the technological core. Management mediates between the environment and the technology of the organization. Management helps find ways of accomodating customers by getting modifications in the organization's technology or getting customers to adapt their demands to what is technically available. Those taking the position that the technological imperative is all-important see that the appropriate span of control, number of organizational levels, and degree of formalization, standardization, and specialization are all to a significant extent determined by the technology of the organization (Filley, House & Kerr, 1976).

Differentiation in the cascading process. Decision units in different locations in the hierarchy may value the same task requirements differently, even though the tasks may clearly be specified in organizational manuals. As a decision process cascades downward in the organization, each decision unit will interpret the relevant information about it in terms of its own information needs (Alexis & Wilson, 1967). (This is an illustration of March and Simon's [1958] uncertainty absorption.) What may be optimal for one decision unit following the same organizational decision tasks may be suboptimal for another unit. Each unit's localized conditions will differentially affect its own problem delineation, search, and choices. For example, departments will perceive the situation differently and react differently if their firm initiates a 10 percent across-the-board cut in budgets. An old, established department with entrenched bureaucratic subunits may be unable to do anything but pass on the 10 percent reduction to its subunits equally across-the-board. Another department may see the cut as an opportunity to eliminate unprofitable subunits. It may eliminate some subunits while maintaining others at full-strength or even expanding some to achieve a totally more profitable outcome for the department as a whole.

ORGANIZATIONAL STRUCTURAL CONSTRAINTS

It is obvious that the organizational structure in which the decision making occurs is likely to affect the decision process. Organizations seem to be characterized by an action versus contemplation dimension. Some have the structures that act quickly upon judgments; others are so structured that they more often than not lose opportunities to act (Katz & Kahn, 1966). The city of Pittsburgh began its first study for a mass transit rail system in 1918 and periodically engaged in such studies in every decade while many other cities built and abandoned mass transit systems between 1920 and 1950.

Tannenbaum (1950) noted the importance that must be attached to the decision maker's *sphere of discretion.* The decision maker is limited by the structure and authority relationships unique to his or her organization. Such constraints form an important part of the decision environment for each organizational position. Katz and Kahn (1977) elaborated:

> The organizational context is by definition a set of restrictions for focusing attention upon certain content areas and for narrowing the cognitive style to certain types of procedures. This is the inherent constraint. To call a social structure organized means that the degrees of freedom in the situation have been limited. (p. 277)

Alexis and Wilson (1967) suggested that the organization impacts on the individual decision maker and channels person-centered behavior toward organization-defined ends by means of the whole collection of experiences and expectations developing out of recurring and nonrecurring situations that form the premises for the individual's decisions.

The organization tries to implant dominating premises to control and regulate the behavior of its members (Simon, 1960). Organizational structures provide status systems with defined roles. These become premises for individual decisions. The organization likewise provides experiences and information through training and communication. These, too, provide premises for decisions to influence individuals toward organizational goals.

Decision-making styles depend on organizational constraints. Heller and Yukl (1969) found that leaders of student organizations engaged much more in joint decision making than did senior business managers. The managers, in turn, were more likely than student leaders to practice delegation of decision making to subordinates. Kumar (1977) studied 40 decisions made in 10 hospitals in each of four different organizational contexts. The centralization of influence in decision making decreased with the increase in technical uncertainty and organizational complexity of the decision context. This was due to the need in this context for decision information sharing, power sharing, and risk sharing. The absolute influence exerted in a given organizational context increased with the increase in technical uncertainty, organizational complexity, technical obstacles and individual resistance to change.

Multiple impact

Embedded in an organization, the individual decision maker is buffeted by demands and influences from a variety of divergent sources within the larger organization. The managerial decision maker is affected by a number of potentially conflicting standards and evaluated by them (Sayles, 1964). For example, Hegarty and Sims (1979) examined unethical decision behavior under different simulated organizational conditions. In a laboratory simulation of a marketing decision, 165 graduate business students made a series of decisions on whether to pay a kickback or not. When students were given a letter from the corporate president supporting ethical behavior, their ethical behavior was higher than for those who received a letter that did not support ethical behavior. While profit goals did not influence ethical behavior, an organizational ethics policy significantly reduced unethical decision behavior.

Organizational structure

The required matching of organizational structure to the demands of the organization's task environment to maximize the organization's effectiveness (Ashby, 1964) also is true about each decision unit within the organization and its operations. The decision unit's structure determines the effectiveness of the decision unit's information processing potential (Duncan, 1972).

Organizations are faced with the dilemma of being both flexible enough to maintain the appropriate match with the shifting environment, and sufficiently reliable to provide the necessary predictabilities to keep the organizations from becoming chaotic. Often, the process of developing stability in organizational functioning prevents the system from having the flexibility to adapt when situations change (Merton, 1940). Weick (1969) suggests that the organization can solve this stability-flexibility dilemma by alternating between flexibility and stability in its structuring of activities and simultaneously expressing these two forms in different parts of the organization. Duncan (1972) found some empirical support for such ability to so alternate. When routine decisions were involved, decision units were highly structured (hierarchical, impersonal, nonparticipative, governed by specified rules and procedures and with labor divided). With less routine decisions, the same units operated with less structure.

Forms of organization. Formal organizations may range in type from the traditional pyramidal hierarchy to the flattened federation of semi-autonomous departments. They may be structured around function, product, or project, geography, or combinations of these and may vary in size, shape (tall or flat), and in centralization or decentralization. Clearly, these organizational variations will systematically constrain the decision processes within the organization.

The structures created to handle decision processes depend on the goals of the organization, its technology, and its environment as well as history, culture, custom, and precedent (Murdia, 1978). Emergency decision making is facilitated by a clear, hierarchical, machine-modeled, chain-of-command; routine decision making, by functional organizations; ill-structured problems, by project teams; flexibility, by matrix organizations; and shared participation in decision making by the linch-pin plan.

The classical, *hierarchial organization* is predicated on the traditional authority structure with downward flows of decisions. Authority originates at the top and spreads in a downward pyramid by delegation. Unity of command and obedience to higher authority is expected so that response to emergencies can be rapid and unquestioning.

Functional organizations are most typical. They are structurally defined by means-end analysis. The members are grouped by the function they perform: production, marketing, purchasing, and so forth. In the functional organization, all unit heads dealing with a function—say manufacturing—report to successively higher heads of manufacturing.

At the top there are parallel heads for other functions such as marketing and employee relations. In the *product organization*, a miniature organization for all functions is repeated for each product line of the larger organization. Replications in different geographical locations, functionally or by product, may also occur as organizations enlarge.

The *functional organization* appears to be most appropriate for carrying out routine, repetitive work. Differentiation in goal orientation is possible. The functional structure also permits a degree of integration sufficient to get the organization's work done. Much of this can be accomplished through paperwork and through the hardware of production. Emerging conflict can be dealt with more safely through the management hierarchy, since the difficulties of resolving conflict are less acute. This is so because the tasks provide less opportunity for conflict and because the specialists have fewer differentiated viewpoints to overcome. This form of organization is less psychologically demanding for the individuals involved (Walker & Lorsch, 1968).

The *project organization* is composed of temporary work groups brought together to accomplish a specific purpose, usually for a few months to a few years. It is disbanded when the project is completed. Studies of high-technology programs have demonstrated that functional organizations, where expertise in specific areas can be maintained, achieve greater technical superiority of output. But, project organizations can meet tighter time and cost schedules (Marquis, 1969).

Walker and Lorsch (1968) suggest that if the task is problem solving, the *product organization* seems to be appropriate, particularly where there is a need for tight integration among specialists. The product organization form allows the greater differentiation in time orientation and structure that specialists need to attack problems. Identifying with a product under a single head encourages employees to communicate openly with each other and to deal constructively with conflict.

In the *matrix organization*, personnel are permanently housed in functional units where they tend to interact with peers having similar skills. But simultaneously, they are temporarily assigned to projects where the budget and schedule are controlled by the project manager. The matrix organization, combining functional and project attachments for its members, creates problems of dual allegiance to the home department versus the project team. However, it is seen to foster more flexibility, better control of projects, lower costs, better customer relations, and shorter development time (Middleton, 1967). Decision-making processes in the matrix organization are likely to be influenced more readily by those with specialized information, informal leadership abilities, and knowledge of how to integrate lateral processes (Knight, 1976).

Likert (1967) introduced a modified hierarchy in which each unit head was also to operate as a member of a group of all his or her peers and their head—the *overlapping groups* or *linch-pin organization*. This was to facilitate vertical communication and wider participation in decision making. Healey (1972), in a laboratory experiment, contrasted an organization with a linch-pin structure and an organization with the more classical line-staff bureaucratic structure to see which would make better nonprogrammed decisions. Initial levels of performance and rates of improvement failed to differ systematically. Lower level personnel in simulations of the traditional hierarchies were less satisfied with the decision-making processes than those with linch-pin structures, but, the top levels in traditional hierarchies were more satisfied with the decision-making processes than their counterparts in the linch-pin structures. However, Likert's numerous field studies (Bass, 1981) provide considerable evidence of the efficacy of the shift of organizations toward the linch-pin arrangement.

Rice and Bishoprick (1971) examined other variations from the typical, pyramidal hierarchy. The *egalitarian model* is based on the voluntary cooperation of the organization's members. Military expeditions of mercenaries who elect their captains and participate for a share of the spoils are illustrative. So are the typical voluntary fraternal and professional organizations. Despite the theoretical equality of membership, most of the decision making is concentrated in the hands of the small, most active, executive committee and the officers at the top.

Federations of autonomous units usually engaged in diverse specializations are illustrated by the business conglomerates with individual profit centers. Management puts the federation together, supplies the units with information, and monitors performance. But most operational decisions take place within the units.

Then there is the *collegial* organization of faculty and administrators. Ideally, technical decisions mainly take place within the units of independent, egalitarian, faculty specialists, limited to their areas of expertise. Housekeeping and support functions lie with the administration which is likely to be organized in a traditional hierarchy. Coordination of decision making is achieved through committees, review boards, administration, dogma, and tradition. Helsabeck (1971) interviewed administrators, faculty members, and students at six small liberal arts colleges about the effectiveness of decision making at the institutions. He concluded that effectiveness would be increased if an overall, highly-participative community senate was responsible for the allocation of resources and authority. But separate, smaller decision-making groups were seen as best suited to deal with decisions requiring special expertise and little spillover to other groups.

Dual hierarchies of technical and commercial direction are standard in German firms. Along with commercial interest, they display a considerably increased concern for technical quality at the highest organizational level. The Spanish Colonial Empire made use of a church hierarchy paralleling civilian and military hierarchies. The redundancy, although generating conflict at lower levels, increased the reliability of the upward flow of information to the top.

Role expectations as constraints

Different organizational structures constrain unit or member decision making in different ways primarily by the role expectations they establish for their members.

> Under *autocracy*, roles are defined by the superior, and the superior directs the activities of the subordinate. . . . there are only two roles. The first is a universally capable subordinate, who can do any job assigned to him, if he has the proper direction. The second is a universally capable superior, who can direct the activities of any subordinate on any job that needs to be done. All wisdom, analytic skill, and knowledge are concentrated in the person of the superior. The model is work oriented, and socio-emotional considerations are ignored. . . .
>
> In a *bureaucracy*, role expectations are . . . embodied in a set of rules, job descriptions, and policies which are then interpreted by the role incumbent. This puts more discretion with the subordinate, and makes the superior more of a planner-judge than a director of operations. It greatly increases the superior's scope, at the expense of his direct control over role performance. (Rice & Bishoprick, 1971, p. 203)

In a *systems* view of organizations, responsibilities for decision making may arise from the demands of one's own job; and from the need to accommodate the interests of superior, peers, subordinates, clients, and regulatory agencies. Some responsibilities are established by policy, others by precedence, custom, or contract with union or government.

In collegial organizations, decision making is dominated by professionalism. The administrative superior, ideally,

> is completely removed from the direction of the professional's job performance, and confines his attention to problems of maintaining the professional's work environment and to utilizing his output. The superior consults the professional as a client, rather than as a work director, and because the professional's role is so well defined, the superior can be confident of the incumbent's behavior. (Rice & Bishoprick, 1971, p. 204)

Bureaucratization

Organizations vary in the degree of their formality and governance by rules. The *bureaucracy* is at one extreme; the *informal* organization is at the other. The rational-legal structure of bureaucracy is characterized by a continuous organization of functions bound by rules. New solutions are not required for each situation. Clients are served in a standardized way.

As long as a situation remains stable, bureaucratic decision-making suffices. When a situation becomes unstable, more flexibility is required. In a study of the decision about continuing the Reserve Officers Training Corps at Stanford University, Benner (1974) examined documents, interviewed personnel, and observed events as they occurred. He concluded that when the issue moves from stable to dynamic, decision making changes from bureaucratic to political.

Each role in a bureaucracy covers a specified sphere of competence, obligation, authority, and responsibility. Decisions of labor and hierarchical control are observed. Ostensibly, bureaucrats fill a position based on their training and knowledge of the technical rules and norms. Authority is given to match merit or skill. Skill includes the ability to deal with technical and ritualistic requirements along with an appropriate set of values (Weber, 1947).

Bureaucracies, with their characteristic formalism, hierarchy, specialization, rules, impersonal relationships, unity of command, limited spans of control, and delegation of routine matters, provide the formal framework for routine decision making by establishing (1) a common set of presuppositions and expectations; (2) subgoals to serve as criteria of choice; and (3) intelligence responsibilities in particular organizational units (Simon, 1960). Nevertheless, although the bureaucracy's officials seek to attain their subgoals consistent with organizational considerations, they have distinct sets of self-interests in power, income, prestige, security, convenience, loyalty, pride in work, and desire to serve the public. They can be typed as climbers, conservers, zealots, advocates, or statesmen. Selective recruitment, indoctrination, and ideology influence their decision making (Downs, 1966).

As a bureaucracy demands increasing reliability of behavior from its members, personal relationships are reduced, the rules of the organization are internalized by its members, and there is an increase in restricted categorization for decision making (Merton, 1936, 1940). That is, each problem is examined in terms of a small number of categories; the first applicable one is chosen. Search is reduced by the restricted categorization. But along with the intended emphasis on reliability and defensibility of individual decision making comes unintended behavioral rigidity, defense of status, difficulty with clients and felt need for defending individual actions. Behavior becomes patterned (March & Simon, 1958). Patterned behavior denies innovative, spontaneous, or opportunistic decision making.

Specialization promotes compartmentalization. The same exact water resources problem is diagnosed differently by bureaucrats in the offices of engineering, economics, and social sciences of the same larger bureaucracy. The goal of optimizing use of the available water is further displaced by personal interests and sets of traditions, whose maintenance become ends in themselves. Displacement also occurs since job performance of incumbents is evaluated by their success in abiding by the rules, not in achieving the functional purposes for which the organization was established.

Informal relations are discouraged making the bureaucracy unable to deal with unforeseen problems and the socioemotional needs of its members (Rice & Bishoprick, 1971).

Yet, bureaucratic (rational-legal) decision making is likely to be more effective than allocating decision making *informally* to specific individuals because they happened to be the most powerful, esteemed, liked, or valued members of the group (Price, 1968). This is seen in street-corner gangs, for example (Caplow & McGee, 1958). Where all members of a decision-making group are of equal status (power of position) as in an initially leaderless discussion, emergence as the leader is a struggle for the temporary position and is associated with personal ability, esteem and likeability (Bass, 1960). Such conflict is avoided or regulated in a bureaucracy where decision making is allocated to roles rather than to individual persons.

Moreover, for the larger organization, the rational-legal bureaucratic style is preferred to authoritarian rule-by-person, in which decision-making power is lodged in "founding fathers," esteemed leaders, or individual entrepreneurs. In such organizations, subordinates are subject to the whims of superiors. Expectations are more easily isolated. Instability is more common although such organizations are able to change more quickly.

Otton and Teulings (1970) found in studying the succession of 34 department heads, that if there was more bureaucratization in a department, there was less likelihood of selecting a "strong" decision maker for successor as department head. But if the successors were outsiders formerly, or were strong leaders, a rebureaucratization process was likely to be initiated by them. (This fits the general proposition that groups lacking structure to complete tasks find structuring leaders more effective.)

Centralization versus decentralization.

Organizations vary in the degree to which they are *centralized* or *decentralized* in decision making. Centralization is greatest when all the decisions are made by a single person in the organization. Centralization is least when each individual unit in the organization shares equally in the making of decisions or makes decisions autonomously. Most organizations lie somewhere in between (Baum, 1961). Decentralization makes more flexible coordination among activities possible. The executives involved are less restricted. Decentralized executives seem to spend less time altogether transmitting or giving orders and decisions (Ebert & Mitchell, 1975).

With decentralization, responsibilities and expectations are a compromise between the requirements of central authority and the demands of local conditions. Host-country nationals who work for multinational firms, for instance, must be versatile and creative in compromise decisions where conflict emerges between parent international company and local institutions. Autonomy frees individual decision-making units to pursue some local goals and still cooperate with other units. The organization benefits in innovation and creativity.

Training opportunities are provided for future top corporate managers with decentralization by giving them increased responsibility and experience in decision making at lower decentralized levels. Also, top management does not have to deal with many smaller problems costly in use of its time. The larger but decentralized organization can work well if objectives are shared and self-discipline is present. Top management can concentrate on goals and strategic decisions; lower levels of management on operational decision making. Top management is consultative, coordinating, and supporting, allowing subordinate executives to pursue self-defined objectives consistent with the larger organizational goals (Rice & Bishoprick, 1971).

Using a computer simulation, Taylor (1976) did find that, as expected, decentralization promoted innovation. And, according to a study of South African and U.S. firms, decentralized decision making with its greater flexibility of response was more effective for those firms facing a highly competitive environment (Orpen, 1978). But Indik (1965) failed to observe the expected relationship.

Centralized decision making requires that the decision-making unit have the information necessary to make the decision, information available at the lower or peripheral levels. The cost, in both time and money, of sending adequate and accurate information to a central place must be weighed against the possible loss of control and coordination when lower-level or peripheral personnel make the decisions.

Centralized decision making is likely to be found when the organization is owned by a parent organization or higher authority. Such was the case in for 116 British, 21 U.S. and 24 Canadian manufacturing firms, as well as for a number of British service organizations. Howes (1963) looked at the effects of centralized decision making in the Cooperative Extension Services of 13 states composed of land-grant institutions at the center of the extension service and county agencies at the periphery. Centralized decision making was more common if funds were centralized at the land-grant institutions. But where decision making was more decentralized, the director could spend more time on public relations and less on internal organizational matters. Staff turnover was less under decentralization but there was less agreement about objectives between field staffs and supervisors.

General Motors has long been touted as the epitome of a large decentralized organization (Drucker, 1946; Sloan, 1965). But more careful scrutiny reveals that increasingly over time decision making was moved to corporate headquarters and away from the divisions.

> . . . decisions as trivial as leg room, and as important as basic styling, body design, advertising, pricing, capital investment, pollution control, and scheduling in factories that assemble cars for several divisions, are not in the division manager's hands. They are made at the top. The division manager is not thereby reduced to the status of a clerk; in an enterprise as large as, say, the Chevrolet division, he has a great deal to do, and the decisions he makes are important ones indeed. But he is not influencing the goals of the organization in any very meaningful sense. General Motors is a highly centralized organization; it just happens to be big and produce a variety of cars, weapons, trucks, locomotives, and so on, so that the density of decision making is correspondingly greater. (Perrow, 1972, pp. 172–73)

Part of the problem may lie in the difficulty in accurately assessing whether an organization really is, or is not, decentralized. It may be for some types of decisions—say marketing decisions—but not about others, such as finance. For example, international firms must depend heavily on local country advertising specialists rather than attempt to dictate advertising copy from parent headquarters. But, at the same time, they may impose highly-centralized production methods everywhere within the multinational organization. Bylsma (1969) found that the introduction of collective bargaining decentralized decision making in six Michigan community colleges but only for some problem areas such as salaries, class size, academic calendar, continuing contract, work load, and time assignment. Other aspects of academic governance such as academic programs remained centralized.

Controls

In some organizations, constraints that automatically trigger decision making are seen in the type and amount of controls imposed by policy, rules, norms, and sanctions. Here, organizational decision making can become automatic. Two types of automatic control systems are *feedforward* and *feedback*. In feedforward control, deviations or variances from standards are predicted. Then, actions are taken in advance to compensate for anticipated deviations. In the more familiar feedback control, an observed deviation, discrepancy, or variance is used to correct the ongoing system. Both types of control are shown in Figure 4.

FIGURE 4   Feedforward and feedback control

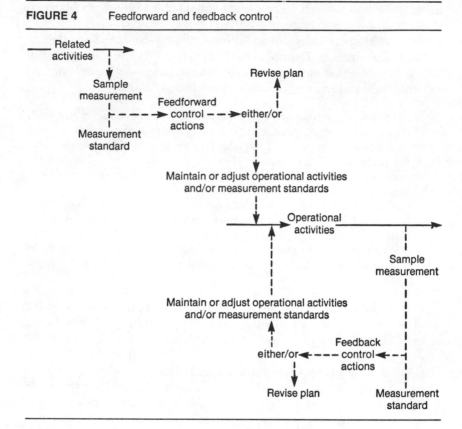

From A. C. Filley, R. J. House, & S. Kerr, *Managerial Process and Organizational Behavior* (Glenview, Ill.: Scott Foresman, 1976,) p. 444.

As sales volume rises or falls, feedforward control can be used to make adjustments in advance of inventories, production volume, purchase schedules, and employment. Adjustments can be made based on sales forecasts to maintain a predetermined relationship of costs and activities to income. Staffing can be based on new sales orders. But strong, well-defined, highly predictable relationships are required for depending on such feedforward controls (Filley, House, & Kerr, 1976).

Among its many uses, feedback is employed to control production quality. Finished goods are sampled by inspectors who compare them against predetermined standards. If deviations are observed, directions are sent to the operators to adjust the production methods to correct the deviations. With extreme deviations, new plans of production may be required.

Feedback must rely upon error as the basis for correction and only begins after an error has taken place. Because there is a time lag between a deviation from standard and the consequent corrective action, actual performance fluctuates around the standard. Feedback speed becomes important.

Unobtrusive controls. The organization does not control decision-making processes as much as the premises upon which the decisions are founded. These premises include the vocabulary that will be used and the preference ordering of goals likely to arise out of negotiations among the subunits of the organization (Simon, 1960).

Perrow (1972), following March and Simon (1958), provided an insightful understanding of how organizational decision making for less well-structured, nonroutine problems is shaped by a complex set of mechanisms rather than merely a set of specified rules, as suggested by conventional wisdom. These mechanisms unobtrusively control the premises upon which the decisions are made. The general argument is that the individual within the organization does not make decisions based on the prescribed rules for the unit; nor are the decisions based on selfless professional judgments. Rather, various mechanisms such as uncertainty absorption, organizational vocabularies, available communication channels, and interdependencies of units and programs, affect organizational behavior by limiting information content and flow, thus controlling the premises available for decisions. These mechanisms also set up expectations which focus on only some aspects of the situation. This further limits the search for alternatives. They indicate the threshold levels at which a discrepancy requires decision making, thus promoting satisficing rather than optimizing behavior (Perrow, 1972).

Formalism as a constraint

Attention to the formalities of the decision-making process is of considerable consequence. Making convincing presentations to management committees is one requirement for the successful executive or sales representative. In France, in particular, "the fetish for an elegant irreproachable presentation is such that . . . 'when a problem is well presented the solution is adopted even if the solution is not as good as the presentation'." (DeGramont, 1969, p. 446–447) Whether "due process" has been observed in the events leading up to a decision will determine the acceptance or rejection of a decision and the legitimacy of actions based on it. Due process is based on custom, on organizational charter and constitution, on contract and on the laws of the land. Organizations with grievance procedures for employees to follow and collegial organizations, for instance, attach great importance to due process as the means for ensuring the fairness with which decisions will be made.

Degree of formalization

Extreme formalization in the organization, as a whole, causes an inability of the organization to deal with its socioemotional problems, particularly in a rapidly changing environment. This was seen in a survey by Gebert (1977) of 600 managers from 30 West German firms. Again, Delaney (1978) observed that organizations more oriented toward form than toward purposes, needs, and capabilities were more likely to adhere to established routines and procedures.

Highly formalized organizations are likely to be relatively inefficient. However, Paulson, (1974) found in data from 135 health and welfare organizations, that formalization coupled with decentralization, did tend to produce more effective bureaucracies, although not necessarily more efficient ones when costs of effectiveness were considered.

Dealing with ambiguity is a key to effective decision-making relationships in highly formalized structures because of the opportunities it offers calculating actors dealing with reciprocity, authority, and jurisdictional relationships. Promotion comes more readily to the individual who can distinguish between form and substance, and favors form over substance (Delaney, 1978). (Contrarily, in the Japanese scheme of things, individual behavior following an agreement is more important than what is written in the agreement.)

Much of the impact of the formal structure is conditioned by how much organizational change is underway. Particularly affected are the middle managers involved in the direction, rate and consequences of such change (Billings, 1974).

THE IMMEDIATE GROUP AS A CONSTRAINT

The small group within the organization plays an important role in the decision process. Top management, as a whole, is seen to operate like a small, informal group (Glickman, Hahn, Fleishman, & Baxter, 1969). At lower levels, individual decision makers are likely to be strongly constrained by the norms and aims of the close associates that make up their immediate group, particularly if the group is highly cohesive. Fortunately, a vast literature is already available on small group decision making (See McGrath & Altman, 1966, for example). More specifically, how individual preferences combine to form the final group decisions is the subject of a variety of lines of investigation. Davis (1973), for instance, has provided a model which builds probability distributions for the group from those of its individual members.

Generally, groups facilitate rather than inhibit effective decision making. A group decision will be better than the decisions of individual members working alone (Bass, 1960). To illustrate, 23 undergraduate teams of 6 to 9 students each took a final multiple choice examination for a class in organizational behavior conducted by the author. They completed the examination first individually, then as teams. Not only were team scores for correct answers, as expected, better than those of the average team member, but for 21 of the 23 teams, the team scores were better than the highest scoring member of the team. Yet, whether committees facilitate or inhibit organizational decisions, according to Decker and Johnson (1976), depends upon their size, their chairperson and members, their working methods, and their secretarial assistance. Obviously, their official and unofficial *raisons d'être* will also make a difference in whether and when they help or hinder organizational decision processes. Hobbs (1976) found it important to distinguish between two patterns emerging in the organizational roles of university committees: the deliberative, collective, decision-making role of member-dominated committees and the one-person advisory role of chairperson-dominated committees.

Depending on the task, there is an optimum number of members, ranging from one to many, that will ensure the highest quality group decision making. Each additional member adds helpful information as well as redundancy and increasing communication complexity. If all the required information to make the quality decision is available with one member alone, then adding members is inefficient. Only when additional members provide more information without more complexity is quality promoted (Bass, 1960).

Bass, McGregor, and Walters (1977) did find that foreign investment decisions of U.S. firms were judged more effective when made by task forces and boards of directors than by the president or individual executive. A survey of several thousand readers of the Harvard Business Review is generally supportive of the need for committees and their positive contributions to the organization (Tillman, 1960). Schoner, Rose, and Hoyt (1974) compared the quality of decisions on three economic problems for individuals, two forms of real five-member groups, and three nominal or synthetic groups designed around specific decision rules. Both types of real groups outperformed individuals. That is, real group decisions were better than those of their average individual member. But as is usually the case, the real group decisions were inferior to those of the best member. Real groups with no previous experience with the problems made better decisions than did groups whose members had previously made individual decisions on the same tasks. Presumably, in groups where members first decided for themselves, it was difficult to move the average member from his or her commitment toward the possibilities of a better group decision. The real groups also made decisions superior to the synthetic group in which a plurality could decide for the group.

Certain theorists such as Steiner (1972), however, have been able to identify group conditions in which instead of an "assembly bonus effect" from group effort, there are accumulated interferences resulting in losses rather than gains over individual performance. Such occurs in brainstorming for instance, where the individuals in nominal groups usually produce more quality and quantity of ideas than they do when assembled in real groups working together (Campbell, 1968). "Groupthink" in organizations has its costs. As Janis and Mann (1977) have documented, when faced with threats, groups of executives within the organization are likely to procrastinate, pass the buck, and bolster each other's rationalizations. The defensive avoidance is maintained by the mutual support members give each other.

Group deliberations remain a fact of organizational life. What is needed is the education of its members as to the beneficial and deleterious constraints it imposes on their decision making. This is particularly true for groups in which consensus, majority vote, or emerging decisions will be made by a leader strongly influenced by consultation with the members such as is likely to occur among professionals expected to work on highly unstructured problems. This will permit the final decision to reflect more of the influence of the most competent and informed members rather than those who merely are higher in level in the organizational hierarchy in which the immediate decision group is embedded.

Types of teams

Delbecq (1967) and Shull, Delbecq, and Cummings (1970) identified four types of teams of specialists and how their processes are dependent or independent of the larger organization. Whether the specialists are cosmopolitans or locals and whether the team task is repetitive or unique are important considerations. Figure 5 displays four types of decision-making teams: routine, engineered, craft, and heuristic. These idealized types of teams are thought to be the optimum matches for the four combinations of task demands and necessary personnel.

In the routine group of technical locals with repetitive tasks, the decision unit is a staff with an appointed leader. It is most system oriented. The group concerns itself with specifying quantity and quality objectives, along with critical control points and sequencing. Economy and efficiency are sought by the group. Higher authority specifies objectives and clarifies contingencies. Control is by control points and individual responsibility.

FIGURE 5   Structures of organizational units

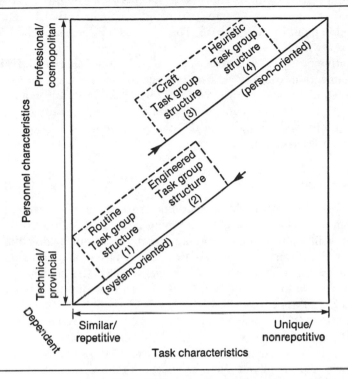

F. A. Shull, Jr., A. Delbecq, and L. L. Cummings, *Organizational Decision-Making* (New York: McGraw-Hill, 1970), p. 192

In the engineer group, when tasks are nonrepetitive, but technical specialists are still required along with a designated project leader, the group process is characterized by control points, periodic review, and specific quantity and quality objectives. There is more independent planning and individual responsibility, with strong emphasis remaining on economy and efficiency. There is more negotiation with higher authority about the inputs and outputs of the project unit. Feedback mechanisms about the adequacy of performance are available.

In the craft group, the "tailor-made" definition and solution of problems reside with the group of skilled personnel. The task may still be somewhat repetitive. The decision team is more likely to engage in independent action, diagnosis, and consultation with peer review. There will be consultations with higher authority for planning and control. Professionalism is the norm.

Finally, in the heuristic teams, faced almost exclusively with non-repetitive, ill-structured tasks, independent analysis and solution with full participation and majority rule (or consensus) is pursued by the team. It is most person oriented. There is open support or disagreement. There is little time constraint. Creativity is sought. Higher authority seldom is involved in planning and control. These are usually accomplished by the group as a whole.

Effective group work is critical to the success of Likert's (1967) linchpin organization. Moving traditional organizations toward more democratic systems was seen to have long-term payoffs in 40 organizations involving over 200,000 employees. Kennedy (1966) sees the emergence of such a scheme for the California State College system. (For a review, see Bass, 1981, pp. 302–308.)

The risky shift

Probably the most highly-researched team effect on decision making has been the risky shift, the tendency of individual members to accept more risk in some problem-solving situations when making the same decision as a group than when acting alone. Discussion and consensus increase the risky shift (Wallach & Kogan, 1965). The shift is increased when responsibility is felt to be diffused and no one member can be blamed for failure (Kogan & Wallach, 1967).

The group makes possible the sharing of persuasive arguments not originally available to individuals alone and gives members more confidence about understanding the alternatives (Bateson, 1966). The risky shift is more pronounced when group members are not in competition with each other (Kogan & Carlson, 1967) and appears greater in more cohesive, and in relatively larger, groups (Teger & Pruitt, 1967). The shift may be due to the fact that the more assertive members also are greater risk takers and as a consequence influence the more cautious, passive members to go along with them (Rim, 1966). It may be due to the greater security produced by the group setting in contrast to being alone.

THE INDIVIDUAL AS A CONSTRAINT

It is obvious that the decision process will be strongly affected by consistent personal differences in values, interests, competencies, personalities, premises, and cognitive and perceptual tendencies among the individuals responsible for the decisions at each stage of the decision process. Also affecting the decision process will be the values, premises, and experiences, which vary as a consequence of the individual decision-maker's role and position in his or her groups, organization, and culture.

To understand the final decisions that emerge from an organization, it may be particularly necessary to determine the premises of the various individuals upon which the decisions are based (March & Simon, 1958).

Individuals will differ in their valuing of the organization's goals, their own ideals, their perceptions of the discrepancies between desired and current states of affairs, what resources they think they have available, in what areas to search for alternatives, in their ability and willingness to innovate, in the weighting given to alternatives and in their optimism or pessimism in estimating risks. These change with experiences, successes, and failures.

Collins and Moore (1964) found in a study of 110 business firms that it was particularly important to distinguish between entrepreneurs and professional managers. The professional managers were more socially mobile and able to make decisions. They were more dedicated to their work, and adapted more easily to authority and interpersonal relations. The entrepreneurs were less sure of themselves, resisted authority, and "wheeled and dealed" in their transactions.

Explicit values and premises

The solution to a promotion problem may be completely determined in advance by an implicit premise, such as no one being promoted into top management in the firm unless he or she is a member of the owner's family. But as Harrison (1981) observed, value judgments and premises could be made quite explicit in every aspect of the organizational decision-making process.

1. In the setting of objectives, it is necessary to make value judgments about selecting opportunities and making necessary improvements within time and resource constraints.
2. In developing a range of relevant alternatives, it is essential to make value judgments about the various possibilities that have emerged from the search activity.
3. At the time of the choice itself, the values of the decision maker, as well as the ethical considerations of the moment, are significant factors in the process.
4. The timing and means for implementing the choice necessarily require value judgments, as well as an awareness of ethical interests.
5. Even in the follow-up and control stage of the decision-making process, value judgments are unavoidable in taking corrective action to ensure that the implemented choice has a result compatible with the original objective. (p. 64)

Implicit values and premises

Nevertheless, more in need of understanding are the implicit values and premises of the individuals in the decision-making process, for they often remain unconscious, below the threshold of awareness. Goals are often selected, gaps identified, alternatives searched for, and choices weighted and selected based on a complex set of implicit values that are unclear to the decision maker. No wonder much of the action takes place after-the-fact. "I decide, then I justify. My choice was value-driven, but I was not aware of this. Now that I have made my choice, I need to find good reasons for it." To increase awareness of one's values in decision making, Leys (1962) suggests that decision makers first try to articulate for themselves a set of relevant but not necessarily completely controlling standards, tests, or criteria. These can be organized in an orderly manner. Pending decisions can be tested against them to increase the match between one's priorities in values and one's judgments.

Kast and Rosenzweig (1970) argue that the effective decision maker must balance valuing harmony and order with valuing survival and effects on others; maximum satisfaction and results (the bottom line) with lawfulness, contracts, and authorizations; and integrity and self-respect with loyalty, institutional, and social demands. The decision maker:

> . . . may have to compromise a particular norm or value in a given situation, but he can be reasonably comfortable if he recognizes that certain other values are enhanced by so doing. He must cope with pressures from individuals and/or groups from inside and outside the organization. Formally and informally, various values are "pushed" at the decision maker, who either discards them or integrates them into his own value system. This is the "balancing act" performed in any judgmental decision process. On balance, what is most important? What tips the scale in this particular situation?
>
> Decision makers in the real world cannot afford the luxury of deciding policy questions in general. This leads to all-encompassing values or standards which do not really apply in specific situations. The decision maker is better advised to develop a sense of the situation and deal with each problem on its own merits. (p. 416)

According to Katz and Kahn (1966) a value dimension of particular importance to understanding organizational decision making is the emphasis on ideology or power, although they see few organizational leaders as pure ideologists or pure power-brokers. Actually, most are likely to accept compromises to achieve power and to attain their ideological goals. On the one hand, President Reagan continued to espouse the conservative ideology of his supporters about importance of national budget balancing and lower taxes. But at the same time he came to support unbalanced budgets and increased taxes to compromise with economic, social, and political considerations.

Systematic differences in values were seen when 245 professional planners and engineers were assessed (unpublished study) in their willingness to permit public participation in selecting a road routing likely to have an effect on the local community. These assessments were found to be related to each individual's values. Public participation was favored by those higher in social and religious values and lower in economic values. At the same time, the professionals, as a whole, were much less concerned with noise and pollution than was the public.

Perceptual and cognitive biases

"To err is human." Understanding, predicting, and controlling such error is a major aspect in the study of organizational decision processes in all its phases. Faced with real portending disaster, the well-known human propensities are to misjudge real conditions in systematic ways as a consequence of perceptual distortions, motivation, and habit. Systematic errors can be observed in how we attribute causation of events which in turn has systematic consequences on organizational decision making. For instance, a supervisor who attributes the poor performance of a subordinate to dispositional tendencies, such as a lack of motivation, will tend to be punitive. If the poor performance is attributed to situational factors such as luck or lack of training, the supervisor is likely to try to help the subordinate (Green & Mitchell, 1979).

Feldman (1981) listed 10 biases that have been found operating in causal attributions: (1) we generally misunderstand the importance of situational factors and overestimate the importance of individual traits ("He failed mainly because he is lazy"); (2) if actors in the situation, we over-emphasize individual traits; (3) if observers of the situation, we see only the most salient features of the environment as the causal factors; (4) we see actions with sentimental or affective consequences to the observer as due to individual traits ("She rejected me because she dislikes intellectuals"); (5) we see people as more responsible for serious acts than for trivial ones; (6) we hold actors more responsible for acts leading to rewards than for acts preventing losses; (7) we pay little attention to common behavior in judging a particular action; (8) we use our own behavior as a standard against which to judge others; (9) we end the search for explanations with the first plausible one and (10) for liked people, we attribute good actions to them rather than to the situation; for disliked people, we attribute good actions to the situation, bad actions to them.

Statistical sources of individual bias. Anchoring effects, failure to consider base rates, mistaken belief in the law of small numbers, and failure to consider the regression towards the mean, are just some of the statistical phenomena that result in systematic bias. Slovic, Fischoff, and Lichtenstein (1977) have listed the consistent biases uncovered in a variety of field studies. They noted, for example, consistent overconfidence in the probability assessments of military intelligence analysts.

Likewise there was consistent underestimation by engineers of repair time for inoperative units. As mentioned earlier, Cyert, Simon, and Trow (1956) showed that objectives motivate estimates. Students acting as sales managers underestimated costs and overestimated sales. As cost analysts they did the reverse. More generally, Fischoff (1976) observed that cost-benefit analysts and those engaged in risk assessments tend to ignore important consequences of possible outcomes reflecting their availability biases—constraints in thinking.

Other errors. Numerous other examples of constraints in perceptual and cognitive processes were enumerated by Katz and Kahn (1966). These errors, while general, are also likely to differ from one individual to another; some persons suffering more than others in their distorted views of reality.

Individual decision makers project their own particular values on others. For example, superiors will see their subordinates as committed to the organization's goals as the superiors are. Individual decision makers will tend to err in oversimplification, and in global and undifferentiated thinking. We see members of other groups as homogeneous. Particularly, if they are remote, we will fail to differentiate among individuals in the group. (If we are not Chinese, all Chinese are seen to look and act alike.)

We tend to view the world in opposing categories, in black or white, with no shades of grey possible. (You must be in one room or another; you cannot be lying across the threshold between the rooms, or standing with one foot in each.)

We tend to respond in cognitive, near-sighted response to the immediate, the visible, the distinct, neglecting aspects of a problem or possibilities that are remote in time and place. We ignore what may be less overt, but more important. The executive attends to the most recent subordinate's complaints rather than to larger organizational needs of more consequence. Oversimplified notions of cause-and-effect are still another source of error. We tend to accept the exciting event as the major cause. We see cause-effect in one direction, not allowing for interaction. Thus, managers are likely to interpret informal restrictions of production by workers as due to a few agitators, or due solely to fears of rate-busting when the restriction may be a complex compromise among workers, shop stewards, and immediate supervisors to meet management-set standards and worker needs. Again, a project's failure may be attributed to the personnel assigned to it rather than to the complex market changes that really lay behind the failure.

Additional individual constraints on effective decision making and erroneous premises, implicit or explicit, have been noted by Elbing (1970). These include the tendency to evaluate rather than investigate;

the tendency to equate new with old experiences which may not be the same; the tendency to deal with problems superficially; the tendency to make decisions based on a single goal; the tendency to confuse symptoms and causes; the tendency to accept an evaluation based on selected variables (particularly if available numerically) rather than the fully relevant elements in the situation; and the tendency to make quick decisions rather than in-depth analysis of the problems. Individual differences in these tendencies can be seen as we look at the effects on decision making of personality and competence.

Furthermore, performance in different phases of the decision-making process will depend on one's intelligence, skill, education, experience, sex, and social status. But effectiveness in one phase does not guarantee effectiveness in another.

Personality and competence

Individuals differing in their personality, competence, and behavior, differ accordingly in dealing with different aspects of the organizational decision process. Some may be better at diagnosis; others, at searching for solutions. Thus, for instance, willingness to make difficult choices was found by Pollay (1970) to be associated with the achievement potential of decision makers.

Individuals differ in their decision-making styles, which in turn may result in organizational misunderstandings and mismatches between organizational needs and individual assignments. Individual decision makers also vary in what information is to be accepted, what sequence of events must be followed, and how many errors subordinates will be permitted to make. They vary in what decision-making rules are made explicit or are never stated; in whether proposals are evaluated on the basis of their intrinsic merit or their political acceptability. They vary in whether change is accomplished within the existing framework, or the rules of the game are changed, or an entirely different *game* is attempted. They vary in how much responsibility they delegate (Harrison, 1981).

Numerous studies attest to the extent a supervisor will be directive or participative in his or her decision-making style as a function of his or her personality. Direction seems to be mainly a matter of one's authoritarian personality; participation is more affected by situational circumstances along with a more equalitarian personality (Farrow & Bass, 1977). Participation, consultation, and delegation are more likely to be found among older managers at higher educational and organizational levels with greater seniority, who are more esteemed by their subordinates, and believe in being fairminded (Heller & Yukl, 1969; Pinder, Pinto & England, 1973; Bass, Valenzi & Farrow, 1977).

Hegarty & Sims (1979) found that foreign nationality, Machiavellianism (Mach V Scale), and economic value orientation (Allport-Vernon-Lindzey Study of Values) were positively related to unethical decision behavior. Using a sample of industrial managers, Taylor and Dunnette (1974), consistent with previous studies, showed that dogmatism was associated with a decision-making strategy characterized by rapid and confidently held decisions following limited information search. Willingness to risk was associated with an information-seeking strategy involving rapid decisions made on the basis of little information, but deliberate information processing. Intelligence was positively related to efficiency in processing information, accurate choices, and caution in changing decisions in the face of adverse consequences.

Cognitive structure. People differ in their cognitive structures—the way they organize their perceptions. Some tend toward complexity; others, towards simplicity. According to a line of investigation by Driver and Streufert (1969) and Harvey, Hunt, and Schroder (1961), search tactics depend strongly on the cognitive structure of the decision makers. In contrast to those with complex cognitive structures, those with simple cognitive structures tend to immediately categorize and stereotype. They depend upon simple, fixed rules of integration reducing the possibility of thinking in terms of continua. They suffer little internal conflict. They generate few alternative relationships. They reach closure quickly. Their behavior depends mainly on external conditions rather than internal processes. For them, a few rules can cover a wide range of phenomena. They make fewer distinctions between separate situations. They are more deterministic. They form fewer compartments for their environment.

The "simplistic" and the "complex" persons differ in the ways they prefer to gather information (Streufert, Suedfeld, & Driver, 1965). The simplistics prefer to request summary information about various characteristics of a problem situation. Those with complex structures prefer to act upon the environment, then observe the resulting response. The simplistics tend to request information about ongoing events, while those with complex structures tend to request information about more novel possibilities (Suedfeld & Streufert, 1966). The complex decision makers spend more time processing information; generate a greater number of interpretations; consider more alternative implications of information; are better able to integrate discrepant information; acquire more information prior to making a decision; and express greater uncertainty about their decisions. They are more tolerant of ill-structured problems and can make use of greater information loads.

When faced with increasing failures, the simplistic decision makers engage in more delegated information search in comparison to the more complex decision makers. Although the amount of self-initiated search is about the same for both simplistic and complex thinkers, dyads of members with complex structures do better in utilizing the information obtained (Streufert & Castore, 1971).

Risk preferences. Risk taking is subject to wide individual differences related to personality, experience, maturity, and organizational location. Rigid and dogmatic personalities are overly confident (Brim & Hoff, 1957) and more willing to take risks (Kogan & Wallach, 1964). In ambiguous situations, women are more averse to taking chances than are men (Wallach & Kogan, 1959). Older managers are less willing to accept risks and place less value on risky decisions (Vroom & Pehl, 1971).

Streufert (1978) concluded from a series of simulation experiments of complex military decisions that officers with several years of experience tended to take smaller risks than did ROTC students. Yet greater risks were taken by college students, in general, than ROTC students. Officers placed in command compared to those without command responsibility were less likely to make risky complex decisions. But, at the same time, they tended to take more risks with simple decisions.

Fifty-one corporate managers were found to differ consistently from each other in their perceptions of the risk and uncertainty in a situation. Perceived environmental variables were less important in contributing to perceived uncertainty than the extent the managers differed from each other in various cognitive processes (Downey, Hellriegel, & Slocum, 1977).

Brim et al. (1962) found that those who tend to be dependent on others will be more optimistic about the outcomes of their actions. But, they will consider fewer such outcomes in examining alternatives and will be less rational when they rank proposed actions. Those who have a stronger desire for certainty tend to make more extreme judgments in evaluating prospective outcomes.

Creativity. Creativity in an organization depends considerably on the extent to which it contains creative persons. According to Berelson and Steiner (1967), intelligence is usually, but not always, necessary for creativity. Creative persons are less likely to be more dogmatic in outlook. They are less likely to be dichotomous thinkers, less conventional and conforming. They are more willing to consider and express their own irrational impulses, and more likely to have a good sense of humor.

But above and beyond these individual differences in personality and competence which constrain the decision process, are constraints imposed by the organizational roles taken by the individual members.

Effects of role

Decision makers within the organization are influenced by their roles in the family, church, and community. Their particular culture and subculture affect their aspirations, attitudes toward authority, orientation toward time and money, and interpretations of what is real and what is important (Thompson, 1967). The values of consequences and their weights will in themselves vary as we move from one culture to another (Bass, Burger, et al., 1979). Such cultural variations may be seen even among organizations in the same country. A case can be made that organizational cultures differ from each other.

The attributes one attaches to one's own organizational role, and how they fit with one's outside roles, affects decisions about continuing participation in the organization (Simon, 1960). Once brought into the organizational situation, the decision-makers' personal life goals may prove to be matched or mismatched with organizational demands placed upon them by their location in the hierarchy, their task demands, and their organizational associates (March & Simon, 1958).

Particularly significant is with whom, and with what roles, the decision makers identify themselves: as women, as MBAs, as Prudential salesmen, as prospective early retirees, as old Californians, or as new Republicans. Dearborn and Simon (1958) showed that managers, when presented with a detailed case with much factual and little evaluative material, tended to focus attention on sales issues if they came from the marketing department. They tended to focus on clarifying the organization if they came from the production department and on human relations issues in the case if they came from the legal, public relations, or industrial relations departments. Bass, Farrow, and Valenzi (1980) noted that such managers saw themselves as much more influenced by external legal, social, and political forces in their organizational decision making if they were in personnel departments rather than finance or production departments. They were also less likely to be seen as directive in decision style by their subordinates if they were in personnel departments.

We tend to view problems from an individual vantage point centered in our own sociopsychological space. U.S. policymakers see left-right conflict in developing countries in terms of presence or absence of Soviet intervention. The company executive and the labor union leader look at the same conflict from completely opposing points of view and remain isolated from each other's ideas, concerns, approaches, and values (Druker, 1946).

Hierarchical level. What decisions will be considered and how they will be processed depends on the level of the decision maker's position in the organization hierarchy. Upper-level managers focus on goals and the development and maintenance of the organization as a whole. At middle-management levels, decisions center on the dividing of broad purposes into more specific ends. The technical and economic problems of action become prominent. At low-management levels, decisions are concerned with what is technologically correct conduct (Barnard, 1938). It follows that what is needed for making decisions, such as the kinds and amounts of information required, depends on one's management level (Kallman, Reinharth & Shapiro, 1980).

Hierarchical level was singled out by Blankenship and Miles (1968) as particularly important in determining a manager's decision-making style. Upper-level managers require more freedom from their superiors. They also show a stronger willingness to delegate, and to rely on their own subordinates in the decision-making process than do managers at lower levels. Middle-level managers tend to involve their subordinates less in the decision-making process. Lower-level managers are more often at the receiving end of initiatives for decisions by their superiors, and more often are expected to consult with their superiors before proceeding on most matters.

Empirical survey support for these propositions about hierarchical level was provided by Heller and Yukl (1969) who found that senior business managers in Britain emphasize delegation as a decision style; second level and first-level managers emphasize making decisions by themselves, then explaining them. But consultation was found most often among middle managers.

Concomitant with rising hierarchical levels are other variables which may actually underlie the observed stylistic decision-making differences. As level increases, subordinates are more highly educated and experienced. Superiors perceive them to be more competent. Trust levels may be higher, hence more subordinates are permitted to participate at higher levels. But middle managers must remain in more conformance to higher authority; they can risk less. While top managers can take more chances and delegate, middle managers maintain greater security by consulting with subordinates but not relinquishing control over the final decisions through delegation. (For more on how hierarchical level influences decision-making style, see Bass, 1981, Chapter 19.)

A longitudinal study of 56 organizational decisions in three Dutch firms by Heller, Drenth and Koopman (1982) found that the extent hierarchical level made a difference in one's participation depended on the phase of the decision. The start-up phase of the decision was dominated by top managers and to a lesser extent by middle managers and professional staff who, in turn, became more important in the developmental phase. Again top managers dominated in the final decision and authorization phase. Workers and first-line supervisors made their greatest contributions in the implementation phase. Correlational analyses with decision outcomes indicated that worker participation in the development phase increased their satisfaction with the process and with its outcomes. In the same way, too much top management influence during the development and implementation phases contributed to frustration and dissatisfaction at lower levels. At the same time, too much influence by lower and middle management and professional staff on the final choice and authorization was seen to reduce the efficiency of the process and the quality of its outcomes.

Interactions among constraints

The interaction among constraints is illustrated by the aforementioned extent to which the phase of the decision process affects the efficacy of participation by organizational members at different levels in the hierarchy. In real life, it is a mix of organizational, group, and individual constraints that moderate the decision process. How much of each is a matter of empirical inquiry determined by an analysis of variance model, which apportions the percent of variance due to each constraint and interaction. Vroom and Yetton's (1974) analysis of managers' responses to case descriptions concluded that the particular decision styles chosen could be attributed somewhat to individual differences, but more to the problem situation and the interactions. Whether decision supports are available may make an even bigger difference in the process.

8

Decision aids and support systems

The purpose of most decision aids is to reduce cognitive overload. They do so by decomposing the decision process into its structurally related parts. The decision maker is asked to deal with each part sequentially rather than the entire process all at once. According to Slovic, Fischoff and Lichtenstein's review of experimental studies (1977), judgment is improved demonstrably when aids can be employed.

Decision supports can systematically facilitate a line manager's problem-solving behavior by: (1) providing more structure to a less well-structured problem; (2) extending the decision-maker's information processing ability; (3) stimulating appropriate concept formation; (4) providing cues to the decision maker of the critical factors in the problem, their importance, and the relations among them; (5) utilizing data which might not have been collected and data which needs to be collected to solve the problem; and (6) breaking out from ineffective mental sets (Hammond, 1974).

Decision aids and support systems range from those which provide complete structure for the decomposed decision process to those which provide only partial structure for transforming the presenting inputs to the problem, to the search for solutions, and to the evaluation and choice. With fully structured supports, the particular set of inputs to the problem completely determines the outputs—as do algorithmic solutions, for example. Outputs are fully determined by the particular set of inputs and the designated transformation operators. Assumptions must be made as explicit as possible. But with partially structured supports for the decomposed decision process, variations in judgment enter into the transformation process so that the same designated set of inputs may result in a variety of different outputs. Many assumptions remain implicit. Whether aids are fully or partially structured match the kinds of search and choice processes possible with well-structured or ill-structured problems. Fully structured aids always produce the same outcomes for a given set of inputs (including the output of random results if the inputs are random). Partially structured aids are guides which don't automatically lead to a particular pattern of outcomes for a particular set of inputs.

Fully structured aids usually provide an explicit programmed set of calculations. Anyone using the completely structured aid properly will reach the same final answer. Partially structured aids provide rules whose efficiency will depend on the judgment of the decision makers. A formula or cookbook is a more structured aid; an agenda for staging the decision-making process is a less structured aid. The problems themselves must be well-structured to make use of highly structured aids; they need be less so, for less structured ones.

Management scientists tend to concentrate on the more highly structured aids and support systems, although, in general, they still see much room for judgment. For one thing, outcomes may still depend on the implicit values of the decision makers, all of which may not be fully made explicit. The final linear program to determine the optimum location for a set of warehouses still will require judgments about values and constraints in the situation. Even after the final deterministic solution has been obtained, most management scientists recommend it be seen as suggestive to decision makers rather than completely controlling their subsequent actions.

Behavioral scientists tend to concentrate on less highly structured supports. *Staging*, for example, is such a support. Decision makers are forced to remain focused on problem identification and diagnosis before starting the search for solutions. Again, choice is delayed until the search process is exhausted. The process is structured, but considerable judgmental variation is possible within each stage of the process.

FULLY STRUCTURED AIDS

Routine decision making can be facilitated by programs, SOP, maps, flowcharts, decision tables, and checklists. For problems that can be reasonably well structured with routine solutions, for which a single objective function can be assumed, and for which risk estimates can be reasonably complete, the mathematical methods of operations research are available to assist the decision maker. Typically, an optimum choice is algebraically determined using accepted assumptions about parameters, variables, and the criterion function. Linear and dynamic programming, decision trees, game theory, team theory, waiting-line theory, and probability theory are the better known mathematical methods and theories employed. A mathematical model is constructed starting from assumptions about how to represent in the model the system of real-world variables to be analyzed. What is to be maximized or minimized—the criterion function—is defined. Empirical estimates are obtained by the numerical parameters in the model that specify the concrete situation to which it is to be applied. Mathematical operations are completed to find the alternative, which for the specified parametric values, results in maximizing the criterion function (Churchman, Ackoff, & Arnoff, 1957).

Operations research forces more logical descriptions of objectives, the making explicit of assumptions, and provides more precise descriptions of a wider array of alternative solutions and the ability to compare them (Shuchman, 1963).

Modeling

Given problems and possible solutions with sufficient structural clarity, models can be constructed symbolically, usually mathematically (and on occasion, physically), to represent the important elements in the real situation. Empirical estimates of the values of the variables in the situation, and empirical estimates of the values of the variables in the model that hold for the particular, concrete situation, can be obtained. An optimization model can be constructed if, in addition, the criterion function is defined so that the expected values of alternatives can be compared using a specified set of decision rules (Alexis & Wilson, 1967). Although model building requires the problem to be well structured, the study of less well-structured problems can be clarified by the attempt to model them. Unfortunately, the attempt may produce oversimplification and distortion of the problem in order to make it amenable to modeling.

Model building. As outlined by Harrison (1981), the model for modeling (Figure 6) begins in the real world with the establishment of objec-

FIGURE 6   The model of modeling

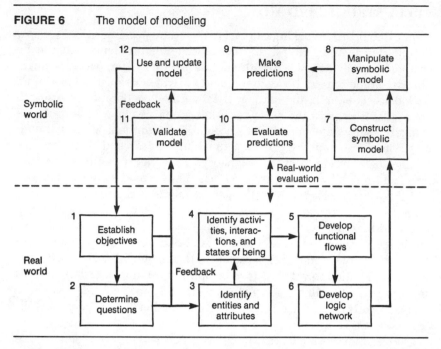

From E. F. Harrison, The managerial decision-making process (2d ed.). (Boston: Houghton Mifflin, 1981) p. 295.

tives, the determination of the problems the model is supposed to solve, the identification of the significant fixed and variable entities, interactions and fixed parameters of consequence, and the mapping of their actual flow and the logic of the flow. From this logic, the symbolic model is constructed. (It could be mathematical or physical.) The model is manipulated to make predictions. The model is validated by the extent the predictions match real world outcomes. The results are used to adjust the model to improve the match of the model with the real world.

Uses.   Modeling assumes that a faithful replica of the problem situation has been constructed. But, of course, its projections will only be accurate to the degree that its premises, parameters, and specified relationships are reasonable approximations of their real-world counterparts. It is particularly useful in dealing with uncertain real situations to see what kinds of reasonable expectations about outcomes a decision maker should entertain for various possible antecedent conditions. It is in this sense, that aids are seen as support systems; for the decision maker, after obtaining a view of what to expect, still must make the final decision.

To illustrate, budgetary models provide a pattern of the task environment of the budgeters and the problems with which they must deal. Such models need to be highly disaggregated to provide understanding of the match between changes in proposed spending to actual spending. By identifying the variables of the task situation that constrain the budget decision makers, modeling can provide a guide to the changes necessary to give more flexibility to budget officers (Bromily, 1981).

Models can be specifically useful for each phase of the decision process. They can help determine the feasibility and effectiveness of various objectives and goals before spending time and effort in search and evaluation. Models can be used in search to uncover a wide range of relevant alternatives at a low cost for the search in contrast to conducting a real search. Alternatives may be evaluated and compared by revising the model until projected outcomes conform to the desired objectives. After the final choice, the model can be used as a control device to monitor how close expected outcomes match real outcomes when the decision is implemented (Harrison, 1981).

Model types

Linear programming models deal with a body of known constraints and variables to find an optimum solution. *Decision trees* reveal a network of possibilities leading to one among alternative outcomes. Dealing optimally with users of services, roads, and facilities is the aim of *queueing* or *waiting line theory*. Wagner (1969) sees these approaches to such well-structured problems as providing for better coordination among marketing and production, better control of what is happening routinely, and what will happen. It makes it possible to organize better systems for transforming materials and providing services.

Models can be highly dynamic, linked to the real world for continuing readjustment of the model itself. Thus, *rolling production schedules* provide an effective decision support in the search for production optimality to meet demand patterns within cost constraints using forecast windows (Baker, 1977). Nevertheless, because these models always leave out some aspects of the real situation, the estimates tend to be overly optimistic. For example, they are likely to overestimate the potential gains from innovation.

Multiattribute utility theory provides a model for determining the utilities and weights for deciding among alternatives with multiple attributes. Products can be compared which are simultaneously different in price, quality, and serviceability. Instead of evaluating several proposed designs, first on the basis of one criterion such as judged safety, then on the basis of estimated costs of development and finally on the basis of marketability, each design is judged simultaneously on all three criteria in combination.

Team theory is a normative explanation of information flows by Marschak and Radner (1972) which deduces how organizational members should make observations about the environment confronting the organization; what communication channels should be employed, what messages communicated, and what actions each organizational member should take based on the information received. In well-structured, simple situations, team theory may provide ways of calculating optimal strategies for dealing with communications about uncertain environments. For less well-structured, more complex situations, it can be used as a conceptual guide to monitor behavior and avoid information-communication failures (MacCrimmon & Taylor, 1976).

Sensitivity analysis

The sensitivity of models can be analyzed. Such an analysis calculates the effect of deviations from the values originally assigned to the various parameters of the model and to what extent the solution departs from optimal as a consequence of such deviations. The analysis checks on whether the optimal solution would be altered if the values assigned to the parameters of the model in the original analysis were changed. If the original solution is unaffected by significant changes in the parameters, it is inferred that the solution is likely to apply over a wide range of conditions. But, if small deviations in the parameters result in major changes in the solution, less confidence can be placed in the choice, or in any substitute alternative, for that matter (Radford, 1981).

Applications

Typical problems to which operations research can be applied include: optimum product mixes, dynamic replenishment of inventories, optimum distribution of goods from a number of different sources to different destinations, optimum assignment of work orders to a number of different machines or people, the shortest routes for production flows, inventory management, and critical path scheduling (Radford, 1981).

Operations research fosters a more rational and systematic attack on decision making. Operating, rather than policy, problems are handled. Nevertheless, operations research has the potential for contributing to the search for answers to strategic questions because it forces common goals to be the basis of decisions in the different units of the organization (Johnson, Kast, & Rosenzweig, 1963). Also, simulation can lay out possible future real-time trends in compressed time, following different assumptions about the interplay of the variables of consequence. This gives the strategic planner a better description of his or her options. In comparison to intuitive approaches, operations research provides better descriptions of assumptions and objectives; a more precise definition of the problem and the importance and relation among the factors involved; the information required to obtain an optimal solution; a precise description of the alternative solutions and their costs and benefits; the ability to compare many more alternatives with considerable confidence; and a basis for predicting the consequences of changes.

Implementation

It is one thing to have a mathematical optimization or near-optimization model. It is another to get managers to use it, even for well-structured problems. As Crum, Klingman, and Tavis (1979), among others, have noted, despite the availability of a variety of mathematical modeling techniques for helping financial decision making; they have not been widely employed by corporate financial managers, partly because of a lack of understanding of the underlying relationships by managers, as well as because of poor communications. Necessary for implementation is the formulation of optimization models that are easier to implement. It also seems difficult to introduce better but more sophisticated decision aids. A survey of the decision aids used by European marketing managers by Wensley (1977) found them bound to traditional aids which they felt were proven effective for practical situations. They had little motivation to shift toward better but more sophisticated and untried aids.

Walker (1973) contrasted cases of attempts to apply operations research techniques to major policy problems in long-range planning for NASA's unmanned planetary exploration program. Early on, the analytic efforts used relatively formal methodologies and concentrated on analysis of scientific, technological, and economic issues. The supports had little or no impact on policy outcomes. There was little acceptance by NASA planners for the analytic techniques used. Only when in the later period of 1968 to 1970, when less formal analytical techniques were employed and careful consideration was given to the organizational, political, and psychological aspects of the surrounding decision process, did the analytic support processes have a significant impact on policy outcomes.

Wagner (1969) finds that a limiting factor in the application of mathematical rigor to organizational decision-making problems is the fact that it must depend on the ingenuity of the professional operations researcher. There are few standard applications. Designing particular applications in designated organizations requires considerable skill. "Model formulations remain tailor-made to a large degree." Systems of decision supports for organizations can include not only the professional operations research staffs themselves, but also the incorporation of their techniques as routines in the management information system for ready routine variance detection, for search and retrieval of data, and for comparative forecasting.

Different arrangements of line personnel, staff specialists, consultants, and clients can be employed in the development of operations research solutions. Many combinations of researchers and executives are possible. For example, a large problem can be broken up into meaningful, smaller problems. The short-run solutions can then be fed to the client until the whole job is completed. The line manager or client can be brought into the project as a team leader or as a team member (Radnor, Rubenstein, & Bean, 1966).

PARTIALLY STRUCTURED AIDS

For those decisions less amenable to complete and clear structuring, partially structured approaches provide ways to increase the orderliness with which the decision makers can deal with a problem. These approaches can be quantitative or qualitative. Quantitative approaches, for example, are various orderly processes for quantitatively pooling inputs. These include the Delphi procedure, nominal group estimating, and regression analyses for capturing policies.

Qualitative, heuristic supports are guidelines to support the increase in the quality of solutions to ill-structured problems. These involve improving the decision process by using special sets to force relationships (synectics) or to encourage free association (brainstorming). Other special guidelines that may also be employed to improve the process include rules for staging, for prioritizing, and for cause-effect interpretations.

Since consistent, repeating patterns are seen in the behavior of real decision makers confronted with specified circumstance, *heuristic computer programs* can be written to reproduce them. A model of reality is constructed and a program of rules is determined which can become a decision aid for novices. For instance, one can increase one's familiarity with chess by playing against a computer model which has been programmed to respond as an expert would, depending on a set of specified rules and the pattern of several previous moves made by the novice and the model.

Among other systematic ways to assist decision makers in dealing with ill-structured problems, *scenarios* can be prepared which detail possible future courses of action and their outcomes in a complex environment. Or *position papers* can be written advocating particular courses of action, the reasons for doing so, and the anticipated outcomes.

Quality of decision making can also be enhanced by organizing for creative conflict among those responsible for the decision. Techniques include using a devil's advocate, dialectic argumentation, and adversary dialogues (discussed later in this chapter). Finally, organizations can be seen to incorporate checking devices to control their irrational tendencies by using computer programming language, voting rules, waiting periods, and expert advisors.

Supports for the decision process as a whole

As Mintzberg et al. (1976) found, decision-processes are unlikely to be orderly if decision makers are left to their own devices when dealing with ill-structured organizational problems. But anything that will promote more orderliness is likely to move managers from satisficing toward more optimal solutions. Thus, making systematic preparations before taking action was seen to be more common among more capable administrators than among those with less administrative knowledge and aptitude (Frederikson, 1962).

Staging. Illustrative of a heuristic to improve decision processes and their outcomes is the rule to separate the stages in decision making rather than to wander back and forth too frequently from problem diagnosis to search, and from search to evaluation. Thus, when groups were forced to separate the stages in decision making they saw themselves as becoming more efficient, more satisfied with outcomes, and more committed to the decisions reached (Goodchilds, Schonfield, & Gibb, 1961).

Maier and Solem (1962) encouraged staging in 96 four-member groups, each trying to solve a problem. Fifty groups served as controls carrying on freely and spontaneously The forced-staging groups were asked to present the problem first to get everyone's views about it. Only then were they to explore and discuss all the important factors in the situation. Finally, at the end of the search and discussion, they were to use the list of factors to synthesize a solution to the problem. Staging promoted higher-quality solutions.

The Delphi technique. Experts individually complete a series of questionnaires about problems, solutions, and choices. The composite information gathered from each questionnaire is shared with the experts and forms the basis for the next questionnaire in the series. The experts are kept apart physically until the end of the process to avoid the dominance of any one of them early on. Many variants are possible (Dalkey & Helmer, 1963). The Delphi technique has been used to delineate problems as diverse as estimating future Soviet military capabilities, stimulating wider search for innovative government policies, and evaluating the quality of life (Cetron & Ralph, 1971). Some evidence exists that the Delphi approach helps improve the accuracy of forecasts (Business Week, 1970) and it is used regularly by a number of U.S. firms (Luthans, 1973).

Supports for problem discovery and diagnosis

Rules for prioritizing, elaborating, and probabilistic information processing are illustrative of supports for problem discovery and diagnosis.

Prioritizing. Setting priorities is of fundamental importance. Guidelines suggest that attention should first be paid to critical activities, then to those of lower importance. At the same time, a balance needs to be achieved between too much concern about threats, and too little concern for opportunities (Drucker, 1963).

Elaborating. To further delineate the problem, Kepner and Tregoe (1965) offer a set of rules to elaborate the nature of the problem in terms of what it is and is not, when it appears and disappears, when it is present and when not, and so on. Causes can be sought at times and locations when changes in the state of affairs occur. MacCrimmon and Taylor (1976) add the directions to examine changes in the environment that have precipitated the problem, to factor complex problems into simpler subproblems, and to establish what is controllable in the situation. They also suggest applying means-end analysis and either working forward or working backward from where one is to where one wants to be. The complexities of the problem can also be reduced by aggregating information available about it. Information can be *chunked* (grouping information into categories and then arranging them in order of importance). Optimal levels of aggregation are to be sought. For instance, day-by-day changes in stock prices may be too fine to deal with; yearly changes may be too coarse. Monthly changes may be best.

The probabilistic information processing system (PIP). PIP aims to improve both speed and accuracy of diagnoses in military and business command-and-control systems. Participants generate hypotheses and estimate likelihood ratios which are then aggregated for Baysian analysis. This enables decision makers to screen and filter information, to weigh different aspects, and to extract what is certain in the information (Edwards, 1962).

Supports for search and innovation

Establishing appropriate sets, along with forced and free association, are examples of supports of the search and design process.

Appropriate set. Appropriate attitudinal sets enhance the search process. A questioning frame of mind helps generate alternatives. A decision maker may systematically ask: Why? Where? When? Who? What? How? What current resource could be adapted? Modified? Substituted? Transformed? Combined? Omitted? Reversed? (Osborn, 1941). Adopting a set to be original increases the creativity of ideas generated. If one tries to discover or invent unique solutions, rather than accepting just any solution, more new alternatives are produced (Maltzman, Bogartz, & Breger, 1958). If one adopts a constructive set rather than a negative or critical set toward ideas, more creative solutions are likely to emerge (Hyman, 1964).

Following MacKinnon (1966) and Corson (1962), Bass and Ryterband (1979) spell out other attitudinal sets of consequence to the search and innovation process:

> The frame of reference the organization sets for its problem solvers is of particular importance. Venturesomeness and wide-ranging research for new and better ways of doing things are likely to be inhibited if emphasis in the organization is always on rules, clearances, and reviews, or if the payoff is to those who maintain stability and order rather than to those who innovate. Search will be inhibited if jurisdictional lines are stressed, so that one executive avoids making suggestions to another about the other's area of responsibility. On the other hand, creativity will be enhanced when the organization approves attempts to experiment, to innovate, and to challenge old ways of operating. (p. 441)

Forced and free association. Arbitrary combinatory searches, and the "black box technique" (what needs to be inside if . . .) depend on forced and free association. A forced search arbitrarily can call forth every permutation and combination of possibilities. Thus, eight alternative designs for a product can be generated by considering it in terms of the eight combinations of low or high price, high or low quality, and high or low serviceability (Zwicky, 1969).

Of particular popularity have been *synectics* and *brainstorming*, each illustrating forced and free association (Fulmer, 1974). Although synectics supports all phases of problem solving, innovative search processes in particular can be especially facilitated (Gordon, 1961). Participants must dismiss their usual ways of thinking about a problem. The participants are required to use analogies, to "make the familiar strange." They play the role of some element in the problem. They may be instructed to imagine that they are the wheel at the head of the driving rod. Then, they may be asked to consider such questions as: "What do you do? What should you do? How do you feel as the wheel?" They are also asked to make direct analogies between the problem and nature; for instance, between the rotation of the wheel and the ability of planets to spin. They consider symbolic analogies using mathematical models. They make fantasy analogies; for example, equating saintly halos and round plates. The synectics approach is more structured than brainstorming. It follows a repeatable set of stages using analogies to generate creative solutions and to choose the most favorable alternative. Alternatives are evaluated as they are generated.

Brainstorming was originated by Osborn (1941) as a group procedure. Participants are directed to freely express ideas, to forgo criticism, and to delay evaluation of any of the ideas until they are all listed collectively.

Nominal versus real groups.   Nominal groups are collections of individual participants whose judgments are pooled to form a collective opinion without any face-to-face interaction among the participants. And, as we have already seen, the Delphi Technique makes use of nominal groups, permitting real group interaction only after the several rounds of individual work have been completed and the results shared. Experimental studies of brainstorming indicate that real groups may inhibit, rather than facilitate, the production of ideas in contrast to the same or comparable nominal groups of individuals working by themselves and mechanically pooling their outputs (as with the Delphi Technique). Brainstorming work periods need to be extended for real groups to do better than nominal groups. In addition, cohesiveness is needed for effective real group performance (MacCrimmon & Taylor, 1976).

An empirical comparison by Van de Ven and Delbecq (1974) of the nominal, Delphi, and real group decision-making processes favored and provided support for the nominal group, and, secondarily, for the Delphi technique, as ways to abstract and organize expert information about the problem.

Delbecq and Van de Ven (1971) offered the following reasons for the usually superior creativity of nominal groups.

1. Noninteracting nominal or Delphi groups do not inhibit the performance of members.
2. Noninteracting groups cannot focus on a single train of thought, as may interacting groups.
3. There is less likely to be early evaluation and the distraction of elaborate comments.
4. Round-robin procedures (such as in Delphi) allow risk takers to state risky problems thus making it easier for the less secure to engage in similar disclosures.

Nominal groups seem likely to be particularly effective in organizations where superiors ordinarily stifle communications upward from subordinates and where subordinates are specialists while their superiors are generalists.

Nevertheless, a combination of nominal group work followed by real group interaction seems most productive. Souder (1977) found that nominal and interacting group processes in combination worked best for achieving both statistical consensus, and high levels of integration of R&D and marketing management trainees. The nine strategic planning groups could achieve consensus statistically in nominal groups but not the required integration. They could do neither in just real groups. But the combination (of nominal and real groups) accomplished both beginning with nominal groups of members working alone, followed by real group interaction. The combination seems best for search and design as well as evaluation and choice.

Supports for evaluation and choice

Numerous qualitative and quantitative approaches are available to assist in evaluating and making choices.

Kepner-Tregoe's rules. Kepner and Tregoe (1965) formalized and popularized a list of rules which decision makers could follow to increase their orderliness in evaluation and choice. Three kinds of actions were posited that can be taken to deal with a problem. The first is interim or temporary action to be taken when the cause of the problem is as yet unclear. Without knowing the reason for increased customer complaints, the organization will order free replacements until the cause is identified. The second is corrective action taken to determine the cause of the problem and eliminate it. Inspection may be improved and other quality control measures taken to keep most defective products from reaching the market. The third action is adaptive. A reevaluation may suggest that the product should be redesigned or abandoned.

To evaluate alternative actions, Kepner and Tregoe suggest listing desired outcomes and how well each alternative is likely to achieve them. "Must" objectives are outcomes that must be achieved. For instance, the battery for the heart pacemaker must be absolutely fail-safe; other outcomes may also be desired but are not critical. A negotiated raise in wages should not increase by more than 10 percent. For each available choice, estimates are made of the extent desired outcomes are likely to be achieved. Along with the critical requirements, they direct the choice of alternatives. The adverse consequences and side effects of the first choice also must be considered before accepting it as final.

Combining judgments. Sawyer (1966) reviewed the predictive accuracy of eight possible ways of combining predictive data about the future performance of applicants or clients. These methods of combining information to form a prediction ranged from global judgments following interviews to statistical syntheses combining collected data and interview judgments. Statistical combining of data, in some manner, generated more accurate predictions than dependence alone on judgments to combine components.

Policy capturing. As noted in Chapter 5, policy capturing which makes use of the lens model (Brunswik, 1955) has been found useful in a variety of applied situations. A set of judges indicate numerically how important each component reason for a choice is, or was, to them. Then they attach a numerical rating to how strongly they do, or did, prefer a particular choice. The beta weights of the multiple regression equation are determined to yield the optimum prediction of the judges' strength of choice from their ratings of each component. The beta weights indicate the proportionate influence of the components on the choice. If we then discover that some component is having an unintended influence, corrective action may be taken. For example, in educational institutions, policy capturing has made it possible to improve policies about student grades, student placement in special education, the hiring of new teaching personnel, and the selection of curricular materials. Again, the initial rating policies that exist within a board of judges have been identified to help the members of such boards to reach consensus and to express their final joint policy in a precise manner.

Strategic assumption making. Mitroff and Emshoff (1979) offer a rational, syllogistic procedure for dealing with ill-structured problems. It requires focusing on the assumptions underlying each proposed course of action, prioritizing them in order of their importance and certainty, then assessing the damage each assumption does to the assumptions of the other alternatives. Resolution of apparent conflicts is then sought. The improved awareness of the assumptions underlying the chosen alternative is seen as fundamental to justifying the final choice.

Combinatory matching. It can also be helpful to evaluation and final choice to do a complete examination of all possible objectives of a designated choice against all possible alternative ways of reaching the objective. Weights can be assigned to indicate the extent to which each alternative meets each of the objectives. Then, the alternative that meets the greatest amount of the total array of objectives can be identified. A decision matrix for the 1962 Cuban missile crisis (Table 2) illustrates such an examination. In an analysis of options, the Naval blockade that actually was instituted was the alternative judged highest in likelihood of meeting the widest assortment of the eight objectives seen to be involved in the crisis. Only the Naval blockade was judged relatively high in meeting all eight objectives (Harrison, 1981).

TABLE 2 Decision matrix: The Cuban missile crisis

	Objectives							
Alternatives	(1) Missiles are removed immediately	(2) World power balance remains in favor of United States	(3) U.S. hemispheric defenses are preserved	(4) World opinion remains favorable toward United States	(5) Sentiment of U.S. public remains favorable toward administration	(6) Sino-Soviet relationship is not strengthened	(7) U.S. relationship with Soviet Union is not worsened	(8) Total point value
Weight (maximum value)	10	10	10	10	10	10	10	70
1. Do nothing	0	1	1	4	2	5	2	15
2. Diplomatic approach to Castro	2	4	1	2	2	5	4	20
3. Diplomatic pressures	2	2	2	4	3	5	4	22
4. Invasion	8	8	8	0	2	2	0	28
5. Air strikes	8	8	3	2	2	2	0	30
6. Blockade	4	6	3	8	10	8	6	50

From E. F. Harrison, *The managerial decision-making process*, 2d Ed. (Boston: Houghton Mifflin, 1981), p. 312.

Such a matrix is particularly useful when a participating decision unit or organization is engaged in an analysis of its strategic options in a competitive environment and an examination of the tactics which would be needed to bring about fruition of a designated strategy (Radford, 1981).

Relationships may be contrived by cataloging, arbitrary listing, and focusing on designated objects, as well as by random juxtapositions of items from different categories and by forcing challenges to accepted assumptions about the outcomes expected from specific actions (De Bono, 1970).

SPAN. The higher the correlation between the influence on the group decision and the competencies of the individual members, the better the group decision will be (Bass, 1960). But it may be difficult for members to accurately estimate the differential competencies of each other. Nevertheless, MacKinnon (1966) proposed exploiting the possibilities by the SPAN technique. Each member starts with an equal number of votes—say 100—which can be allocated directly by the member among the alternatives or the votes can be given to members to allocate who are judged as more knowledgeable about the issue. SPAN transfers votes not between the alternatives, but to those members who are deemed experts on the problem, so that the correlation is increased between judged member expertise and member influence on the final outcome.

The uses of contrived conflict

Organized dissent can facilitate consideration of a wide range of alternatives. F. D. Roosevelt was said to have used this device repeatedly. He set up competing subordinates to argue out a final position which he could accept.

Constructive conflict. Mason (1969) studied two approaches, the *devil's advocate* and *dialectic argumentation*. The devil's advocate presents a diametrically opposed point of view to the favored alternative under consideration. This brings to the surface the possible biases and false assumptions that provide support for the favored alternative. The devil's advocate (Herbert & Estes, 1977) legitimatizes taking an adversary stand and providing criticism of the favorite alternative when none might be forthcoming. But, it may focus too much attention on finally choosing an alternative that can withstand all possible petty criticisms. For Hegelian dialectic argumentation (Hegel, 1964), decision makers examine a situation logically from two opposing points of view. First, an alternative and its underlying assumptions are presented. Next, another plausible alternative or counterplan is considered. A debate follows. The case for each alternative must interpret all available information as supporting evidence. Out of this should come a synthesis which includes the best elements of both alternatives. The dialectic approach forces equal time and consideration for the popular and apparent alternative with opposite points of view. A creative synthesis can emerge.

Stanley (1981) has listed a number of other formalized adversary roles that promote fuller examination of problems, alternatives, and evaluations. These include the leader of the opposition in the British House of Commons who is paid to lead the "loyal opposition."

Efforts continue to provide legal protection to "whistle-blowing" and responsible dissent by employees in government agencies. Private organizations need also to encourage bona fide responsible dissent when, for example, sanctions against bypassing the chain of command usually stifle attempts to question organizational policies. Stanley notes that

> just as a surgeon controls both clotting and hemorrhaging during an operation, an organization's homeostasis does require constraint of reckless, malicious, unfounded public exposure by self-serving members, . . . (but it must) allow . . . for ventilating of *ultra vires* acts and other mis- or malfeasant acts or omissions. (p. 16)

Mason (1969) found that using a devil's advocate was helpful to management decision makers because it gave them a broader grasp of the planning problem with which they were confronted. Cosier (1978) went further, finding in a series of experiments on strategy planning greater effectiveness on decision outcomes by objective, nonemotional devil's advocates as contrasted to "carping critics," dialectical inquiry, and expert advice from consultants. In a simulated financial decision-making experiment, subjects were asked to predict price-earnings ratios for three profit centers. They were aided by information about each centers' P/E ratio, inventory turnover, and debt-to-equity ratio. The objective, nonemotional devil's advocate was found particularly better than other approaches (Schwenk & Cosier, 1980).

But Schwenk and Cosier (1980) also reported that when the state of the world conforms to the assumptions underlying a plan, the expert approach was superior to using the devil's advocate. When the state of the world was opposite to the assumptions in the plan, the reverse was true. The devil's advocate was superior. When the state of the world was midway between the assumptions of the plan and counterplan, again the objective, nonemotional devil's advocate was better.

Systematic checks on organizational irrationality. Katz and Kahn (1966) see that casting organizational problems into computer language in itself forces one to be clear about the variables and parameters involved, the priority with which different criteria of decision making will be applied, and the process of inference by which decisions are to be made. Undefined terms must be eliminated. Complete stability is built in from one decision making situation to another.

> . . . if the essential data and procedures for decision-making can be programmed, many of the erratic and fallible elements in organizational decisions are eliminated. (p. 295)

Numerous guides and rules are instituted to help reduce irrationality and impulsive decision making. Formal periods of waiting or deliberation are required before policies can be changed. Minorities may be protected by requiring more than a simple majority to decide on an issue. An assembly is required to vote on the same issue more than once before its passage. Two houses of a legislature must both approve a bill for it to become a law. Executives are given the power to veto; legislatures to override executive vetoes.

Experts are called in for consultation. However, proper identification and role requirements need to be carefully considered. Experts need to be located who are not redundant in attitudes and information with legislators or in-house personnel.

Impact of education and training

With typical business and professional education programs and specialized decision-making training programs making it increasingly likely that the modern manager will have some appreciation about what is now known about the decision-making process and ways to make it more effective, the question is whether the following summarization from March and Simon (1958) needs to be qualified.

The original reads:

> Because of the limits of human intellective capacities in comparison with the complexities of the problems that individuals and organizations face, rational behavior calls for simplified models that capture the main features of a problem without capturing all its complexities. . . . (1) Optimizing is replaced by satisficing—the requirement that satisfactory levels of the criterion variables be attained. (2) Alternatives of action and consequences of action are discovered sequentially through search processes. (3) Repertories of action programs are developed by organizations and individuals, and these serve as the alternatives of choice in recurrent situations. (4) Each specific action program deals with a restricted range of situations and a restricted range of consequences. (5) Each action program is capable of being executed in semiindependence of the others—they are only loosely coupled together. (March & Simon, 1958, p. 169)

It is not unreasonable to assume that the limits of human intellectual capacities have been expanded by the increased availability of knowledge about the decision process and aids to improve it. As a consequence, it would follow that: (1) satisficing levels may be attracted upward to a displaced ideal of the optimal; (2) alternatives may not only be generated sequentially but by contiguity of time and place, of perceived cause-and-effect, by deliberate contrast efforts, and other special tactics; and (3) managers can adopt a systematic point-of-view dealing with multiple objectives and multiple constituencies in a single decision process. Mathematics have become available for better-structured multiple criterion problems. Computers make feasible what were once impossibly lengthy calculations of interactions among multiple variables. Whether or not decisions are coupled varies with the competence, motivation and experience of the decision makers and the support systems available to them.

Research specifically focused on how much managers with modern management educations can, and do, operate at levels of effectiveness beyond that posited a quarter of a century ago would seem warranted.

9

Unanswered questions and unresolved issues

Unanswered questions and unresolved issues in organizational decision making will be generated from two sources: (1) the gaps, incompleteness, and missing links suggested in our preceding discussions; and (2) the need for empirical verification of a model (to be presented) of the organizational decision-making process. The model attempts to summarily capture much of what we have presented so far.

The ability to answer unanswered questions about the decision-making process and to resolve unresolved issues depends on one's view of the process. The optimist points to the public rather than private character of organizational decisions. Observable and recordable interactions between people must take place. But a complete, individual decision-making process can occur with no external manifestation. The pessimist points to the relative difficulty in conducting controlled experiments on organizational decision making in contrast to the ease with which one can replicate or extend a finding in individual decision making. The pessimist cites the complexity of the organizational decision process. The optimist counters by showing how a few simple rules can often account for a large percentage of what happens. Nevertheless, there continues to be a relative paucity of hard data about organizational decisions. A large number of intriguing hypotheses generated by March and Simon (1958) still remain untested. The Mintzberg et al. (1976) study is difficult and expensive to replicate or extend. Thus, we often must depend on anecdotal understandings of case outcomes when more questions than answers remain about what happened.

The pathology of organizational decision processes remains underresearched. While controlled experimentation is unlikely, business historians and investigative journalists can provide insight into many of these situations by their skillful articulation and their ability to dig comprehensively into the wide range of facets involved in complex organizational decisions. But it is difficult for the analyses to emerge free of errors and subjective biases.

Xerox decided to move its corporate headquarters to Stamford, Connecticut, from Rochester, New York—the site where the firm originated, and its main manufacturing center. At least six reasons for the decision circulated in the community:

1. Top management needed to be closer to Wall Streets' financial markets.
2. Top management needed to develop some space between itself and manufacturing operations to operate more as an international company with multiple marketing objectives.
3. Operations management could be free from the heavy hand of top management.
4. Top management could privately profit by moving from New York, which had an income tax, to Connecticut, which did not.
5. The wives of top managers of Xerox, a new company, never felt fully accepted by the older, established Rochester society.
6. Top management (and spouses) wanted to be closer to the New York entertainment world.

Even if one was privy to all the discussions and arguments that transpired before the decision to relocate, it would be impossible to separate the business justifications from the personal rationalizations. The personal advantages might have been seen only after the idea for moving was first broached. On the other hand, personal dissatisfactions may have sparked the initiative to investigate the organizational benefits and costs of such a move. Asking the actors to recall what happened would only provide partially valid evidence. Such recall could not recapture subconscious motivations, hidden, or blind agendas.

The example illustrates the difficulty of trying to move from conceptualizing what is involved in an important organizational decision to obtaining an empirically valid understanding of the decision process. We are blessed with a surplus of organizational theories and theorists replete with concepts and models of organizational decision making, but we have little hard data to provide the support for them.

March and Simon (1958) laid out over a hundred propositions, yet a quarter of a century later—while much reference and comment about them continues—relatively few empirical tests have been made of most of them. Similarly, the experimental results from tests of hypotheses derived from behavioral decision theory need to be replicated in organizational settings (March & Shapira, 1982).

Decision flow. We have little understanding on how decisions flow and change as they move through organizations. The linkages between strategic decision making at the top and operational decisions below call for more empirical study (Mintzberg et al., 1976). This is most clearly seen in the political arena. Elections result in changes in the political leadership. The new leaders try to change old programs or to introduce new programs. Nevertheless, the cadres, bureaucracies, and civil servants who must operationalize and administer these programs remain in office. This considerably constrains implementation of programmatic changes. The new Administration could not replace the whole operational apparatus even if it wanted to. One of its key problems becomes how to ensure that its new policies are translated into new practices. A similar unresolved issue is how decisions about organizational operations, aimed to promote the organization's immediate efficiency, interact with decisions about the long-term survival of the organization (Spray, 1976). This, in turn, expands into the question of why some organizations grow while other remain small.

Growth. Clearly, organizational decision making is systematically affected by an organization's position in its development history. Small businesses have different decision processes than large corporations. But the issue is still hardly explored. As an organization grows, matures, and declines, its decision processes are likely to be different. What kinds of decisions occur in some small businesses so that they just succeed in maintaining themselves? In contrast, what decisions lead other small businesses to develop into large corporations (Dandridge, 1979)?

Decision priorities. When should one decision be made relative to others? What decisions should be made today rather than tomorrow? Better-structured, interconnected problems can be dealt with by analysis of pathways and decision trees; less well-structured and unconnected problems require a different approach to establishing their priorities. The intermingling of planning and operations requires more than simple sequential ordering of decisions. The setting of decision-making priorities needs attention. Roberts and Hanline (1975) suggest building the schedule of decision making around the judged potential gain from each decision. A more complex set of judgments is probably needed for dealing with various attributes of the set of problems to be faced. Do they emerge from narrow or wide scans? Are they accute or chronic problems? How much information is likely to be available? Is there organizational slack to permit simultaneous attack on several problems?

Methods and models

For 2,500 years decision making, as conceived by Western philosophy, was an orderly, forward-moving, causal means-to-ends. Cyclical thinking was more characteristic of Oriental approaches. In the last three decades' consideration of organizational decision making, description has come to be required before prescription; the fixed, ideal goal has been replaced by a readjusted, displaced objective; the logic-driven complete search has become limited; the infinite perfection of information has been rejected as infeasible; rationalization has become as important as rationality; and disorderliness, incrementalism, serendipity, and contiguity have been elevated to key aspects of the organizational decision process.

A summary model. Figure 7 is a model of the possible causal linkages between the idealized phases of organizational decision making. The linkages are as follows: (a) Scanning alerts decision makers to possible discrepancies outside or inside the organization; (a') the diagnosis lacks completeness—more detailed scanning is requested; (b) the completed diagnosis directs where to search and/or innovate; (b') the search results in a modification of the aspirations in the diagnosis; (c) the alternatives found or invented need to be evaluated so a choice can be made; (c') the choice is already made and search proceeds to justify it; (d) the choice must be authorized and implemented; (d') authorization is rejected or implementation failure forces reevaluation, redesigning (d''), or redefinition of the problem (d'''); (e) the problem diagnosis completely defines the solution—any search is preempted; (e') the problem diagnosis is reshaped to fit the choice—a choice is made on what can be done, not on solving the precipitating problems; (f) implementation, either a failure or a success, refocuses scanning.

Links a, b, c, d, e, and f are the more commonly expected cause-effect relations but links a', b', c', d', d'', d''', and e' may appear more often than supposed. The model is a description of what is possible. It provides a basis for empirical study of what is likely to be most efficient and most effective. If one is willing to make further assumptions about the nature

FIGURE 7   Potential causal linkages in organizational decisions

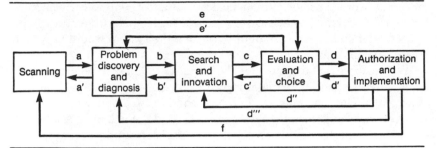

Causal linkages

a. Scanning detects a possible opporunity, threat, variance or disturbance.
a.' Diagnosis calls for more detailed information.
b. Discovery and diagnosis determines the direction and location of search.
b.' Search and innovation produce redefinitions of the problem, changes in level of aspiration, and displacement of the ideal.
c. Search and innovation provide what is to be evaluated and chosen.
c.' Evaluations and choices foreclose on what will be sought. Search is conducted to justify what has already been chosen as a solution.
d. Evaluation and choice must be authorized before being implemented.
d.' Rejected authorization or failed implementation forces reevaluation; (d") redesign or (d''') redefinition.
e. Problem diagnosis determines the evaluation and choice. Search is eliminated. The solutions to the problem are given by the diagnosis.
e.' The evaluation and choice result in modifying the diagnosis. What we want to do leads to our articulating that we have problems.
f. Implementation experience changes scanning focus.

of the decision process, specific deductions can be drawn. For example, if one accepts as an axiom that forward cause-effect linkages such as a, b, c, and d need to be balanced in speed and amount by parallel backward linkages such as a', b', c', d', then it follows that decision outcomes will be more effective if such balance is observed.

It seems reasonable to suggest that all of these cause-effect linkages are likely to be observed, but in differing amounts and in varying significance. It is likely that effective organizational decision processes will tend to display more of some linkages than others. Effective decisions will be described by patterns of linkages different from ineffective decisions. For example, organizations that exclusively focus on search for justification, where managers must primarily be naive advocates rather than naive scientists, are likely to be in a state of decay. But organizations that demand only naive scientists to the exclusion of the naive lawyers, also do so at their own peril. It becomes a matter of how much of each causal linkage is present, not the absolute amount. We are likely to find a direct relation between how much of each is present and the organization's effectiveness. Some degree of contiguity in time or place is mandatory for easy process flow. We can take advantage of contiguity by making it easier for certain executives to be closer together in time and space. But total dependence on contiguity to drive the system would make for organizational disaster.

We speculate that organizational decisions are likely to be most effective if characterized by stronger forward linkages (a, b, c, d) with bursts of accompanying backward linkages (such as c′, b′, and a′) and some stronger backward linkages (particularly d‴ and f). Such linkage analysis may be an important guide to developing decision support systems and improving organizational decision effectiveness. We may be able to relate missing or inadequate linkages to the effectiveness of decision outcomes and satisfaction with them.

In the Garbage Can model of Cohen, March, and Olsen (1972), applicable to organizational anarchies, preferences are ill-defined, inconsistent, unclear, uncertain, or problematic. The means the organization uses are unclear and misunderstood by their own members. Learning and precedents are a matter of accidental trial-and-error. Participation in the decision process is fluid; the mix of decision makers changes capriciously.

> . . . such organizations can be viewed . . . as collections of choices looking for problems, issues and feelings looking for decision situations in which they might be aired, solutions looking for issues to which there might be an answer, and decision makers looking for work. (p. 1)

Such an organizational anarchy is characterized by weakened linkages in the model of Figure 7. Thus, ill-defined preferences are conceived to imply fuzzy evaluations. Misunderstood means imply fuzzy search mechanisms. Fluid participation results in fluctuating scanning, diagnosis, search, and evaluation. This weakens all linkages. Boundaries between the problem, search, and evaluation processes are also weakened to the point that much overlapping occurs.

The Kepner-Tregoe, or Maier staging-trained, rational organizations can be conceived in the model as maintaining strong, direct, forward linkages from problem to search to evaluation (a, b, c).

The romantic, mystic, political, rationalizing organizations can be conceived as maintaining strong backward linkages from evaluation to search to problem (c′, b′, a′).

Some other possible but highly ineffectual linkages are not shown in Figure 7. For instance, a threat picked up in scanning might lead to bypassing diagnosis and search to achieve a much too hasty choice.

Cultural effects should be considered. One wonders which links Cartesian-intoxicated French are likely to emphasize as compared to Japanese who pursue nonWestern logic.

Effective versus ineffective decisions. A concern for theory and a concentration on describing departures from optimality have probably undercut useful empirical studies of effective and ineffective organizational decision processes that use the standard approaches of personnel psychology, such as the critical incidents technique. We should focus more attention on the central question of what differentiates effective from ineffective decision processes. Curtis (1976), for instance, used the critical incidents technique in interviews with 45 randomly selected school superintendents. The conclusion reached was that effective rather than ineffective decisions were more likely if team rather than individual decision making was employed; if adequate time was allowed; and if a plan of action emerged from the process.

Some alternative methods. Particularly promising is the combination employed in field work by Heller, Drenth and Koopman (1982) of tracing documentary evidence and retrospections of informants integrated with observation of the decision process as it continues forward to completion.

The use of verbal protocols has been a major approach to studying human information processing, particularly for complex tasks (Clarkson, 1962; Newall & Simon, 1972). But it would seem preferable to use Bloom's stimulated recall method (Bloom & Broder, 1950) to study the process with less potential interference of the method with the activity under study. As the audiotape or videotape of a decision-making experience is played back, a second tape is running to record the participant's recall of events. This ought to stimulate more salient material as well as enhance the reliability and validity of the recall.

Perrow (1972) suggested a way to assess how much decision making is required in a designated situation. Organizational members are asked how often they face problems for which there are no ready solutions. Unfortunately, distorted answers are expected. It would be useful to find indirect ways to ask this same question.

There is a paucity of completed multistage and organizational decision-making experiments because of the inherent difficulties found in such research. A method, probably using an interactive computer program in which a few simple premises suffice for handling the task, is necessary.

Problem discovery and diagnosis

In the ideal, problems emerge as reactions to true gaps between the actual and desired state of affairs; they are the result of variances from expectations. But regardless of the true state of affairs, there are proactive individual decision-makers who will always find or even invent problems—like the small boy who, given a hammer, will find things to use it on. A veteran of 30 years in the federal service quipped that one could always find problems to solve. If organizations are apart, they need to be put together. If they are together, they need to be separated. This will make for a long career as a federal executive. Change for change's sake is advanced as an argument for determining that a problem exists and that decisions are required about what changes to institute. Nevertheless, most managers state that they would like to be more proactive, more alert to possible problems than they actually are (Bass & Burger, 1979). How to promote such proactivity is an important, unresolved issue.

If not started by a crisis, the sensed gap between current and desired states seems to wax in urgency. Then, in a good many instances, if search and choice processes do not follow, it is likely to wane. We know very little about such aborted organizational problems. Some obviously don't go away and failure to attend to them leads to a worsening of the situation. But there are many problems that, if left unsolved, do tend to go away. How can we detect which problems will be best handled by being abandoned rather than solved?

Keep in mind that the current load of problems is likely to determine the extent executives are open to considering new ones. A manager facing crises does not look for additional problems; one faced with a few mild problems is likely to search for opportunities. The threshold for reacting to a problem will shift depending on the executive's work load and the number and type of decisions currently being faced (Radomsky, 1967).

While March and Shapira (1982) see the contiguity in time and place of persons, problems, and solutions as central causal factors, Perrow (1972) finds it hard to accept the Cyert and March (1963) idea that organizational goals emerge primarily as a fortuitous process based on the "disorganized file drawers of goals" each organizational constituent maintains for use in negotiated trade-offs. Solutions are developed by decision units looking for problems. Perrow suggests the determination of organizational goals is and can be much more intentional and rational. We are dealing here with empirical questions. No doubt, one can find many organizations in which Cyert and March's model applies, and many in which much more deliberation and orderliness is the rule. How much spontaneity and how much deliberation is near optimum is an unanswered question, probably strongly dependent on the decision task required.

Incrementing. The individual decision maker is seen by Lindbloom (1969) to make successive limited comparisons, taking small steps from the current to the desired state of affairs. Even strategic planning can be incremental (Quinn, 1979). What happens in a chain of decision makers? Under what conditions does a brushfire starting at one end of the chain reach the other end as a conflagration? Organizations can be the victims of "creeping error." Uncertainty is absorbed. But one can also see errors being magnified as they move through successive decision units. Presumably, previous organizational history produces such processes. What are the differences in the way decisions moving up the organizational ladder are modified as compared to those moving down? Downward movement is much faster, supposedly, than upward movement.

Comparable questions can be posed about the cascade of decisions from the center to the boundaries of the organization or from the boundary units to the center. Whether the environment is stable or turbulent, uniform or heterogeneous, is likely to affect the warping of the decisions. A change in a uniform, stable environment which produces problems and tentative solutions at the organization's boundaries is likely to affect central-policy decision making more than a change in a turbulent, heterogeneous environment which prompts one unit at the boundary to decide to modify its procedures.

Timing. The same organizational problem can repeatedly surface to reality before the threshold of awareness and reaction is reached. The threshold of awareness may be reached many times and, as indicated before, actions may be avoided until the problem goes away. Whether or not organizational problems receive attention will depend on a variety of external and internal factors unrelated to the nature of the problem itself. For instance, whether an executive happens to read a magazine article or meet an old friend, may affect the decision to cross the threshold to take action. Although there is usually no scarcity of problems, only a portion are likely to capture the attention of executives. Some problems will be crowded out by others. Firms can continue to engage in much foolishness until hit by a downturn in the business cycle or the appearance of severe competition; suddenly they can no longer afford the slack in their systems. The same cries of alarm will go unheeded in some firms until crisis conditions appear. Executives learn to time their cries of alarm. Some of Etzioni's (1967) suggestions for continuing wider and narrow scanning mechanisms seem appropriate here. Safire (1981) notes that after each new U.S. president is inaugurated, the White House staffs must first focus on policies, then on operations. Early on, more power resides with those responsible for policy considerations. In time, the operations, and those in charge of operations, come to dominate. Presumably, the kinds of problems which originally attract the most attention are about policies; those that later attract most attention are about operations.

Buffers or amplifiers. Some individual executives and decision units absorb uncertainties. They muffle alarms. Problems, in general, have to be severe to be passed on from their unit. Other executives and units tend to amplify concern for any problems which have reached their attention. We could use a lot more information about the consistency of these tendencies and what contributes to them.

Surprises. One thing seems to be certain for most policy decision makers. Surprises are going to occur. How do organizations best prepare for unforeseen contingencies?

Recategorizations. A single piece of inconsistent evidence tends to be discounted in an overall impression. This is particularly true if the single bit of evidence is highly discrepant from the rest. Yet, such a discrepancy is also the basis of problem recognition, of reevaluating the evidence from a benign input to one that triggers an awareness of a problem. Threshold studies are needed to examine how the same objective discrepancies are seen as either conforming to current plans and expectations or as variances requiring attention (Feldman, 1981). In a world with multiple objectives, decision makers are faced with balancing desired outcomes. One outcome could be maximized only at the expense of seriously reducing achievement of the others. The balancing depends on the values of the decision makers and is likely to result in differences in what they see as important discrepancies calling for action. One executive may see a slight decline in sales as traumatic; another with more interest in product quality and service may see the same objective event as of little consequence. Each executive is likely to be unaware of how his or her own values affect the weight they attach to different kinds of variances. Many values are implicit. Executives seldom consciously introspect enough to identify their own value system (Kast & Rosenzweig, 1970) and the impact of their values on their attention to variances. Values are more likely to surface to consciousness and be made explicit in the choice phase (and, secondarily, in the search phase) of the decision process.

Diagnosis. Mintzberg et al. (1976) were surprised by the lack of research attention paid to problem diagnosis. They regard it as the single most important phase in the decision process, for it determines to a major degree the courses of action that will be taken. It seems to be a highly underresearched phase of the organizational decision-making process. One reason for the lack of attention by American research to organizational diagnosis may be that American managers seem to pay less formal attention to the diagnostic phase than, for instance, Japanese managers appear to do (Drucker, 1971).

Structuring. Much of our argumentation has centered around whether problems are well structured or ill structured as given. Yet how well a problem is structured is variable in itself and is modifiable. For instance, when we try to make use of a computer to assist in dealing with a problem, the programming requires a careful increase of the quantity and quality of the problem's structure. We are forced to be more explicit and more systematic. We need to research how readily we can accurately move problems from the category of ill structured to the category of well structured. We need to learn what is lost in the process, as well as what is obviously gained in terms of the ability to use the available algorithms which result from the improved problem structure. Structure is man-made simplification of reality. One can reach precise but erroneous solutions to what in reality are complex problems. Body counts are poor indicators of an enemy's morale and willingness to persist.

Decision making for a closed system can pursue optimum solutions. Where the system remains open, one can only establish criteria of good decisions based on perceived improvement over past performance or by comparison with performance in similar organizations. To the degree that the system for which the decisions are being made could move realistically toward more closure (for example, by increased control of the organization's environment), decision making could move further toward optimality. Obviously, the costs and threats might be much greater than the benefits of moving from satisficing with an open system toward optimization and closure with a less open system. Nevertheless, there may be considerable overall benefit from, for example, reductions in the openness of a system or a subsystem by vertical integration of all the units in the organization, or by making long-term agreements with suppliers or buyers.

Goal clarity.   This is associated repeatedly in management surveys with organization satisfaction and effectiveness (Bass, 1981). Never-theless, March and Shapira (1982) suggest that ambiguous preferences permit exploration and development of more attractive goals. Establish-ing a single, clear goal toward which everyone must work may produce less satisfaction when conflicts of interest are present than "creative obfuscation" and sequential attention. Again, the decision tasks may determine which direction is best to take.

Simplification.   Structuring, closing the system, and clarifying goals are all seen as simplifications by organizations of the decision process. The decision process does not search for and evaluate all possible alter-natives. Multiple goals are handled sequentially. What we know about how rumors and individual perceptions and cognitions are simplified can also be examined for relevance to the organizational situation.

Search and design

Search and innovation depend on the source of the discrepancies which alert the decision makers to the existence of a problem. Four types of benchmarks provide anchors, against which departures signal the emergence of possible problems and the direction search or innovation should take. First are criterion checks (such as territorial sales). Second are repetitive procedures (such as annual performance ratings). Third are policy statements. Fourth are other decision units inside or outside the organization. Ference (1970) suggests that deviations from explicit criteria and from routines are likely to stimulate search in the immediate area of the problem and among solutions already available. But departures from policy are expected to result in more extended search and design efforts.

With reference to the impact of others, either inside or outside the organization, some regularities of consequence may be found. For example, one may speculate that in the absence of clear criterion checks, the impact of other decision units on problem awareness and the instituting of search is heightened. Furthermore, decision makers will set different weights on the various units in the organization. A dean practicing management-by-exception may institute search and choice based on the complaints of one student whose complaint has been ignored by the allegedly offending faculty member.

Design alternatives. Organizational design still seems to be a matter of art and personal preference. "By their organizational designs, ye shall know them." We need simple studies of how executives would like to organize those around them as well as how they actually do so. A set of standard cases could be developed for use in discriminating among executive preferences for, say, more or less hierarchy or more or less structure. Studies of transferred executives could determine how they actually introduce their particular, favored approaches to organizational designs as opportunities to do so are made available.

Overload. Increasingly, computer technology expands the load of information available to decision makers. How do they deal with overloading? By temporarily ignoring portions? By processing the more accessible portions? By declining in receptivity as a function of fatigue? By using waiting-line tactics? By filtering to simplify? By organizing to receive generally fewer broad lumps rather than more detailed inputs? By using parallel processing channels? By withdrawing altogether? (See Miller, 1960.)

Sequential or parallel? For Simon (1955), search is sequential; each successive alternative is judged for its satisfactoriness until a threshold is reached. For Soelberg (1967), search generates parallel alternatives whose explicit comparisons against an implicit favorite await the end of search. For Soelberg, there is more rationalization and justification in the search and choice process. It is probable that both rationality and rationalizing are occurring. How much of each is an empirical question no doubt affected by the constraints and contingencies of the situation and the decision makers.

Speed of decision. Search is divergent; choice is convergent. Early choice shuts off possibilities of wider search and likely innovative alternatives. Tradeoffs exist between rapid decision making, cost of search, creative innovations, and higher quality solutions. Can decision makers be taught the conditions under which search should be extended and choice delayed?

Character of evoked alternatives. We still have only a modest amount of understanding about the character of the array of alternatives that will emerge.

Along with areas of control, the impact of the diagnosis, and the outcomes sought, the alternatives generated depend on a variety of additional exogeneous variables. March and Simon (1958) suggested a number of such variables including the objective availability of external alternatives, one's felt participation in decision making, organizational inhibitors, task complexity, and decision makers' competencies. Many have commented on the abstractness of Simon's bounded rationality argument that decision makers search "locally." What is meant by this? More generally, what else limits the search process, apart from the problem diagnosis and the intended outcomes? It is suggested that decision makers start by focusing on those variables over which they have control (Emory & Niland, 1968). It would follow that ordinarily they would focus next on those variables over which their decision unit, then their organization, has control. Finally, they would consider environmental conditions over which they usually have little control.

Sources of information. Ference (1970) suggested that information will be sought informally for ill-structured problems. Furthermore, information sources will be selected according to substantive needs, not the prescribed organizational rules, and from sources used frequently rather than infrequently. Consistent with this, Klauss and Bass (1982) were surprised to find in large scale surveys of engineering project personnel that as much as 85 percent of the employees' information came from interpersonal, face-to-face, or telephone contact rather than by written documents and memos.

Presumably, with the advent of management information systems, the computer is becoming an ever-increasing source. Also, the size of the organization, the functions of the manager, and the type of decisions are obviously likely to affect which sources are selected. But the issue of information sources remains underresearched. The sources are likely to differ on such important dimensions as their credibility, availability, saliency, and comprehensiveness.

Evaluation and choice

Research is needed on how information and the structure of the situation in which it is embedded are used to make choices (Slovic & Lichtenstein, 1971). Again, relatively little is known about the interplay of what is required in a choice situation and the particular biases of the decision makers. On the one hand, the decision makers' statistical knowledge, skill, tolerance for ambiguity, motivation, and familiarity with the choice situation make a difference in the choice made. On the other hand, choice will be a function of situational factors such as failure and the importance of the decision. For example, more risky choices are likely to be taken when decisions are less important. We are willing to take bigger risks when the stakes are low.

A list of questions about risk in environmental, health, and safety decision making includes: How do we determine how safe is safe enough? How are implicit estimates of risk translated into decision making? What are the institutional constraints associated with decision making in the face of risk and uncertainty? How are individual perceptions of risk aggregated to social (and organizational) perceptions of risk? Are some risks unacceptable no matter what the expected benefits? (PRA, 1979–80.)

Exploitation versus exploration. Organizational decision making often can be seen to lie on a dimension ranging from conservative exploitation to exploratory gambling. Exploitation usually yields relatively lower, but more certain, payoffs than does exploration which in turn yields relatively less certain but higher payoffs. Exploitation is preferred if less risk can be tolerated, but many more conditions generate exploitation rather than exploration or vice versa and would seem well worth examining. Time preferences as to when money outcomes are to be achieved have been computed, but, the numbers obtained do not necessarily mirror a decision maker's true time preferences (Weingartner, 1969).

Simulations, such as Exercise Koloman (Thiagarajan, 1975) and Exercise Venture (Link, Thiagarajan, Trbovich, & Vaughan, 1975), are available for the study of exploitation versus exploration. MacCrimmon (1974) suggests that for quick decisions the more adventurous gambling strategy should be preferred. Presumably, those preferring exploitation have concave utility functions against increasing uncertainty; those preferring exploration have convex ones.

While utility functions seem relatively stable over time (Grayson, 1960), the interplay among executives with different-shaped utility functions seen by Swalm (1966), would be well worth further study. One interesting question is: If one is in a chain-of-command, how will one's utility function be modified knowing that one's decisions are to be reviewed by higher authority? Results of the vertical interplay of decision-making units are likely to be quite different in an organization with an open, trusting climate than one which is closed and untrusting. The risk of taking risks is magnified when trust is absent. Unfortunately, direct methods of measuring individual utilities are likely to be highly distorted (Sen, 1970; MacCrimmon, 1974). We need to develop or use indirect measurement methods of utility such as error choice, sentence completion, or even projective techniques. Better yet, we need to study actual investment or purchasing behavior as risks are varied.

Strategic assumptions. Promising—but untested—is Mitroff and Emshoff's (1979) approach to the evaluation of a designated strategy by working backward to the data supporting it, then from the supporting data to the diagnostic assumptions. The data are conceived as minor premises; the assumptions as major premises; and the strategy as the consequence of a syllogistic argument. Focus moves far back to the assumptions about the conditions, events, or attributes that must be true about the problem.

Bayesian analysis. Bayesian analysis permits one to adjust subjective probability estimates about the likelihood of an outcome on the basis of newly acquired data. Many questions about the application and applicability of Bayes' theorem remain unanswered. For what kinds of choice situations is the Bayesian approach best suited? How can we obtain accurate subjective probability assessments? What is the best way to revise prior probabilities on the basis of new information? What procedure should be followed to revise prior probabilities from a complex of information from different kinds of inquiries such as market tests, product-use tests, and surveys?

How can the Bayesian approach be applied when the decision-making unit is a group? How can it be combined for a cascade of decisions involved among line executives, or specialists, and other staff personnel? (Newman, 1971.)

Effects of failure. Theories about the impact of trouble on the willingness of organizations to increase their risk seeking generally have not been supported by research findings. Both increased chances for survival and for complete failure seem to result in failing organizations increasing their risk seeking (March & Shapira, 1982). What may be needed is a theory about changes in risk taking that accompany fast growth and success as well as decline and threat of failure.

Unintended consequences. Organizational decision making is replete with examples of choice solutions producing both intended and unintended consequences. March and Simon (1958) contrasted Merton's (1936) and Gouldner's (1954) models of how the demand by the organization for control not only results in intended consequences such as emphasis on reliability, use of impersonal rules, and visibility of power relations, but also in many possible unintended consequences such as interpersonal tension and felt need for defensibility. How much attention is paid, and how much should be paid, to unintended consequences when making choices is unknown.

Conflict and authorization

Relatively little research has been completed on this phase conceived by Mintzberg et al. (1976) as the final acceptance or rejection of the proposed solution including its going forward or upward in the organization. For instance, we know little about how socioemotional factors in the earlier phases of the decision-process affect acceptance or rejection. Much more attention has been paid to the implementation of decisions as a function of developed commitment.

Coalition formation studies have focused on outcomes rather than processes involved and so the latter, in particular, remains less well understood. Nevertheless, Davis, Loughlin, and Komorita (1976) have been encouraged by the agreement of predictions from descriptive and normative theories about the union of weaker persons against the single stronger person in the behavioral experimental studies generated by economic and mathematical theories.

Legitimacy. What makes a decision process legitimate? Legitimacy is attached to a decision which is reached by due process. The process follows a course prescribed by agreed upon rules, by custom, or by law—it is due course of process. March and Shapira (1982) offer two propositions. To be legitimate, the process is sensitive to the concerns of relevant people. The right people have influenced the process. (But who the right people are remains a big question.) It would seem worthwhile to fully explore and expand this important contribution to acceptance, authorization, and commitment.

Constraints

How close decision making should be to the scene of the action is a general subject of continuing inquiry. Can effective marketing policies for a foreign subsidiary be made at the international headquarters of the parent multinational firm? Can top management make effective planning decisions for worker-supervisor configurations? Self-planning decisions come closest to optimal. But when self-planning is not possible, many suggestions have been offered for offsetting the separation of planning from doing. For instance, planners should maintain close consultation with operators as the plans are developed. Frequent feedback of success or failure should be built into the plans. Providing for operator discretion may also help (Bass, 1977).

How to organize effective decision making in respect to the technology of the organization remains a central research question. Much of the argument in favor of hierarchy as the "natural law of organizations" is as polemical as the argument for power equalized systems. Conceptualizations of technology that directly suggest the kinds of organizational decision processes that will approach nearer to optimality are still needed. How, and in what ways, should we depart from hierarchy for various newer kinds of technologies to come closer to better decision making? What designs will be most effective for man-computer-equipment team networks? What designs can achieve better decision making in retirement communities?

It seems obvious that organizational decisions will be more effective the greater the participation and influence of those decision makers with more relevant information. The more correlated information and authority are in a decision-making system, the more likely that the decision outcome will be effective (Bass, 1960).

The impact of organizational constraints on the tendencies of individual decision makers to filter and to pigeonhole information has yet to be studied comprehensively. Nor do we know much about why they use certain heuristics and not others (Ungson, Braunstein & Hall, 1981).

Informal organization. Although it is well known (see Dalton, 1959, for instance) that the informal channels of communication and other informal links between organizational members deviate from the formal channels of authority and control, we still have little appreciation of how the amount and direction of such deviations systematically affect the decision-making process. Presumably, conflict increases with increasing deviation (or increasing deviation reflects increasing conflict and blockage in the formal organization).

Individual biases and reeducation. What happens when decision makers become aware that they possess biases which fly in the face of reality? The continuing success of one-armed bandits and lotteries with high but improbable payoffs suggests that intellectual understanding of one-to-ten versus ten-to-one odds on bets does not produce much change in continued preference of the majority for the long shot. Statistically astute psychologists are still victimized by the erroneous law of small members. As Slovic, Fischoff, and Lichtenstein (1977) noted, experts often do no better—and sometimes worse—in making decisions in the face of uncertainty. As experts, they often suffer from overconfidence and do particularly poorly even in comparison to a random strategy implying no knowledge about the process. Can such decision making be improved by attention to the socioemotional as well as the intellectual aspects of decision-making in uncertain situations? How should such reeducation be developed and evaluated?

Katz and Kahn (1966) suggest bringing together for planning upper level managers concerned about long-range objectives and lower level managers responsible for carrying out the actions required by the plans. Fisch (1961) proposed closing the distance by declaring that the line-staff concept is obsolete. Early in product development, for instance, a team of basic experts in R&D, marketing technology, and so forth, are responsible for decisions. As the product idea progresses, some basic people are dropped from the team; developmental engineers and technicians are added. In later development, the final production and service managers who will actually conduct operations join the team with the developers dropping off.

Many of the devices of self-management and other forms of industrial democracy are legislated efforts to close the distance between decision making and decision execution. (See Bass, 1981, pp. 203–206.)

Contiguity. March and Romelaer (1976) find contiguity in time and place of problems, solutions, and decision makers more important to decision outcomes than hierarchical or consequential means-end analyses. If they are correct, much can be done with network studies, physical layouts, and man-team-computer-linkages to determine how much weight should be given to contiguity over rationality in understanding decision processes.

Decision aids and support systems

EDP. Electronic data processing as a decision support system is rapidly expanding in terms of its potential applications and effects on organizational life. Alter's study of 56 EDP decision support systems (1976) revealed six ways in which they provide support: (1) retrieving isolated data items; (2) providing a way for ad hoc analysis of data files; (3) obtaining prespecified aggregations of data in the form of standard reports; (4) estimating the consequences of proposed decisions; (5) proposing decisions; and (6) making decisions. We need to detail Alter's (1976) parallel discovery of the many unintended consequences of these support systems. He found that the users valued the EDP support systems for a variety of reasons completely different from the intended purposes of the systems. A wide range of such purposes were seen. The support systems were valued as aids to improving interpersonal communication, problem solving, individual learning, and organizational control.

The support systems were also seen to provide managers with vehicles for persuasion, and organizations with a common vocabulary and discipline to facilitate negotiations among decision units.

The advent of the computer has been a great leap forward in information processing. It should make relevant, detailed information available as needed. It can provide much of the necessary scanning, signaling only when human intervention is necessary. It can draw together what is needed for improved diagnoses. It can widen and intensify the search process exponentially. It can facilitate the evaluation and choice process by improved displays which promote human understanding. It can broaden the choice process by generating synthetic alternatives and alternative futures.

Nevertheless, there remain great discrepancies between the promise of what computer technology can offer and its effectiveness in supporting organizational decision making (Milutinovich, Lipson, & Naumes, 1976). Presumably, many of the unanswered questions about organizational decision making in the decades ahead will center on interactions between computers, individuals, and organizations. The required, correct information must get to the right person and place at the right time (Brink, 1971).

Each year that passes sees further strides in hardware and software development. Earlier difficulties disappear. Nevertheless, with computer technology, information may be plentiful without being relevant. It may be extensive but inadequate. It may be detailed but not precise. "Its seeming comprehensiveness (can be) illusory and, although it flows in without respite, it (may) not (be) timely. In short, it (may be) less a help than a hindrance to effective decision making and control." (Hertz, 1969, p. 30)

For effective decision making, middle management usually needs more than original summaries of transactions during a given period. The data may need to be rearranged, resummarized, and restructured. One manager may need output displays quite different from those required by another manager.

Established schedules for data gathering and printouts may completely fail to serve the need for a rapid decision at a particular point in time. The executive may have to fall back on less desirable but available data bases.

Despite the rapid advances in computer technology, particularly in microcomputers, which has increased the ease with which managers can learn to use computers to support their decision making, management attitude and lack of education still seems to hinder the potential use of the computer in planning and forecasting. "Most managers cannot easily communicate their experience and judgment into machine readable actions" (Milutinovich, Lipson & Naumes, 1974.) The challenge for both research and education is to develop human capabilities to measure up to the technological capabilities of the computer and to reshape organizations and their policies to facilitate the process.

Nominal groups. We need to explore the conditions under which nominal groups do better than real groups and vice versa (Hoyt, 1974). Further, no one has yet invented a way to determine which member of a group (either nominal or real) has the best answer, since group results continue to be better than that of the average member but not as good as that of the best member. If one could estimate in advance who was the best member, and if groups accepted this estimation, group results could be moved further toward optimality by differentially weighting votes of individual members according to their estimated expertise—the SPAN technique.

The effectiveness of nominal groups, brainstorming, synectics, and so on, needs to be explored as part of a larger decision process. Comparisons among these aids will be useful.

MAUT. Numerous questions remain to be answered about the validity and applicability of Multiple Attribute Utility Theory. These include what assessment procedures to use; the impact of missing or neglected attributes; the direct or indirect assignment of weights; whether and where the theory can be applied; and how to go about validating the theory (Slovic, Fischhoff, & Lichtenstein, 1977).

Elegance. Like Gresham's Law, simpler but less adequate analytical aids appear to forestall the use of more complex, more valid ones. Consider a common decision that finance officers are called upon to make: namely, how to evaluate equities. According to a survey by Bing (1971), despite the more elegant approaches taught in academic institutions, three-fourths of practitioners tended to concentrate on only three simple procedures: comparing price-earnings multiples with norms, comparing price multiplied by estimated future earnings, and comparing p/e multiples and growth with industry norms. Yet a rich academic literature is available (e.g., Brealey & Myers, 1981) on the theories and techniques of finance, providing both deductive and empirical validations of more sophisticated alternatives to making effective decisions.

In the same way, DeVall, Bolas, and Tang (1976) have shown that implementation by management of applied research is hindered rather than helped by research results that are supported by elegant, rather than simple, statistics, conceptualizations, and research designs.

One reason for the continued, greater use of simpler aids is greater familiarity and experience with them. But another reason for the wide gap found between academic research and real world practice as pointed out by Bing (1971) and Carleton (1977) among others, is that process issues play an important role in determining such decision making and its effectiveness.

Even after coaching, decision makers may reject the underlying premises on which a complex aid is based. They also often see the aid as too complicated and unrealistic. Even if the aid is used, the conclusions reached with it may be rejected as too difficult to explain or justify to receive authorization from higher-ups. The quality of that conclusion depends on the quality of the judgments put into the analysis by the decision makers, no matter how sophisticated the analysis. How sensitive decision aids are to errors in problem structuring is unknown. Equally unknown is how much a decision aid is worth (Slovik, Fischhoff, & Lichtenstein, 1977).

A systems view. A rich, unmined area for study will accrue from Keene and Martin's (1978) conception of the decision support as part of a larger system of decision maker and decision support. The decision support is a model of reality to be used by the decision maker to examine various alternative futures for which different parameters, variables, and assumptions are entered into the model. As these futures are displayed, the decision maker's cognitive map of reality is modified. The decision maker's final choice of alternative emerges from comparisons among these displayed futures. The changes in these maps during the course of interaction between decision maker and model may be a particularly informative way to open up new understanding of the organizational decision process. But this is only one among the wealth of opportunities for empirical research on organizational decisions. Such research will contribute to better understanding of human decision making in organizations as well as more effective utilization of organizational resources.

References

Abelson, R. P. Script processing in attitude formation and decision making. In J. S. Carroll & J. W. Payne (Eds.) *Cognition and social behavior*. Hillsdale, N.J.: Erlbaum, 1976.

Ackoff, R. L. Management misinformation systems. *Management Science*, 1967, *14*, B-147-56.

Aguilar, F. J. *Scanning the business environment*. New York: Macmillan, 1967.

Aiken, M., & Hage, J. Organizational interdependence and intra-organizational structure. *American Sociological Review*, 1968, *33*, 219–230.

Alexander, E. R. Choice in a changing world. *Policy Sciences*, 1972,*3*, 325–337.

Alexander, E. R. The limits of uncertainty: A note. *Theory and Decision*, 1975, *6*, 363–370.

Alexander, E. R. The design of alternatives in organizational contexts: A pilot study. *Administrative Science Quarterly*, 1979, *24*,382–404.

Alexis, M., & Wilson, C. Z. *Organizational decision-making*. Englewood Cliffs, N.J.: Prentice Hall, 1967.

Allen, H. T. An empirical test of choice and decision postulates in the Cyert-March Behavioral Theory of the Firm. *Administrative Science Quarterly*, 1966, *11*, 405–413.

Alter, S. L. How effective managers use information systems. *Harvard Business Review*, 1976, *54*, 97–104.

Anderson, N. H. Algebraic models in perception. In E. C. Carterette & M. P. Friedman (Eds.), *Handbook of perception*. New York: Academic Press, 1974.

Ansoff, H. I. *Corporate strategy*. New York: McGraw-Hill, 1965.

Aram, J. D. *Dilemmas of administrative behavior*. Englewood Cliffs, N.J.: Prentice-Hall, 1976.

Arbel, A., & Strebel, P. The neglected small firm effects. *Financial Review*, in press.

Argyris, C. *Integrating the individual and the organization*. New York: Wiley, 1964.

Arrow, K. J. *The limits of organizations*. New York: Norton, 1974.

Arrow, K. J. Public and private values. In S. Hook (Ed.), *Human values and economic policy*. New York: New York University Press, 1967.

Ashby, W. R. *An introduction to cybernetics*. London: Methuen, 1964.

Ashton, R. M. The robustness of linear models for decision-making. *Omega*, 1976, *4*, 609–615.

Atkinson, J. W. *An introduction to motivation*. Princton, N.J.: Van Nostrand, 1964.

Baker, K. R. An experimental study of the effectiveness of rolling schedules in production planning. *Decision Sciences*, 1977, *8*, 19–27.

Baldridge, J. V. *Power and conflict in the university*. New York: Wiley, 1971.

Barnard, C. I. *The functions of the executive*. Cambridge, Mass.: Harvard University Press, 1938.

Barnard, C. I. Elementary conditions of business morals. *California Management Review*, 1958, *1*, 1–13.

Bass, B. M. When planning for others. *Journal of Applied Behavioral Science*, 1970, *6*, 151–171.

Bass, B. M. Utility of managerial self-planning on a simulated production task with replications in twelve countries. *Journal of Applied Psychology*, 1977, *62*, 506–509.

Bass, B. M. *Stogdill's handbook of leadership (Rev. ed.)*. New York: Free Press, 1981.

Bass, B. M., Burger, P. B., et al. *Assessment of managers: An international comparison*. New York: Free Press, 1979.

Bass, B. M., Farrow, D. L. & Valenzi, E. R. A regression approach to identifying ways to increase leadership effectiveness. Technical Report 77–3, University of Rochester, 1977.

Bass, B. M., & Ryterband, E. C. *Organizational psychology (2d ed.)*. Boston: Allyn & Bacon, 1979.

Bass, B. M., McGregor, D. W., & Walters, J. L. Selecting foreign plant sites: Economical, social, and political considerations. *Academy of Management Journal*, 1977, *20*, 535–551.

Bass, B. M., & Rosenstein, E. Integration of industrial democracy and participative management: U.S. and European perspectives. In King, B. T., Streufort, S. S. & Fiedler, F. E. (Eds.), *Managerial control and organizational democracy*. Washington, D. C.: Victor Winston & Sons, 1977.

Bateson, N. Familiarization, group discussion, and risk taking. *Journal of Experimental Social Psychology.* 1966, *2*, 119–129.

Baum, B. M. *Decentralization of authority in a bureaucracy.* Englewood Cliffs, N.J.: Prentice-Hall, 1961, 21–29.

Behling, O. & Schriesheim, C. *Organizational behavior.* Boston: Allyn & Bacon, 1976.

Benner, R. V. The strategy and structure of change in the university: Theory and research on decision making in complex organizations. *Doctoral dissertation, Stanford University,* 1974.

Benson, R., Coe, W., & Klasson, C. A multiple criteria optimization algorithm. *Proceedings of American Institute for Decision Sciences,* 1975, 255–257.

Berelson, B., & Steiner, G. A. *Human behavior.* New York: Harcourt, Brace & World, 1967.

Billings, C. R. The psychological effect of change on middle management personnel and on the decision-making process within organizations. *Doctoral dissertation, California School of Professional Psychology,* San Francisco, 1974.

Bing, R. A. Survey of practitioners' stock evaluation methods. *Financial Analysts Journal,* 1971, May–June, 55–60.

Blankenship, L. V., & Miles, R. E. Organizational structure and managerial decision behavior. *Administrative Science Quarterly,* 1968, *13*, 106–20.

Blau, P.M. *The dynamics of bureaucracy.* Chicago: University of Chicago Press, 1955.

Bloom, B. S., & Broder, L. S. Problem-solving processes of college students. *Supplement Educational Monograph,* 1950, *73*.

Bobbitt, H. R., Breinholt, R. H., Doktor, R. H., & McNaul, J. P. *Organizational behavior.* Englewood Cliffs, N. J.: Prentice-Hall, 1974.

Bowman, J. S. Managerial ethics in business and government. *Business Horizons,* October 1976, *19*, 48–54.

Brealey, R., & Myers, S. *Principles of corporate finance.* New York: McGraw-Hill, 1981.

Brehmer, B. Hypotheses about relations between scaled variables in the learning of probabilistic inference tasks. *Organizational Behavior and Human Performance,* 1974, *11*, 1–27.

Brehmer, B., Kuylensticrna, J., & Liljergren, J. Effects of function, form and cue validity on subjects' hypotheses in probabilistic inference tasks. *Organizational Behavior and Human Performance,* 1974, *11*, 338–354.

Brickman, P. Optional stopping on ascending and descending series. *Organizational Behavior and Human Performance,* 1972, *7*, 53–62.

Brim, O. G., Jr. et al. *Personality and decision processes.* Stanford: Stanford University Press, 1962.

Brim, O. G., Jr., & Hoff, D. B. Individual and situational differences in desire for certainty. *Journal of Abnormal and Social Psychology,* 1957, *54*, 225–229.

Brink, V. A. *Computers and management: An executive viewpoint.* Englewood Cliffs, N.J.: Prentice-Hall, 1971.

Broadbent, D. E. *Decision and stress.* London: Academic Press, 1971.

Brody, N. The effect of commitment to correct and incorrect decisions on confidence in a sequential decision task. *American Journal of Psychology*, 1965, 78, 251–256.

Bromiley, P. Task environments and budgetary decision making. *Academy of Management Review*, 1981, 6, 277–288.

Browning, L. D. Diagnosing teams in organizational settings. *Group and Organization Studies*, 1977, 2, 187–197.

Brunswik, E. Representative design and probabilistic theory in a functional psychology. *Psychological Review*, 1955, 62, 193–217.

Burns, T. On the plurality of social systems. In J. R. Lawrence (Ed.), *Operational Research and the Social Sciences*. London: Tavistock, 1965.

Business Week. Forecasters turn to group guesswork. March 14, 1970, pp. 130–134.

Bylsma, D., Jr. Changes in locus of decision making and organizational structure in selected public community colleges in Michigan since 1965. *Doctoral dissertation, University of Michigan*, 1969.

Campbell, A. C. On introducing supraminimal data to items whose solution demands the use of indirect procedures. *British Journal of Psychology*, 1968, 59, 211–217.

Campbell, J. P. Individual versus group problem solving in an industrial sample. *Journal of Applied Psychology*, 1968, 52, 205–210.

Caplow, T., & McGee, R. J. *The academic market place*. New York: Basic Books, 1958.

Carleton, W. An agenda for more effective research in corporate finance. *Financial Management*, 1978, 7–10.

Caro, R. A. *The power broker: Robert Moses and the fall of New York*. New York: Knopf, 1974.

Carroll, A. B. Managerial ethics: A post-Watergate view. *Business Horizons*, April 1975, 18, 75–80.

Carter, E. E. The behavioral theory of the firm and top level corporate decisions. *Administrative Science Quarterly*, 1971, 16, 413–428.

Cetron, M. J., & Ralph, C. A. *Industrial applications of technological forecasting*. New York: Wiley, 1971.

Churchman, C. W., Ackoff, R. L., & Arnoff, E. L. *Operations research*. New York: Wiley, 1957.

Clarkson, G. *Portfolio selection: A simulation of trust investment*. Englewood Cliffs, N.J.: Prentice-Hall, 1962.

Clarkson, G. P. E., & Pounds, W. F. Theory and method in the exploration of human decision behavior. *Industrial Management Review*, 1963, 5, 17–27.

Cohen, M., & Collins, J. N. Some correlates of organization effectiveness. *Public Personnel Management*, 1974, 3, 493–499.

Cohen, M. D., March, J. G., & Olsen, J. P. A garbage can model of organizational choice. *Administrative Science Quarterly*, 1972, 17, 1–25.

Coleman, P. Leadership and loyalty: The basic value dilemmas of the educational administrator in the 70s. *R. I. E.*, November 1975.

Collins, D. F., & Moore, D. G. *The enterprising man*. East Lansing: Michigan State University, 1964.

Conrath, D. W. Organizational decision making behavior under varying conditions of uncertainty. *Management Science*, 1967, 13, 487–500.

Coombs, C. H. Portfolio theory and the management of risk. In M. F. Kaplan, & S. Schwartz (Eds.) *Human Judgment and Decision Process*. New York: Academic Press, 1975.

Corbin, R. M., Olson, C. L., & Abbondanza, M. Context effects in optional stopping decisions. *Organizational Behavior and Human Performance*, 1975, *14*, 207–216.

Cosier, R. A. The effects of three potential aids for making strategic decisions on prediction accuracy. *Organizational Behavior and Human Performance*, 1978, *22*, 295–306.

Cravens, D. W. An exploratory analysis of individual information processing. *Management Science*, 1970, *16*, B-656–670.

Crozier, M. *The bureaucratic phenomenon*. Chicago: University of Chicago Press, 1964.

Crum, R. L., Klingman, D. D., & Tavis, L. A. Implementation of large-scale financial planning models: Solution efficient transformations. *Journal of Financial and Quantitative Analysis*, 1979, *14*, 137–152.

Culbert, S. A. & McDonough, J. J. *The invisible war: Pursuing self-interests at work*. New York: Wiley, 1980.

Curtis, G. L. Correlates of effective decision-making in critical incidents in public school systems. *Doctoral dissertation, University of Missouri*, Columbia, 1976.

Cyert, R. M., Dill, W. R., & March, J. G. The role of expectations in business decision making. *Administrative Science Quarterly*, 1958, *3*, 307–340.

Cyert, R. M., Feigenbaum, E. H., & March, J. G. Models in a behavioral theory of the firm. In J. M. Dutton & W. H. Starbuck (Eds.), *Computer simulation of human behavior*. New York: Wiley, 1971.

Cyert, R. M., & March, J. G. *A behavioral theory of the firm*. Englewood Cliffs, N.J.: Prentice-Hall, 1963.

Cyert, R. M., March, J. G., & Starbuck, W. H. Bias and conflict in organizational estimation. *Management Science*, 1961, *7*, 254–264.

Cyert, R. M., Simon, H. A., & Trow, D. B. Observation of a business decision. *Journal of Business*, 1956, *29*, 237–248.

Dalkey, N., & Helmer, O. An experimental application of the Delphi method to the use of experts. *Management Science*, 1963, *9*, 458–467.

Dalton, M. *Men who manage*. New York: Wiley, 1959.

Dandridge. T. C. Children are not "Little grown-ups": Small business needs its own organizational theory. *Journal of Small Business Management*, 1979, *17*, 53–57.

Davis, J. H. Group decision and social interaction. A theory of social decision schemes. *Psychological Review*, 1973, *80*, 97–125.

Davis, J. H., Laughlin, P. R., & Komorita, S. S. The social psychology of small groups: Cooperative and mixed-motive interaction. *Annual Review of Psychology*, 1976, *27*, 501–541.

Dearborn, D. C., & Simon, H. A. Selective perception: A note on the departmental identifications of executives. *Sociometry*, 1958, *21*, 140–144.

De Bono, E. *Lateral thinking: Creativity step by step*. New York: Harper and Row, 1970.

De Gramont, S. *The French: Portrait of a people*. New York: Putnam, 1969.

Decker, C. R., & Johnson, R. H. How to make committees more effective. *Management Review*, 1976, *65*, 34–40.

Delaney, W. A. Form vs. substance: Some guidelines for managers. *Management Review*, 1978, *11*, 46–48.

Delbecq, A. L. The management of decision making within the firm: Three strategies for three types of decision making. *Academy of Management Journal*, 1967, *10*, 329–339.

Delbecq, A. L., & Van de Ven, A. H. A group process model for problem identification and program planning. *Journal of Applied Behavioral Science*, 1971, *7*, 466–492.

Dent, J. K. Organizational correlates of the goals of business managements. *Personnel Psychology*, 1959, *12*, 365–396.

Diesing, P. Noneconomic decision making. In M. Alexis & C. Z. Wilson (Eds.), *Organizational decision making*. Englewood Cliffs, N.J.: Prentice-Hall, 1967.

Dill, W. R. Decision making. *Sixty-third Yearbook of the National Society for the Study of Education, Behavioral Science and Educational Administration*, 1965, 200–202.

Donovan, J. C. *The policy makers*. New York: Pegasus, 1970.

Downey, H. K., Hellriegel, D., & Slocum, J. W. Individual characteristics *as* sources of perceived uncertainty variability. *Human Relations*, 1977, *30*, 161–174.

Downs, A. *Bureaucratic structure and decision making*. Santa Monica, Calif.: Rand, 1966.

Driscoll, J. M., & Lanzetta, J. T. Effects of two sources of uncertainty in decision making. *Psychological Reports*, 1965, *17*, 635–648.

Driver, M. J., & Streufert, S. Integrative complexity: An approach to individuals and groups as information-processing systems. *Administrative Science Quarterly*, 1969, *14*, 272–285.

Drucker, P. F. *Concept of the corporation*. Boston: Beacon Press, 1946.

Drucker, P. F. *The practice of management*. New York: Harper & Row, 1954.

Drucker, P. F. Managing for business effectiveness. *Harvard Business Review*, 1963, *43*(3), 53–60.

Drucker, P. F. *The effective executive*. New York: Harper & Row, 1967.

Drucker, P. F. What we can learn from Japanese management. *Harvard Business Review*, 1971, *49*, 110–122.

Dunbar, R. L. M., & Goldberg, W. H. Crisis development and strategic response in European corporations. *International Institute of Management*, Berlin, Germany, 1978.

Duncan, B. The implementation of different decision-making structures in adapting to environmental uncertainty: An expansion of contingency theories of organization. *Proceedings of the Academy of Management*, 1971, 39–47.

Duncan, R. B. Characteristics of organizational environments and perceived environmental uncertainty. *Administrative Science Quarterly*, 1972, *17*, 313–327.

Duncan, R. B. Multiple decision-making structures in adapting to environmental uncertainty: The impact on organizational effectiveness. *Human Relations*, 1973, *26*, 273–291.

Ebert, R. J. Environmental structure and programmed decision effectiveness. *Management Science,* 1972, *19,* 435–445.

Ebert, R. J., & Mitchell, T. R. *Organizational decision processes: Concepts and analysis.* New York: Crane & Russak, 1975.

Edwards, W. The theory of decision making. *Psychological Bulletin,* 1954, *51,* 380–417.

Edwards, W. Man and computers. In R. M. Gagne (Ed.), *Psychological principles in system development.* New York: Holt, Rinehart & Winston, 1962, 75–114.

Einhorn, H., & Hogarth, R. Behavioral decision theory. *Annual Review of Psychology,* 1981, *32,* 53–88.

Elbing, A. O. *Behavioral decisions in organizations.* Glenview, Ill.: Scott, Foresman, 1970.

Emery, F. E., & Trist, E. I. The causal texture of organizational environments. *Human Relations,* 1963, *18,* 20–26.

Emery, J. C. Organizational planning and control systems. New York: Macmillan, 1969.

Emory, C. W. & Niland, P. Making management decisions. Boston: Houghton Mifflin Co., 1968.

Etzioni, A. Mixed scanning: A third approach to decision making. *Public Administration Review,* 1967, *27,* 385–392.

Farrow, D. L., Bass, B. M., & Valenzi, E. R. A manager's tendencies to be participative associated with his perceptions of the environment outside his organization. *Proceedings of the Academy of Management,* 1977.

Farrow, D. L., Valenzi, E. R., & Bass, B. M. A comparison of leadership and situational characteristics within profit and nonprofit organizations. *Proceedings of the Academy of Management,* 1980.

Farrow, D. L., Valenzi, E. R., & Bass, B. M. Managerial political behavior, executive success and effectiveness. *Proceedings of the Academy of Management,* 1981.

Feldman, J., & Kanter, H. E. Organizational decision making. In J. G. March (Ed.), *Handbook of Organizations.* Chicago: Rand McNally, 1965.

Feldman, J. M. Beyond attribution theory: Cognitive processes in performance appraisal. *Journal of Applied Psychology,* 1981, *66,* 127–148.

Feldman, M. S., & March, J. G. Information in organizations as signal and symbol. *Administrative Science Quarterly,* 1981, *26,* 171–186.

Ference, T. P. Organizational communications systems and the decision process. *Management Science,* 1970, *17,* B-83–96.

Festinger, L. *Conflict, decision and dissonance.* London: Tavistock, 1964.

Feyerabend, P. *Against method: Outline of an anarchistic theory of knowledge.* London: NLB, 1975.

Filella, J. Influence patterns among three levels of managers. Unpublished manuscript. Undated.

Filley, A. C., House, R. J., & Kerr, S. Managerial process and organizational behavior. Glenview, IL.: Scott, Foresman, 1976.

Fisch, G. G. Line-staff is obsolete. *Harvard Business Review,* 1961, *39*(5), 67–79.

Fischhoff, B. Cost-benefit analysis and the art of motorcycle maintenance. *ORI Research Monograph.* 16(1). Eugene: Oregon Research Institute, 1976.

Fleming, T. *1776: Year of illusions*. New York: Norton, 1975.

Flippo, E. B. *Management: A behavioral approach*. Boston: Allyn & Bacon, 1966.

Forward, J., & Zander, A. Choice of unattainable group goals and effects on performance. *Organizational Behavior & Human Performance*, 1971, *6*, 184–199.

Fox, F., & Staw, B. M. The trapped administrator: The effects of job insecurity and policy resistance upon commitment to a course of action. *Administrative Science Quarterly*, 1979, *24*, 449–471.

Frederikson, N. In-basket tests and factors in administrative performance. In Guetzkow, H. (Ed.), *Simulation in Social Science: Readings*. Englewood Cliffs, N.J.: Prentice-Hall, 1962.

Friedlander, F. The relationship of task and human conditions to effective organizational structure. In Bass, B., Cooper, M. R., & Haas, J. A. (Eds.), *Managing for accomplishment*. Lexington, Mass.: D. C. Heath, 1970.

French, J. R. P., & Raven, B. The bases of social power. In D. Cartwright (Ed.), *Studies in social power*. Ann Arbor: University of Michigan, Institute for Social Research, 1959.

Fulmer, R. M. *The new management*. New York: Macmillan, 1974.

Gameson, W. A. A theory of coalition formation. *American Sociological* Review, 1961, *26*, 373–382.

Gebert, D. Adaptation of decision-making autonomy of situational variables: Survey of managers in West Germany. *Psychologie und Praxis*, 1977, *21*, 145–154.

Gettys, C. F., Kelly, C. III, & Peterson, R. The best guess hypothesis in multistage inference. *Organizational Behavior and Human Performance*, 1973, *10*, 364–373.

Giuliano, T., Appelman, A., & Bazerman, M. H. Escalation in individual and group decision making. *Proceedings of the American Psychological Association*, 1981.

Glickman, A. S., Hahn, C. P., Fleishman, E. A., & Baxter, B. *Top management development and succession: An exploratory study*. New York: Macmillan, 1969.

Glueck, W. F. *Business policy: Strategy formation and management action*. New York: McGraw-Hill, 1976.

Goodchilds, J., Schonfield, J., & Gibb, J. R. Some effects of group problem solving of an enforced separation of problem solving stages. ONR Technical Report 8, Washington, D. C.: National Training Laboratories, 1961.

Gordon, W. J. J. *Synectics*. New York: Harper & Row, 1961.

Gore, W. J. Administrative decision making in federal field offices. *Public Administration Review*, 1956, vol. 17, 281–291.

Gouldner, A. W. Patterns of industrial bureaucracy. Yellow Springs, Ohio: Antioch Press, 1954.

Gouran, D. S. The Watergate cover-up: Its dynamics and its implications. *Communication Monographs*, 1976, *43*, 176–186.

Grayson, C. J. *Decisions under uncertainty*. Cambridge: Harvard University Press, 1960.

Green, S. G., & Mitchell, T. R. Attributional processes of leaders in leader-member interactions. *Organizational Behavior and Human Performance*, 1979, *23*, 429–458.

Griffiths, D. E. Administration as decision making. In A. Halpin (Ed.), *Admin-*

istrative theory in education. Chicago: Midwest Administration Center, 1958.

Halaby, C. N. Organizational decision-making structure: The case of promotion decisions. Doctoral dissertation, Cornell University, 1976.

Halpin, S. M., Streufert, S., Steffey, J., & Lanham, N. Information load, proportion of relevance, and relevance perception. *Psychonomic Science,* 1971, *23,* 403–406.

Hammond, J. S. The roles of the manager and management scientist in successful implementation. *Sloan Management Review,* 1974, *15*(2), 1–24.

Hammond, K. R. (Ed.) *The psychology of Egon Brunswik.* New York: Holt, Rinehart & Winston, 1966.

Harrison, E. F. *The managerial decision-making process* (2d ed.). Boston: Houghton Mifflin, 1981.

Harvey, O. J., Hunt, D. E., & Schroder, H. M. *Conceptual systems and personality organization.* New York: John Wiley, 1961.

Healey, R. J. A laboratory experiment to test the effect of structure upon organizational decision making. Claremont, Calif.: Claremont, 1972.

Hegarty, W. H., & Sims, H. P. Organizational philosophy, policies, and objectives related to unethical decision behavior: A laboratory experiment. *Journal of Applied Psychology,* 1979, *64,* 331–338.

Hegel, G. W. F. *The phenomenology of mind.* London: George Allen & Unwin, 1964.

Heller, F. A. The role of business management in relation to economic development. *International Journal of Comparative Sociology,* 1969, *10,* 292–298.

Heller, F. A. The role of longitudinal method in managerial decision making studies. Seventh Biennial Leadership Symposium, Oxford, England, 1982.

Heller, F. A., Drenth, P.J.D., & Koopman, P. L. An analysis of 56 decisions in three Dutch organizations. *Journal of Occupational Psychology,* 1982, *54.*

Heller, F. A., & Yukl, G. Participation, managerial decision making, and situational variables. *Organizational Behavior and Human Performance,* 1969, *4,* 227–241.

Helsabeck, R. E. The relationship between decision-making structure and organizational effectiveness: A comparative case study in college governance. Doctoral dissertation, Indiana University, 1971.

Herbert, T. T., & Estes, R. W. Improving executive decisions by formalizing dissent: The corporate devil's advocate. *Academy of Management Review,* 1977, *2,* 662–667.

Hertz, D. B. *New power for management.* New York: McGraw-Hill, 1969.

Heynes, R. W. Factors determining influence and decision satisfaction in conferences requiring pooled judgments. *Proceedings of the Administrative Conference.* University of Michigan, Ann Arbor, 1950.

Higbee, K. L., & Streufert, S. Group risk taking and attribution of causality. ONR Technical Report 21, Purdue University, 1969.

Hillier, F. S., & Lieberman, G. J. *Introduction to operations research.* New York: Holden-Day, 1967.

Hinings, C. R., Hickson, D. J., Pennings, J. M., & Schneck, R. E. Structural conditions of intraorganizational power. *Administrative Science Quarterly,* 1974, *19,* 22–44.

Hobbs, W. C. Organizational roles of university committees. *Research in Higher Education,* 1975, *3,* 234–242.

Hogarth, R. M. *Judgment and choice: The psychology of decision,* New York: Wiley, 1980.

Houston, S. R. (Ed.) Judgment analysis: Tool for decision makers. *R. I. E.,* 1975.

Howard, R. A. Proximal decision analysis, *Management Science,* 1971, *17,* 507–541.

Howes, M. L. Centralization of decision making and organizational effectiveness in the cooperative extension service. Doctoral dissertation, University of Wisconsin, Madison, Wis., 1963.

Hyman, R. Creativity and the prepared mind: The role of information and induced attitudes. In C. Taylor (Ed.), *Widening horizons in creativity.* New York: Wiley, 1964.

Indik, B. P. Organizational size and member participation: Some empirical tests of alternative explanations. *Human Relations,* 1965, *18,* 339–350.

Jackson, J. Consensus and conflict in treatment organizations. *Hospital & Community Psychiatry,* 1966, *68,* 161–167.

Janis, I. L., & Mann, L. *Decision making.* New York: Free Press, 1977.

Johnson, R. A., Kast, F. E., & Rosenzweig, J. E. *The theory and management of systems.* New York: McGraw-Hill, 1963.

Kallman, E. A., Reinharth, L., & Shapiro, H. J. How effective companies manage their information. *Business,* 1980, *30*(4), 35–39.

Kast, F. E., & Rosenzweig, J. E. *Organization and management: A systems approach.* New York: McGraw-Hill, 1970.

Katona, G. Rational behavior and economic behavior. *Psychological Review,* 1953, *60,* 307–318.

Katz, D., & Kahn, R. L. *The social psychology of organizations.* New York: Wiley, 1966.

Keene, P., & Martin, M. S. *Decision support systems: An organizational perspective.* Reading, Mass.: Addison Wesley, 1978.

Kefalas, A., & Schoderbek, P. P. Scanning the business environment—some empirical results. *Decision Sciences,* 1973, *4,* 63–74.

Kelley, H. H., & Michela, J. L. Attribution theory and research. *Annual Review of Psychology,* 1980, *31,* 457–501.

Kennedy, R. E. An emerging model for effective decision making in the California state colleges (1862–1965). Doctoral dissertation, Claremont Graduate School, 1966.

Kepner, C. H., & Tregoe, B. B. *The rational manager.* New York: McGraw-Hill, 1965.

Khandwalla, P. N. Mass output orientation of operations technology and organization structure. *Administrative Science Quarterly,* 1974, *19,* 74–97.

Kilmann, R. H. Towards a systematic methodology for evaluating the impact of interventions on organizational effectiveness. *Academy of Management Review,* 1976, *1,* 87–98.

Kimberly, J. R., & Evanisko, M. J. Organizational innovation: The influence of individual, organizational, and contextual factors in hospital adoption of technological and administrative innovations. *Academy of Management Journal*, 1981, *24*, 689–713.

Klauss, R., & Bass, B. M. *Interpersonal communication style: Effects on credibility, satisfaction, and effectiveness*. New York: Academic Press, 1982.

Kleinmuntz, B. (Ed.), *Formal representation of human judgment*. New York: Wiley, 1968.

Knight, F. H. *Risk, uncertainty, and profit*. New York: Harper, 1920.

Knight, K. Matrix organization: A review. *Journal of Management Studies*, 1976, *13*, 111–130.

Kogan, N., & Carlson, J. Group risk taking under competitive and noncompetitive conditions in adults and children. *Research Bulletin, ETS*, RB-67–21, Princeton, N.J., 1967.

Kogan, N., & Wallach, M. A. *Risk taking: A study in cognition and personality*. New York: Holt, Rinehart & Winston, 1964.

Kogan, N., & Wallach, M. *New directions in psychology: Group decision involving risk*. New York: Holt, Rinehart & Winston, 1967.

Koontz, H., & O'Donnell, C. *Principles of management*. New York: McGraw-Hill, 1968.

Krouse, C. G. Complex objectives, decentralization, and the decision process of the organization. *Administrative Science Quarterly*, 1972, *17*, 544–554.

Lacho, K. J. An empirical analysis of the product addition decision process in the food broker using the Cyert-March theory of organization decision making. Doctoral dissertation, Washington University, 1969.

Lawrence, P., & Lorsch, J. *Organization and environment*. Homewood, Ill.: Irwin, 1969.

Learned, E. P., & Sproat, A. T. *Organization theory and policy*. Homewood, Ill.: Irwin, 1966.

Leblebici, H. Organizational decision making: An exploration of binary choice situations in bank loan decisions. 147 pages. Unpublished doctoral dissertation, University of Illinois, Urbana-Champaign, 1975.

Levine, J. M., & Samet, M. G. Information seeking with multiple sources of conflicting and unreliable information. *Human Factors*, 1973, *15*, 407–419.

Levi, A. Escalating commitment and risk taking in dynamic decision behavior. *Proceedings of the American Psychological Association Meeting*, 1981.

Lewin, K. Behavior and development as a function of the total situation. In L. Carmichael (Ed.), *Manual of child psychology*. New York: Wiley, 1946.

Leys, W. A. R. The value framework of decision making. In S. M. Mailick & E. H. Van Ness (Eds.), *Concepts and Issues in Administrative Behavior*, Englewood Cliffs, N.J.: Prentice-Hall, 1962.

Lichfield, N., Kettle, P., & Whitbread, M. *Evaluation in the planning process*. Oxford: Pergamon, 1975.

Likert, R. *The human organization*. New York: McGraw-Hill, 1967.

Lindblom, C. E. "The science of 'muddling through'," *Public Administration Review*, 1959, *19*, 79–99.

Link, J. R., Thiagarajan, K. M., Trbovich, N., & Vaughan, J. A. *Exercise Venture*. Scottsville, N. Y.: Transnational Programs Corporation, 1975.

Locke, E. A. Toward a theory of task motivation and incentives. *Organizational Behavior and Human Performance*, 1968, *3*, 157–189.

Luthans, F. *Organizational behavior: A modern behavioral approach to management.* New York: McGraw-Hill, 1973.

MacCrimmon, K. R. Descriptive and normative implications of the decision theory postulates. In K. Borch & J. Mossin (Eds.), *Risk and Uncertainty.* London: Macmillan, 1968.

MacCrimmon, K. R. Managerial decision making. In J. W. McGuire, *Contemporary management.* Englewood Cliffs, N.J.: Prentice-Hall, 1974.

MacCrimmon, K. R., & Taylor, R. N. Decision making and problem solving. In M. D. Dunnette (Ed.), *Handbook of Industrial and Organizational Psychology.* Chicago: Rand McNally, 1976.

MacKinnon, W. J. Elements of the SPAN technique for making group decisions. *Journal of Social Psychology,* 1966, *70,* 149–164.

Mackenzie, K. D. *A Theory of Group Structures.* University of Kansas, 1975.

Maier, N. R. F. *Problem solving discussions and conferences.* New York: McGraw-Hill, 1963.

Maier, N. R. F. *Psychology in industry.* Boston: Houghton Mifflin, 1965.

Maier, N. R. F., & Hoffman, L. R. Quality of first and second solutions to group problem solving. *Journal of Applied Psychology,* 1960, *44,* 278–283.

Maier, N. R. F., & Solem, A. R. Improving solutions by turning choice situations into problems. *Personnel Psychology,* 1962, *15,* 151–157.

Maltzman, I., Bogartz, W., & Breger, L. A procedure for increasing word association originally and its transfer effects. *Journal of Experimental Psychology,* 1958, *56,* 392–398.

Mandelbaum, M. Flexibility in decision making: An exploration and unification. Doctoral dissertation, University of Toronto, 1978.

March, J. G., & Olsen, J. P. (Eds.), *Ambiguity and choice in organizations.* Bergen, Norway: Universitetsforlaget, 1976.

March, J. G., & Romelaer, P. Position and presence in the drift of decisions. In J. G. March and J. P. Olsen (Eds.), *Ambiguity and choice in organizations.* Bergen, Norway: Universitetsforlaget, 1976.

March, J. G., & Shapira, Z. Behavioral decision theory and organizational decision theory. In G. Ungson & D. Braunstein (Eds.), *New Directions in Decision Making: An Interdisciplinary Approach to the Study of Organizations.* Boston: Kent, 1982.

March, J. G., & Simon, H. A. *Organizations.* New York: Wiley, 1958.

Marquis, D. G. Ways of organizing projects. *Innovation,* 1969, *5,* 26–33.

Marschak, J. Actual versus consistent decision behavior. *Behavioral Science,* 1964, *9,* 103–110.

Marschak, J. Decision making: Economic aspects. *International Encyclopedia of the Social Sciences,* 1968, *4,* 42–55.

Marschak, J. Economics of information systems. *Journal of the American Statistical Association,* 1971, *66,* 192–219.

Marschak, J., & Radner, R. *Economic theory of teams.* New Haven, Conn.: Yale University Press, 1972.

Martin, N. H., & Sims, J. H. Thinking ahead: Power tactics. *Harvard Business Review,* 1956, *34(6),* 25–36, 140.

Mason, R. O. A dialectical approach to strategic planning. *Management Science,* 1969, *15,* B403–B414.

McCleery, R. Communication patterns as basis of systems of authority and power. *Social Science Research Council,* No. 15, New York, 1960.

McGrath, J. E., & Altman, I. *Small group research: A synthesis and critique.* New York: Holt, Rinehart & Winston, 1966.

McGregor, D. *Human side of enterprise.* New York: McGraw-Hill, 1960.

McGuire, J. W. Theories of business behavior. Englewood Cliffs, N.J.: Prentice-Hall, 1964.

McWhinney, W. H. Organizational form, decision modalities and the environment. *Human Relations,* 1968, *21,* 269–81.

Mechanic, D. Sources of power of lower participants in complex organizations. *Administrative Science Quarterly,* 1962, *7,* 349–364.

Merton, R. K. The unanticipated consequences of purposive social action. *American Sociological Review,* 1936, *1,* 894–904.

Merton, R. K. Bureaucratic structure and personality. *Social Forces,* 1940, *18,* 560–568.

Middleton, C. J. How to set up a project organization. *Harvard Business Review,* 1967, *65,* 73–82.

Miller, G. A. The magical number seven, plus or minus two: Some limits on our capacity for processing information. *Psychological Review,* 1956, *63,* 81–97.

Miller, J. A. Information input overload and psychopathology. *American Journal of Psychiatry,* 1960, *116,* 695–704.

Milutinovich, J. S., Lipson, D. S., & Naumes, W. The computer resource as a barrier to effective executive decision making. *Proceedings of the American Institute for Decision Sciences,* 1974.

Mintzberg, H., Raisinghani, D., & Thoret, A. The structure of "unstructured" decision processes. *Administrative Science Quarterly,* 1976, *21,* 246–275.

Mitroff, I. I., & Emshoff, J. R. On strategic assumption making: A dialectical approach to policy and planning. *Academy of Management Review,* 1979, *4,* 1–12.

Morlock, H. The effect of outcome desirability on information required for decisions. *Behavioral Science,* 1967, *12,* 296–300.

Morlock, H. C., Jr., & Hertz, K. J. Effect on the desirability of outcomes on decision making. *Psychological Reports,* 1964, *14,* 11–17.

Murdia, R. Task structures and management processes in human services organizations. *Indian Journal of Social Work,* 1978, *39,* 273–286.

Narayanan, V. K., & Fahey, L. The micro-politics of strategy formulation. *Academy of Management Review,* 1982, *7,* 25–34.

Newell, A., & Simon, H. A. *Human problem solving.* Englewood Cliffs, N.J.: Prentice-Hall, 1972.

Newman, J. W. *Management applications of decision theory.* New York: Harper & Row, 1971.

Newstrom, J. W., & Ruch, W. A. The ethics of management and the management of ethics. *MSU Business Topics,* 1975 (Winter), 29–37.

New York Times. America in captivity: Point of decision. *New York Times Magazine, Special Issue,* 1981.

Nicolaidis, N. The case method as a research tool in administrative theory. In Sherwood, F. P. (Ed.), *Teaching and research in public administration: Essays on the case approach.* John W. Donner Memorial Fund, No. 16, University of Southern California, 1960.

Office of the Chief of Military History. Department of the Army. *Command decisions.* New York: Harcourt, Brace, 1959.

O'Reilly, C. A. Individuals and information overload in organizations: Is more necessarily better? *Academy of Management Journal,* 1980, *23,* 684–696.

Orpen, C. Market conditions, decentralization, and managerial effectiveness in South African and American corporations. *Management International Review,* 1978, *18,* 61–68.

Osborn, A. F. *Applied imagination: Principles and procedures of creative thinking.* New York: Scribner's, 1941.

Otton, A. J. W., & Teulings, A. W. M. Buitenstaanders en krachtfiguren. *Mens en Onderneming,* 1970, *24,* 296–313.

Parsons, T. *Structure and process in modern societies.* Glencoe, Ill.: Free Press, 1960.

Patchen, M. The locus and basis of influence on organizational decisions. *Organizational Behavior and Human Performance,* 1974, *11,* 195–221.

Paulson, K. Causal analysis of interorganizational relations: An axiomatic theory revised. *Administrative Science Quarterly,* 1974, *19,* 319–337.

Payne, J. W. Task complexity and contingent processing in decision making; an information search and protocol process. *Organizational Behavior and Human Performance,* 1976, *16,* 366–387.

Payne, R., & Pugh, D. S. Organizational structure and climate. In M. D. Dunnette (Ed.), *Handbook of industrial and organizational psychology.* Chicago: Rand-McNally, 1976.

Perrin, E. C., & Goodman, H. C. Telephone management of acute pediatric illnesses. *New England Journal of Medicine,* 1978, *208*(3), 130–135.

Perrow, C. *Complex organizations: A critical essay.* Glenview, Ill.: Scott, Foresman, 1972.

Peters, A. J. Cost accounting for effective management decision making, Doctorial dissertation, University of Michigan, Ann Arbor, 1973.

Peterson, C. R., & Beach, L. R. Man as an intuitive statistician. *Psychological Bulletin,* 1967, *68,* 29–46.

Pettigrew, A. M. *The politics of organizational decision-making.* London: Tavistock, 1973.

Pfeffer, J. Size and composition of corporate boards of directors: The organization and the environment. *Administrative Science Quarterly,* 1972a, *17,* 219–228.

Pfeffer, J. Merger as a response to organizational interdependence. *Administrative Science Quarterly,* 1972b, *17,* 382–394.

Pfeffer, J. Interorganization influence and managerial attitudes. *Academy of Management Journal,* 1972c, *15,* 317–330.

Pfifner, J. M. Administrative rationality. School of Public Administration. University of Southern California, 1960.

Phillips, J. S., & Rush, M. C. Schematic memory biases in decision-making research. Unpublished manuscript.

Pickle, H., & Friedlander, H. Seven societal criteria of organizational success. *Personnel Psychology,* 1967, *20,* 165–178.

Pinder, C., Pinto, P. R., & England, G. W. Behavioral style and personal characteristics of managers. *Technical Report, Center for the Study of Organizational Performance and Human Effectiveness,* University of Minnesota, 1973.

Pollay, R. W. The structure of executive decisions and decision terms. *Administrative Science Quarterly,* 1970, *15,* 459–471.

PRA. Addendum to the program announcement for extramural research, (NSF 78-78), *Division of Policy, Research and Analysis, National Science Foundation,* 1979–1980.

Price, J. L. *Organizational effectiveness: An inventory of propositions.* Homewood, Ill.: Irwin, 1968.

Pruitt, D. G. Informational requirements in making decisions. *American Journal of Psychology,* 1961, *74,* 433–39.

Quinn, J. B. Technological innovation, entrepreneurship, and strategy. *Sloan Management Review,* 1979, *20,* 19–30.

Radford, K. J. *Modern managerial decision-making.* Reston, Va: Reston, 1981.

Radnor, M., Rubenstein, A. H., & Bean, A. S. Integration and utilization of management science activities in organizations. *Proceedings of The Operations Research Society,* 1966.

Radomsky, J. The problem of choosing a problem. *M.S. thesis,* Massachusetts Institute of Technology, 1967.

Raiffa, H. *Decision analysis.* Reading, MA: Addison-Wesley, 1968.

Rapoport, A. A logical task as a research tool in organization theory. In M. Haire (Ed.), *Modern Organizational Theory.* New York: Wiley, 1959.

Rapoport, A., & Tversky, A. Choice behavior in an optimal stopping task. *Organizational Behavior and Human Performance,* 1970, *5,* 105–120.

Reeser, C. The use of sophisticated analytical methods for decision making in the aerospace industry. *MSU Business Topics,* 1971, *19,* 63–69.

Rice, G. H., & Bishoprick, D. W. *Conceptual models of organization.* New York: Meridith, 1971.

Rim, Y. Machiavellianism and decisions involving risk. *British Journal Socioclinical Psychology,* 1966, *5,* 30–36.

Roberts, R. M., & Hanline, M. H. Maximizing executive effectiveness: Deciding about what to decide. *Management Review,* 1975, *64* (6), 25–32.

Roth, C. A multiperson theory of organizational decision making. Doctoral dissertation. Yale University, 1974.

Rothenburg, A., & Hausman, C. R. *The creativity question.* Durham, N.C.: Duke University Press, 1976.

Rowen, H. H. *John de Witt, Grand Pensionary of Holland, 1625–1672.* Princeton, N. J.: Princeton University Press, 1978.

Roy, B., & Vinke, P. Multicriteria analysis: Survey and new directions. *European Journal of Operational Research,* 1981, *8,* 207–218.

Russo, J. E., & Rosen, L. D. An eye fixation analysis of multialternative choice. *Memory and Cognition,* 1975, *3,* 267–276.

Safire, W. Of Meese and men. *New York Times,* October 22, 1981, p. A27.

Sawyer, J. Measurement and prediction, clinical and statistical. *Psychological Bulletin,* 1966, *66,* 178–200.

Sayles, L. R. *Managerial behavior.* New York: McGraw-Hill, 1964.

Schaefer, J. E. A general theory of organizational decision making. Doctoral dissertation, Marquette University, 1971.

Scheff, T. J. Control over policy by attendants in a mental hospital. *Journal of Health and Human Behavior,* 1961, *2,* 93–105.

Schelling, T. C. *The strategy of conflict.* Cambridge, Mass: Harvard University Press, 1960.

Schoner, B., Rose, G. L., & Hoyt, G. C. Quality of decisions: Individual versus real and synthetic groups. *Journal of Applied Psychology,* 1974, 59, 4, 424–432.

Schroder, H. M., Driver, M. J., & Streufert, S. *Human information processing.* New York: Holt, Rinehart & Winston, 1967.

Schwartzman, R. Crisis decision-making. *MBA Thesis,* McGill University, 1971.

Schwenk, R., & Cosier, R. A. Effects of the expert, devil's advocate, and dialectical inquiry methods on prediction performance. *Organizational Behavior and Human Performance,* 1980, *26,* 409–424.

Selznick, P. *Leadership in administration: A sociological interpretation.* Evanston, Ill.: Row, Peterson, 1957.

Sen, A. *Collective choice and social welfare.* San Francisco: Holden-Day, 1970.

Shapira, Z. Expectancy determinants of intrinsically motivated behavior. Doctoral dissertation. University of Rochester, 1974.

Shaw, M. E. Communication networks. In R. Berkowitz (Ed.), *Advances in experimental social psychology.* New York: Academic Press, 1964.

Shuchman, A. Scientific decision making in business. New York: Holt, Rinehart & Winston, 1963.

Shull, F. A., Jr., Delbecq, A., & Cummings, L. L. *Organizational decision making.* New York: McGraw-Hill, 1970.

Simon, H. A. A behavioral model of rational choice. *Quarterly Journal of Economics,* 1955, *69,* 99–118.

Simon, H. A. *Administrative behavior.* New York: MacMillan, 1957, 1960.

Simon, H. A. Decision rules for production and inventory controls of sales. *ONR Research Memorandum,* Carnegie Institute of Technology, 1958.

Simon, H. A. Theories of decision making in economics and behavioral science. *American Economic Review,* 1959, *49,* 253–83.

Simon, H. A. The new science of management decision. New York: Harper & Row, 1960.

Simon, H. A. On the concept of the organizational goal. *Administrative Science Quarterly,* 1964, *9,* 1–22.

Simon, H. A. *The sciences of the artificial.* Cambridge, Mass.: The M.I.T. Press, 1969.

Simon, H. A., & Newell, A. Human problem solving: The state of the theory in 1970. *American Psychologist,* 1971, *26,* 145–159.

Simpson, R. L., & Gulley, W. H. Goals, environmental pressures, and organizational characteristics. *American Sociological Review,* 1962, *27,* 344–351.

Sloan, A. P. *My years with General Motors.* New York: MacFadden-Bartell, 1965.

Slovic, P., Fischoff, B., & Lichtenstein, S. Behavioral decision theory. *Annual Review of Psychology,* 1977, *28,* 1–39.

Slovic, P., & Lichtenstein, S. Comparison of Bayesian and regression approaches to the study of information processing in judgment. *Organizational Behavior and Human Performance,* 1971, *6,* 649–744.

Slovic, P., & Tversky, A. Who accepts Savage's axiom? *Behavioral Science,* 1974, *19,* 368–373.

Snyder, R. C., & Paige, G. D. The United States decisions to resist aggression in Korea: The application of an analytical scheme. *Administrative Science Quarterly:* 1958, *3,* 341–378.

Soelberg, P. O. Unprogrammed decision making. *Industrial Management Review,* 1967, *8,* 19–29.

Souder, W. E. Effectiveness of nominal and interacting group decision processes for integration R&D and marketing. *Management Science,* 1977, *23,* 595–605.

Spray, S. L. Organizational effectiveness: The problem of relevance. *Organization and Administrative Sciences,* 1976, *7,* 165–173.

Stagner, R. Corporate decision making: An empirical study. *Journal of Applied Psychology,* 1969, *53,* 1–13.

Stanley, J. D. Dissent in organizations. *Academy of Management Review,* 1981, *6,* 13–19.

Starbuck, W. H. Organizations and their environments. In M. D. Dunnette (Ed.) *Handbook of industrial and organizational psychology.* Chicago: Rand-McNally, 1976.

Staw, B. M. Knee-deep in the Big Muddy: A study of escalating commitment to a chosen course of action. *Organizational Behavior and Human Performance,* 1976, *16,* 27–44.

Staw, B. M. The escalation of commitment to a course of action. *Academy of Management Review,* 1981, *6,* 577–587.

Steiner, I. D. *Group process and productivity.* New York: Academic Press, 1972.

Streufert, S. Complexity and complex decision making: Convergences between differentiation and integration approaches to the prediction of task performance. *Journal of Experimental Social Psychology,* 1970, *6,* 494–509.

Streufert, S. Complex military decision making. *Naval Research Review,* 1978, *23,* 12–19.

Streufert, S., & Castore, C. H. Information search and the effects of failure: A test of complexity theory. *Journal of Experimental Social Psychology,* 1971, *7,* 125–143.

Streufert, S., & Taylor, E. A. Objective risk levels and subjective risk perception. *ONR Technical Report,* 1971, *40,* Purdue University.

Streufert, S., Suedfeld, P., & Driver, M. J. Conceptual structure, information search, and information utilization. *Journal of Personality and Social Psychology,* 1965, *2,* 736–740.

Stricklin, W. D. Toward a theory of organizational decision making. Doctoral dissertation, University of Southern California, 1966.

Suedfeld, P., & Streufert, S. Information search as a function of conceptual and environmental complexity. *Psychonomic Science*, 1966, *4*, 351–352.

Sutherland, J. W. *Administrative decision making*. New York: Van Nostrand Reinhold, 1977.

Swalm, R. O. Utility theory-insights into risk taking. *Harvard Business Review*, 1966, *44*, 123–138.

Tannenbaum, R. Managerial decision making. *Journal of Business*, 1950–1951, *23–24*, 22–39.

Taylor, B. W. III, & Davis, K. R. Approaches to the multiple objective evaluation of public resource projects. *Proceedings of American Institute For Decision Sciences*, 1975, 166–168.

Taylor, D. W. Decision making and problem solving. In J. G. March (Ed.), *Handbook of organizations*. Chicago: Rand McNally, 1965.

Taylor, M. L. W. A computer simulation of innovative decision making in organizations. Doctoral dissertation, University of Kentucky, 1976.

Taylor, R. N., & Dunnette, M. D. Influence of dogmatism, risk-taking propensity, and intelligence on decision-making strategies for a sample of industrial managers. *Journal of Applied Psychology*, 1974, *59*, 420–423.

Teger, A. I., & Pruitt, D. G. Components of group risk taking. *Journal of Experimental Social Psychology*, 1967, *3*, 189–205.

Thiagarajan, K. M. *Exercise Kolomon*. Scottsville, N. Y.: Transnational Programs Corporation, 1975.

Thomas, K. W., Walton, R. E., & Dutton, J. M. Determinants of interdepartmental conflict. In M. Tuite, R. Chisholm, & M. Radnor (Eds.), *Interorganizational decision-making*. Chicago: Aldine, 1972.

Thompson, J. D. *Organizations in action*. New York: McGraw-Hill, 1967.

Thompson, J. D., & Tuden, A. Strategies, structures, and processes of organizational decision. In J. Thompson, P. Hammond, R. Hawkes, B. Junker, & A. Tuden (Eds.), *Comparative studies in administration*. Pittsburgh: University of Pittsburgh Press, 1959.

Thompson, J. E., & Carsrud, A. L. The effects of experimentally induced illusions of invulnerability and vulnerability in decisional risk taking in triads. *Journal of Social Psychology*, 1976, *100*, 263–267.

Tillman, R., Jr. Problems in review: Committees on trial. *Harvard Business Review*, 1960, *38* (2), 7–12, 162–172.

Tosi, H. L., & Carroll, S. J. *Management: contingencies, structure, and process*. Chicago: St. Clair Press, 1976.

Treddenick, J. M. Cost-effectiveness in defence expenditure. *Omega*, 1979, *7*, 459–467.

Tropman, J. E. The effective committee chair: A primer. *Directors & Boards*, 1980, *5*, (2), 27–33.

Trull, S. G. Some factors involved in determining total decision success. *Management Science*, 1966, *12*, 270–280.

Tullar, W. L., & Johnson, D. F. Group decision making and the risky shift: A transnational perspective. Management Research Center. Report 48, University of Rochester, 1972.

Tversky, A., & Kahneman, D. Availability: A heuristic for judging frequency and probability. *Cognitive Psychology*, 1973, *5*, 207–232.

Tversky, A., & Kahneman, D. Judgment under uncertainty: Heuristics and biases. *Science*, 1975, *185*, 1124–1131.

Ungson, G. R., Braunstein, D. N., & Hall, P. D. Managerial information processing: A research review. *Administrative Science Quarterly*, 1981, *26*, 116–134.

Vaidya, C., Lloyd, R. F., & Ford, D. L., Jr. Organizational information flow characteristics: A selected review and suggestions for future research. *Proceedings of Academy of Management*, 1975, 372–374.

Van de Vall, M., Bolas, C., & Tang, T. S. Applied social research in industrial organizations: An evaluation of functions, theory, and methods. *Journal of Applied Behaviorial Science*, 1976, *12*, 159–177.

Van de Ven, A. H., & Delbecq, A. L. The effectiveness of nominal, delphi, and interacting group decision-making process. *Academy of Management Journal*, 1974, *17*, 605–621.

Vazsonyi, A. Decision support systems: The new technology of decision making. *Interfaces*, 1978, 9, 72–77.

Vroom, V. H. *Work and motivation*. New York: Wiley, 1964.

Vroom, V. H., & Pehl, B. Relationship between age and risk taking among managers. *Journal of Applied Psychology*, 1971, 55, 399–405.

Vroom, V. H., & Yetton, P. W. *Leadership and decision making*. New York: Wiley, 1974.

Wagner, H. M. *Principles of operations research*, Englewood Cliffs, N.J.: Prentice-Hall, 1969.

Walker, A., & Lorsh, J. W. Organizational choice: Product vs. function. *Harvard Business Review*, 1968, *46*, (6), 129–138.

Walker, J. A. Using analysis effectively in complex decision process planning NASA's planetary programs. *Doctoral dissertation*, Harvard University, 1973.

Wallach, M. A., & Kogan, N. Sex differences and judgment processes. *Journal of Personality*, 1959, 27, 555–564.

Wallach, M. A., & Kogan, N. The roles of information, discussion, and consensus in group risk taking. *Journal of Experimental Social Psychology*, 1965, *1*, 1–19.

Walton, R. E. Interorganizational decision making and identity conflict. In M. Tuite, R. Chisholm, & M. Radnor (Eds.) *Interorganizational decision-making*. Chicago: Aldine, 1972.

Weber, M. The theory of social and economic organization. New York: Oxford University Press, 1947.

Webster, E. (Ed.) Decision making in the employment interview. Montreal: Fagel, 1964.

Weick, K. E. *The social psychology of organizing*. Reading, Mass.: Addison-Wesley, 1969.

Weingartner, M. Some new views on the payback period and capital budgeting. *Management Science*, 1969, *15*, B-594–607.

Wensley, J. R. C. Effective decision aids in marketing. *European Journal of Marketing*, 1977, *11*, 62–71.

Witte, E. Field research on complex decision-making processes: The phase theorem. *International Studies of Management and Organization*, 1972, 2, 156–182.

Woods, D. H. Improving estimates that involve uncertainty. *Harvard Business Review,* 1966, *44* (4), 91–98.

Woodward, J. *Industrial organization: Theory and practice.* Oxford: Oxford University Press, 1965.

Wotruba, T. R., & Mangone, R. More effective sales force reporting. *Industrial Marketing Management,* 1979, *8,* 236–245.

Wright, P. The harassed decision maker: Time pressures, distractions, and the use of evidence. *Journal of Applied Psychology,* 1974, *59,* 555–561.

Yu, P. L. A class of solutions for group decision problems. *Management Science,* 1973, *19,* 936–946.

Zander, A., Forward, J., & Albert, R. Adaptation of board members to repeated failure or success by their organization. *Organizational Behavior and Human Performance,* 1969, *4,* 56–76.

Zeleny, M. Descriptive decision making and its applications. *Applications of Management Science,* 1981, *1,* 327–388.

Zimbardo, P. G., & Ebbesen, E. B. Influencing attitudes and changing behavior. Reading, Mass.: Addison-Wesley, 1969.

Zwicky, F., Discovery, invention, research through the morphological approach. New York: Macmillan, 1969.

Index

A

Abbondanza, M., 60
Abelson, R. P., 65, 90
Acceptance, as criteria of effective decision making, 72
Accommodation, 100
Accommodation and adaption, model of, 80–81
Accountability, 91
Ackoff, R. L., 13, 64, 153
Activity, distribution of, in organizational decision making, 8–9
Administrative rationality, 74–75
Adversary dialogues, 159
Aguilar, F. J., 65
Aiken, M., 85
Albert, R., 43
Alexander, E. R., 59, 60, 61, 84
Alexis, M., 30, 36, 37n, 54, 57, 62, 65, 95, 108, 121, 124, 125, 153
Algorithms, 15, 28
Allen, H. T., 119
Allport, G., 146
Alter, S. L., 188
Alternatives
    criteria for evaluation of, 71–73
    designing of, 60
    justification of chosen, 94–95
Altman, I., 136
Ambiguity, dealing with, 136
American Revolution, 41
Amplifiers, 179–80
Annual performance ratings, 182
Ansoff, H. I., 51
Anticipated utility of outcome, 73–74
Appellate decisions, 50
Appleman, A., 60

Applications, of operations research, 156–57
Appropriate set, 161
Aram, J. D., 15
Arbel, A., 88
Arbitration, 99, 110
Argyris, C., 16, 113
Arnoff, E. L., 153
Arrow, K. J., 42, 79
Ashby, W. R., 117, 126
Ashton, R. M., 23
Assembly bonus effect, 138
Atkinson, J. W., 43
Audiotape, use of, to record decision making, 177
Authority, role of, in resolving conflict, 103–5
Authorization, 93–94, 186
Autocracy, 129
Automobile industry, decision making in, 2
Availability heuristic, 89

B

Bacon, Francis, 94
Baker, K. R., 155
Baldridge, J. V., 121
Bargaining, 110, 111
Barnard, C. I., 15–16, 18, 29, 41, 49–50, 56, 59, 72, 149
Bass, B. M., 6, 12, 30, 42, 50, 65, 70, 75, 96, 104, 128, 131, 137, 140, 145, 148, 149, 161, 166, 178, 181, 183, 187, 188
Bateson, N., 140
Baum, B. M., 131
Baxter, B., 136
Bayes' Theorem, 90, 90n
Bayesian analysis, 160, 185

Bazerman, M. H., 60
Beach, L. R., 90
Bean, A. S., 158
Behavioral research, 22
Behavioral theories of the firm, 31–38
Behling, O., 24, 42, 46, 70
Bell Laboratories, 116
Benner, R. V., 130
Benson, R., 121
Berelson, B., 147
Biases
  cognitive, 143
  individual, 143–44, 187–88
  perceptual, 143
Billings, C. R., 136
Bing, R. A., 7, 23, 190, 191
Bishoprick, D. W., 12, 29, 55, 74, 128, 129,
  131, 132
Black box technique, 161
Blankenship, L. V., 149
Blau, P. M., 44
Bloom, B. S., 25, 177
Bobitt, H. R., 86, 117
Bogartz, W., 161
Bolas, C., 95, 190
Boundary spanners, 119–20
Bounded rationality, 183
  model of, 74–78
Bowman, J. S., 102
Brainstorming, 138, 161–62, 162
Braunstein, D. N., 13, 62, 187
Breadth versus depth search, 15
Brealey, R., 190
Breger, L., 161
Brehmer, B., 93
Breinholt, R. H., 86, 117
Brickman, P., 60
Brim, O. G., 147
Brink, V. A., 189
Broadbent, D. E., 64
Broder, L. S., 25, 177
Brody, N., 78
Bromily, P., 155
Browning, L. D., 26
Brunswik, E., 48, 91, 164
Buck passing, 100
Buffering, 17, 86–87, 118, 179–80
Bureaucratization, 44, 129–31
Burger, P. B., 42, 75, 148, 178
Burns, T., 108
Business Week, 160
Bylsma, D., Jr., 133

C

Campbell, A. C., 63
Campbell, J. P., 138
Caplow, T., 131
Carleton, W., 191

Carlson, J., 140
Caro, R. A., 105
Carping critics, 167
Carroll, A. B., 102
Carroll, S. J., 14, 40, 78
Carsrud, A. L., 84
Carter, E. E., 11
Carter, Jimmy, 2
Cascading, 12, 45, 124
Castore, C. H., 147
Categorization, 42
Cause-effect relations, 48, 88, 105, 144,
  174
Centralization versus decentralization,
  131–33
Cetron, M. J., 160
Change, as source of conflict, 102
Choice; *see* Evaluation and choice
Choice behavior, 89
Chunked information, 160
Churchman, C. W., 153
Clarkson, G., 27, 177
Classical management theory, 4, 40, 46,
  104
Coalition formation, 9, 32, 33, 105, 186
Coe, W., 121
Cognitive biases, 143
Cognitive dissonance, 94, 95
Cognitive structure, effect of, on decision
  making, 146–47
Cohen, M., 36, 38, 82, 89, 96, 176
Coin tossing, 6, 103
Coleman, P., 108
Collegial organization, 128, 129
Collins, D. F., 141
Collins, J. N., 96
Combinatory matching, 164
Combining judgments, 163–64
Common sense, 77
Compartmentalization, and specialization,
  130–31
Competence, effect of, on decision making,
  145–46
Complete rationality, model of, 73–74
Comprehension cycles, 7, 8
Compromise, 100
Computer, in decision making, 132, 169,
  180–81, 183–84, 189, 190
Conflict, 99–100, 186
  generation of, 99
  individual versus organization, 101–2
  quasi-resolution of, 33
  resolution of, 9, 103–14
  settlement of, 99
  sources of, 100–103
Consequences, unintended, 186
Conservatism, 90
Conservative focusing, 56

Constraints, 186–87
  definition of, 115–16
  environment as, 117–20
  formalism as, 135–36
  immediate group as, 136–40
  individual as, 140–50
  interactions among, 150
  organizational goals as, 45, 120–21
  organizational structure as, 124–36
  role expectations as, 129
  sources of, 116
  tasks as, 121–24
  technology as, 121–24
Contiguity, in organizational decision making, 6, 188
Contingency planning, 6
Continuous processing, 122–23
Contrived conflict, uses of, 166–68
Controls, 133–35
Coombs, C. H., 74
Coordinators, 99
Corbin, R., M., 60
Correlational analysis, 149–50
Cosier, R. A., 167
Cost-benefit analysis, 70, 97–98, 144
Craft decision-making teams, 139
Cravens, D. W., 57
Creative obfuscation, 181
Creativity, 58–59, 147
Creeping error, 179
Crisis decision, 7–8
Criterion checks, 182
Critical decisions, 16
Crozier, M., 108, 118
Crum, R. L., 157
Cue utilization policy, 91
Culbert, S. A., 16, 113
Cummings, L. L., 3, 12, 50, 56, 97, 138, 139n
Curtailment, 90–91
Curtis, G. L., 177
Cyert, R. M., 2, 14, 28, 29, 32, 33, 34n, 41, 44, 45, 53, 56, 57, 75, 83, 108, 110, 119, 144, 178

D

Dalkey, N., 159
Dalton, M., 187
Dandridge, T. C., 173
Davis, J. H., 109, 136, 186
Davis, K. R., 97
Dearborn, D. C., 148
DeBono, E., 166
Decentralization, versus centralization, 131–33
Decision aids and support systems, 7, 28, 151, 188–91
  applications, 156–57

Decision aids and support systems—*Cont.*
  appropriate set, 161
  combinatory matching, 164, 166
  combining judgments, 163–64
  delphi technique, 159–60
  elaborating, 160
  electronic data processing, 188–90
  elegance of, 190–91
  forced association, 161–62
  free association, 161–62
  fully structured, 153–58
  implementation of, 157–58
  Kepner-Tregoe's rules, 163
  MAUT (Multiple Attribute Utility Theory), 190
  modeling, 153–56
  nominal groups, 162–63, 190
  partially structured, 158–69
  policy capturing, 164
  prioritizing, 160
  probabilistic information processing system (PIP), 160
  purpose of, 151
  range of, 152
  real groups, 162–63
  sensitivity analysis, 156
  SPAN, 166, 190
  staging, 159
  strategic assumption making, 164
  systematic checks on organizational irrationality, 167–68
  systems view of, 191
  use of contrived conflict, 166–67
Decision flow, 173
Decision integration, 118
Decision making, definition of, 4; *see also* Organizational decision making
Decision matrix, 165
Decision priorities, 173–74
Decision tree, 54, 59, 153, 155
Decision value attributes, 30
Decision-making unit, 11
  cascading or multistaged, 12
  supervisor as, 11–12
Decisions, need for, 40
Decker, C. R., 137
Defensive avoidance, 138
DeGramont, S., 135
Delaney, S., 136
Delbecq, A. L., 3, 12, 50, 56, 97, 138, 139n, 162
Delegation, 149
Delphi technique, 159–60, 162
Dent, J. K., 44
Design; *see* Search and design
Design alternatives, 182
Devil's advocate, 159, 166–67
de Witt, John, 8

Diagnosis, 47–49, 180
Dialectic argumentation, 159, 166–67
Diesing, P., 8, 75
Differentiation, 118
Dill, W. R., 2, 29, 51
Discrepancy, as trigger for decision making, 40–41
Displaced ideal, model of, 78–80
Displacement, 45–47, 79, 131
Dogmatism, 146
Doktor, R. H., 86
Downey, H. K., 147
Downs, A., 130
Drenth, P. J. D., 149, 177
Driscoll, J. M., 54, 58
Driver, M. J., 118, 146
Drucker, P. F., 41, 133, 148, 160, 180
Dual hierarchies, 128–29
Due process, 135–36
Dunbar, R. L. M., 119
Duncan, B., 14
Duncan, R. B., 87, 118, 126
Dunnette, M. D., 146
Dutton, J. M., 101
Dynamic programming, 153

E

Earley, James, 31
Ebbeson, E. B., 105
Ebert, R. J., 17, 18, 27, 57, 64, 65, 117, 122, 123, 132
Economic theory
  of the firm, 27–31
  of teams, 67–68
Education, impact of, on decision making, 168–69
Edwards, W., 28, 160
Effectiveness, of decision making, 177
Egalitarian model, 128
Ego involvement, 102
Elaborating, 160
Elbing, A. O., 144
Electronic data processing (EDP), 62, 188–90
Emery, E. I., 117
Emery, J. C., 67
Emory, C. W., 57, 183
Empire building, 44
Empirico-inductive methods, for studying organizational decision making, 24–27
Emshoff, J. R., 13, 102, 103, 164, 185
Engineer decision-making teams, 139
England, G. W., 145
Entrepreneurial manager, 101
Entrepreneurs, 141
Environment
  boundary spanners, 119–20
  consequences of failure to adapt, 118–19

Environment—*Cont.*
  as constraint, 117–20
  four ideal types of, 117–18
  impact of complexity, 118
  organization needs to match, 117–18
Error checking, 64
Escalation, 90–91
Estes, R. W., 166
Etzioni, A., 35, 36, 42, 179
Evaluation and choice, 184
  anticipated utility of outcome, 73
  Bayesian analysis, 185
  and commitment, 89–94
  criteria for evaluation of alternatives, 71–73
  and dealing with uncertainty, 83–89
  effects of failure, 185–86
  exploitation versus exploration, 184–85
  as hard to separate, 69–71
  ideal as anchor, 78–80
  and justification of chosen alternative, 94–95
  model of bounded rationality, 74–78
  model of complete rationality, 73
  model of displaced ideal, 78–80
  model of objectives orientation, 81–83
  of obtained outcomes, 95–98
  political solution, 80–81
  satisficing outcomes, 74–78
  strategic assumptions, 185
  strategic striving, 81–83
  unintended consequences, 186
Evanisko, M. J., 58, 116
Evoked alternatives, character of, 183
Exercise Kolomon, 89–90, 184–85
Exercise Venture, 184–85
Expediency, 81
Experts, calling in, for consultation, 168
Explicit values and premises, 141
Exploitation, 184–85
Exloration, 184–85
Expressive stakes, 110–11
Eye-movement paralleling decision processes, 25

F

Fahey, L., 100, 109
Failure, effects of, 185–86
Failure cycles, 7, 8
Farrow, D. L., 145, 148
Federations of autonomous units, 128
Feedback, 12, 133, 134, 139–40
Feedback delays, 7, 8
Feedback loop, 97
Feedforward, 133, 134
Feedforward controls, 42
Feigenbaum, E. H., 57
Feldman, J., 57, 116

Feldman, J. M., 84, 143, 180
Feldman, M. S., 3–4, 42
Ference, T. P., 55, 65, 182, 183
Festinger, L., 94
Feyerabend, P., 54
Filella, J., 105
Filley, A. C., 47, 48, 49, 66, 122, 124, 134, 134n
Filtering, 64
Firm
  behavioral theories of the, 31–38
    criticisms of, 38
  economic theory of the, 27–29
    criticisms of, 29–31
Fisch, G. G., 188
Fischhoff, B., 74, 89, 90, 92, 143, 144, 151, 188, 190, 191
Fleishman, E. A., 136
Fleming, T., 41
Flippo, E. B., 41
Focus-gambling strategy, 56
Forced association, 161–62
Ford, D. L., Jr., 61
Formalism, as a constraint, 135–36
Forward, J., 43
Fox, F., 60
Frederikson, N., 159
Free association, 161–62
French, J. R. P., 16
Friedlander, F., 14
Friedlander, H., 44
Fulmer, R. M., 161
Functional organization, 126–27

G

Gambits, 109
Game theory, 153
Gameson, W. A., 109
Garbage Can model, 38, 176
Gebert, D., 136
General Motors, 133
Gestalt processes, 59
Gettys, C. F., 93
Gibb, J. R., 159
Giuliano, T., 60
Glickman, A. S., 136
Glueck, W. F., 116
Goals, 42–43
  clarity of, 44, 181
  consistency between subgoals and, 44
  operational versus nonoperational, 43–44
  organizational, as sets of constraints, 45
  stability and change of, 43
Goldberg, W. H., 119
Goldman, H. C., 78
Goodchilds, J., 159
Gordon, W. J. J., 161

Gore, W. J., 9
Gouldner, A. W., 186
Gouran, D. S., 2
Grayson, C. J., 185
Green, S. G., 143
Gresham's Law, 190
Griffiths, D. E., 3
Groupthink, 138
Growth, effect of, on organizational decision making, 173
Gulley, G. W., 85
"Gut" feelings, 77

H

Hage, J., 85
Hahn, C. P., 136
Halaby, C. N., 16
Hall, P. D., 13, 62, 187
Halpin, S. M., 63
Hammond, J. S., 92, 151
Hammond, K. R., 91
Hanline, M. H., 40, 51, 174
Harrison, E. F., 66, 70, 73, 77, 80, 82, 84, 102, 117, 141, 145, 153, 154, 154n, 155, 164, 165n
Harvard Business Review, 137
Harvey, O. J., 146
Hausman, C. R., 59
Healey, R. J., 128
Hegarty, W. H., 125, 146
Hegel, G. W. F., 166
Heller, F. A., 25, 50, 61, 78, 125, 145, 149, 177
Hellriegel, D., 147
Helmer, O., 159
Helsabeck, R. E., 128
Henry IV, King, 81
Herbert, T. T., 166
Hertz, D. B., 189
Hertz, K. J., 77
Heuristic decision-making teams, 139–40
Heuristic programming, 15, 158
Heuristic training, 14, 15
Heuristics, 54, 56
Heynes, R. W., 61
Hickson, D. J., 104
Hierarchial level, 126, 148–50
Higbee, K. L., 89
Hillier, F. S., 74
Hinings, C. R., 104
Hobbs, R. M., 137
Hoff, D. B., 147
Hoffman, L. R., 48, 95
Hogarth, R. M., 18n, 31
House, R. J., 47, 48, 49, 66, 122, 124, 134, 134n
Howard, R. A., 51
Howes, M. L., 132

Hoyt, G. C., 137, 190
Hunt, D. E., 146
Hyman, R., 161

I

Ideal, as anchor, 78–80
Idealism, 34
Identity-denying responses, 111
Immediate group, as a constraint, 136–40
Implementation, 95–96, 157–58
Implicit favorite, 77–78, 93
Implicit favorite model, 95
Implicit values and premises, 141–43
In-basket techniques, 25
Incremental approach, 80
Incrementalism, 34–35, 36
Incrementing, 178–79
Independence of Irrelevant Alternatives,
    79–80
Indifference curves, 74
Indik, B. P., 132
Individuals
    biases of, 143–44, 187–88
    as a constraint, 140–50
    dicision-making styles of, 145–46
    integration of, with organization, 113–14
Industrial espionage, 58
Industrial pyramid, 104
Information
    availability of, 62–64
    cost of, 66–67
    distortion of, 65–66
    failure of, 76–77
    flow of, 101
    overload, 62–64, 66, 182
    relevance of, 64–65
    reliability of, 65
    sources of, 183–84
Information systems, 61–68, 183
Innovative solutions, design of, 59–60
Innovative teams, 114
Innovations, 58, 116
Institutional core, decisions in, 17
Instrumental stakes, 110–11
Instrumental uncertainty, 84
Intelligence, effect of, on decision-making,
    146
Interactive human-computer systems, 25
Interagency planning, 110
International firms, 133
Interrupts, 7–8
Intuition, 23, 77
Inventories, 86–87
Involvement, in decision process, 49–51
Iran, American hostage crisis in, 2
Isolation, 86

J

Jackson, J., 104

Janis, I. L., 81, 100, 138
Johnson, D. F., 90
Johnson, R. A., 156
Johnson, R. H., 137
Joint problem solving
    improving, 111–13
    versus negotiating, 109–14

K

Kahn, R. L., 16, 40, 44, 72, 77, 81, 94, 95,
    97, 102–3, 124, 142, 144, 168, 188
Kahneman, D., 64, 79, 89
Kallman, E. A., 149
Kanter, H. E., 57, 116
Kast, F. E., 1, 76, 142, 156, 180
Katona, G., 47
Katz, D., 16, 40, 44, 72, 77, 81, 94, 95, 97,
    102–3, 124, 142, 144, 167, 168, 188
Keene, P., 191
Kefalas, A., 57–58
Kelley, H. H., 47
Kelly, C., III, 93
Kennedy, R. E., 140
Kepner, C. H., 40, 160, 163, 176
Kerr, S., 47, 48, 49, 66, 122, 124, 134, 134n
Kettle, P., 61
Khandwalla, P. N., 85, 122
Kilmann, R. H., 96
Kimberly, J. R., 58, 116
Klasson, C., 121
Klauss, R., 65, 183
Kleinmuntz, B., 64
Klingman, D. D., 157
Knight, F. H., 83
Knight, K., 127
Kogan, N., 140, 147
Komorita, S. S., 109, 186
Koontz, H., 72
Koopman, P. L., 149, 177
Krouse, C. G., 12
Kuyenstierna, J., 93

L

Lacho, K. J., 55
Lanham, N., 63
Lanzetta, J. T., 54, 58
Laughlin, P. R., 109, 186
Lawrence, P., 85
Learned, E. P., 38, 81
Leblebici, H., 118
Legitimacy, of decision process, 186
Lens model, 91
Levi, A., 47, 90
Levine, J. M., 58
Lewin, K., 41
Leys, W. A. R., 142
Lichfield, N., 61
Lichtenstein, S., 23, 74, 89, 90, 92, 143,
    151, 184, 188, 190, 191

Lieberman, G. J., 74
Likert, R., 127, 128, 140
Lilgergren, J., 93
Linch-pin organization, 127–28, 140
Lindblom, C. E., 4, 34, 35, 178
Linear cue, 92n
Linear equations, 92
Linear models, 23
Linear programming, 7, 7–8, 28, 153, 155
Linear regression, 23n
Linear regression models, 23, 91–92, 91n
Linear weighting, 72
Link, J. R., 184
Linkage, 82
Linkage analysis, 176
Linked choices, 82–83
Lipson, D. S., 189, 190
Lloyd, R. F., 61
Locke, E. A., 43
Long-linked technology, 122
Lorsch, J. W., 85, 127
Lotteries, 6–7
Loughlin, P. R., 186
Luthans, F., 13, 31, 58, 160

M

MacCrimmon, K. R., 3, 5, 15, 22, 51, 55, 56, 66, 67, 71, 72, 73, 74, 83, 87, 88, 97, 110, 156, 160, 162, 184, 185
Machine model of organizations, 29
Mackenzie, K. D., 123
MacKinnon, W. J., 161, 166
Maier, N. R. F., 48, 72, 95, 159
Maltzman, I., 161
Management-by-exception, 182
Management information systems (MIS), 63, 183
Management Neanderthalism, 2
Managerial core, decisions in, 17
Mandelbaum, M., 81
Mangone, R., 64
Mann, L., 81, 100, 138
March, J. G., 2, 6, 18, 29, 32, 33, 34n, 36, 38, 41, 43, 44, 45, 46, 53, 56, 57, 62, 66, 75, 82, 83, 87, 108, 110, 119, 124, 130, 135, 140, 148, 168, 172, 173, 176, 178, 181, 183, 185, 186, 188
Marquis, D. G., 59, 127
Marschak, J., 66, 67, 73, 156
Martin, M. S., 191
Martin, N. H., 7
Mason, R. O., 166, 167
Mathematical game theory, 28
Mathematico-deductive methods, for studying organizational decision making, 23–24
Matrix organization, 127
MAUT (Multiple Attribute Utility Theory), 190

Maximax strategy, 71
McCleary, R., 103
McDonough, J. J., 16, 113
McGee, R. J., 131
McGrath, J. E., 136
McGregor, D. W., 11, 30, 137
McGuire, J. W., 27
McNaul, J. P., 86
McWhinney, W. H., 117
Means-end chain, 76
Means-ends adjustment, 80
Means-ends analysis, 15, 56, 126–27, 160
Means-ends interaction, 60
Means-ends theory, 4, 6, 10, 60, 174
Mechanic, D., 104
Mediating technology, 122
Merton, R. K., 126, 130, 186
Metaphor, 25
Michela, J. L., 47
Middleton, C. J., 127
Miles, R. E., 149
Military History, Office of the Chief of, 56
Miller, G. A., 63
Miller, J. A., 65, 182
Milutinovich, J. S., 189, 190
Minimax strategy, 71
Minimum Resource Theory, 109
Mintzberg, H., 5, 7, 8, 26, 35, 41, 58, 59, 70, 93, 159, 172, 173, 180, 186
Mitchell, T. R., 17, 18, 27, 57, 64, 65, 117, 122, 123, 132, 143
Mitroff, I. I., 13, 102, 103, 164, 185
Mixed scanning, 35–36, 42
Mixed strategy, 71
Modeling, 153
    building of models, 153–54
    types of models, 155–56
    uses of, 154–55
Monitoring, 86–87
Moore, D. G., 141
Morlock, H., 77
Moses, Robert, 105
Multiattribute utility theory, 155–56
Multiple Attribute Utility Theory (MAUT), 190
Multiple cue probability learning, 92
Multiple impact, 125
Multiple objectives, 76
Multiple regression, 23, 164
Multiple regression analysis, 116
Multistaged decision making, 12
Murdia, R., 126
Myers, S., 190

N

Narayanan, V. K., 100, 109
Naumes, W., 189, 190
Negotiating, 100
    compromises in, 101

Negotiating—*Cont.*
 versus joint problem solving, 109–14
Newell, A., 15, 48, 54, 177
Newman, J. W., 185
Newstrom, J. W., 102
New York Times, 2
Nicolaidis, N., 101
Niland, P., 57, 183
Nominal groups, 158, 162–63, 190
Nonlinear regression, 23
Nonprogrammed decision processes, 14
Nonroutine decision making, 31–32
Nonzero sum game, 109
Normative models, of organizational decision making, 22

O

Objective performance standards, 40
Objectives, multiplicity of, 44–45
Objectives orientation, model of, 81–83
O'Donnell, C., 72
Olsen, J. P., 36, 38, 82, 176
Olson, C. L., 6, 60
Operations research, applications of, 156–57
Opportunity planning, 113
Optimality, 99
Optimism, 77
Optimizing, 77
Options markets, 22
O'Reilly, C. A., 63
Organization
 formality of, 187
 intergration of, with individual, 113–14
Organization learning, 33
Organizational decision making
 alternatives of choice in, 3
 behavioral theories of the firm, 31–38
 cascade in, 12, 45, 124
 constraints on, 99–114, 186–88
 decision aids and support systems, 151–69, 188–91
 distinguishing between personal and organizational goals in, 15–16
 distribution of activity in, 8–9
 economic theory of the firm, 27–31
 empirico-inductive methods for studying, 24–27
 evaluation and choice, 69–98, 184–86
 goals in, 15–16, 120–21
 and human decision making, 18–19
 importance of, 2
 interdependence of, among organization cores, 17–18
 mathematico-deductive methods for studying, 23–24
 methods and models of, 21–38, 174–77
 normative models of, 22

Organizational decision making—*Cont.*
 power and politics in, 9–11
 prescription versus description in, 21–22
 problem discovery and diagnosis, 39–52, 177–84
 as problem solving, 3–4
 process of, 4–11
 role of theory in, 27
 search and design, 53–68, 181–82
 structure of problems in, 13–15
 substantive sources of differences in, 16–18
 supervisor as decision-making unit, 11–12
 types of, 17
 units in, 11–12
Organizational goals, as constraints, 120–21
Organizational irrationality, systematic checks on, 167–68
Organizational mapping, 25
Organizational structure, 125–29
Organizational structure constraints, 124–36
Orpen, C., 132
Osborn, A. F., 161, 162
Otton, A. J. W., 131
Outcomes
 anticipated utility of, 73–74
 criteria for evaluating obtained, 16–97
 evaluation of obtained, 95–98
 satisficing, 74–78
Overlapping group organization, 127–28

P

Paige, G. D., 26
Parallel search, 182–83
Paramutual betting, 22
Parsons, T., 17
Participation, in decision process, 49–51
Patchen, M., 16, 104, 106n
Paulson, K., 136
Payne, J. W., 25
Pehl, B., 147
Pennings, J. M., 104
Perceptual biases, 143
Perrin, E. C., 78
Perrow, C., 57, 58, 64, 133, 135, 177, 178
Personality, effect of, on decision making, 145–46
Persuasion, 105
PERT, 7–8
Peters, A. J., 97
Peterson, R., 90, 93
Pettigrew, A. M., 99, 103, 111
Pfeffer, J., 8, 62, 75, 76, 81, 85
Phillips, J. S., 26
Pickle, H., 44

Pinder, C., 145
Pinto, P. R., 145
PIP (Probabilistic information processing system), 160
Polarization, 102
Policy capturing, 91–92, 164
Policy statements, 182
Policymaking, 10, 16–17
Political decision making, 2, 80–81
Politics, importance of, in organizational decision making, 9–11
Pollay, R. W., 145
Portfolio planning, 113–14
Position papers, 158
Pounds, F. W., 27
Power
    importance of, in organizational decision making, 9–11
    role of, in resolving conflict, 103–5
Power brokers, 105, 109, 142
PRA, 184
Pragmatism, 34
Premature closure, 60, 60–61
Priorities, establishment of, for decisions, 51
Prioritizing, 160
Probabilistic functionalism, 48
Probabilistic information processing system (PIP), 160
Probability theory, 30–31, 153
Problem complexity, dealing with, 57
Problem discovery and diagnosis, 177–78
    amplifiers, 179–80
    buffers, 179–80
    categorization, 42
    diagnosis, 47–49, 180
    discrepancy as trigger, 40–41
    displacement, 45–47
    goal clarity, 181
    goals, 42–45
    incrementing, 178–79
    objectives, 42–45
    participation and involvement in decision process, 49–51
    problems and dilemmas, 39–40
    recategorizations, 180
    scanning, 42
    screening, 42
    simplification, 181
    structuring, 180–81
    surprises, 180
    timing, 179
Problem uncertainty; see Uncertainty
Problemistic search, 3
Procrastination, 100
Product organization, 127
Professional managers, 141
Profit, as a constraint, 120–21

Programmed decisions, 14
Project organization, 127
Pruitt, D. G., 78, 140

Q–R

Quality, as criteria of effective decision making, 72
Queueing, 155
Quinn, J. B., 101, 114, 178
Radford, K. J., 48, 51, 74, 82, 89, 97, 156, 166
Radner, R., 67, 156
Radnor, M., 158
Radomsky, J., 51, 178
Raisinghani, D., 5, 7, 8, 26, 35, 41, 58, 59, 70, 93, 159, 172, 180, 186
Ralph, C. A., 160
Rapoport, A., 40, 60
Rate busting management, 57
Raven, B., 16
Reagan, Ronald, 142
Real groups, 162–63
Recategorizations, 180
Recycling, 4
Reeducation, 187–88
Regression analysis, 158
Reinharth, L., 149
Requisite variety, 117
Research & Development, and conflict, 102
Rice, G. H., 12, 29, 55, 74, 128, 129, 131, 132
Rim, Y., 140
Risk, 184
    preferences, of individuals, 147
    and uncertainty, 83, 88–89
Risky shift, 140
Roberts, R. M., 40, 51, 174
Role, effect of, on decision making, 148–50
Role expectations, as constraints, 129
Rolling production schedule, 155
Romelaer, P., 6, 36, 38, 188
Roosevelt, F. D., 166
Rose, G. L., 137
Rosen, L. D., 25
Rosenstein, E., 50
Rosenzweig, J. E., 1, 76, 142, 156, 180
Roth, C., 36
Rothenburg, A., 59
Routine decision-making teams, 138
Rowen, H. H., 8
Roy, B., 24
Rubenstein, A. H., 158
Rubik's Cube, 93
Ruch, W., 102
Rush, M. C., 26
Russo, J. E., 25
Ryterband, E. C., 6, 70, 161

S

Safire, W., 179
Samet, M. G., 58
Satisficing, 74–78, 80, 82
Sawyer, J., 163
Sayles, L. R., 27, 125
Scanning, 42, 51, 174
Scenarios, 88, 158
Schaefer, J. E., 27
Scheduling delays, 7–8
Scheff, T. J., 104
Schelling, T. C., 79
Schneck, R. E., 104
Schoderbek, P. P., 58
Schoner, B., 137
Schonfield, J., 159
Schriesheim, C., 24, 42, 46, 70
Schroder, H. M., 118, 146
Schwartzman, R., 7–8
Schwenk, R., 167
Screening, 42
Search and design, 53, 58–59, 181–82
    as anticipatory behavior, 56
    character of evoked alternatives, 183
    conceptualizations about stimulation of, 54–55
    design alternatives, 182
    as either sequential or parallel, 182–83
    heuristics of, 56–58
    information sources, 183–84
    information systems, 61–68
    innovative solutions, 59–60
    overload, 182
    speed of decision, 183
    stimulation of, 54–55
    termination of, 60–61
    theories on, 53–55
    as ubiquitous and dynamic, 55–56
Seat of the pants judgment, 13
Self-interest, importance of, to organizational decision making, 16
Self-planning decisions, 187
Selznick, P., 16
Sen, A., 185
Sensitivity analysis, 74, 156
Sequential attention, 181
Sequential search, 182–83
Shapira, Z., 6, 18, 43, 62, 149, 173, 178, 181, 185, 186
Shaw, M. E., 55
Shuchman, A., 153
Shull, F. A., Jr., 3, 12, 50, 56, 97, 138, 139n
Side payments, negotiating of, 110
Simon, H. A., 3, 13, 14, 15, 18, 22, 28, 29, 32, 35, 43, 45, 46, 48, 53, 54, 58, 63, 66, 75, 76, 87, 120–21, 124, 125, 130, 135, 140, 144, 148, 168, 172, 173, 177, 182, 183, 186

Simpson, R. L., 85
Sims, H. P., 7, 125, 146
Skunkworks, 114
Sloan, A. P., 133
Slocum, J. W., 147
Slovic, P., 22, 23, 74, 89, 90, 92, 143, 151, 184, 188, 190, 191
Snyder, R. C., 26
Social visibility, 49
Soelberg, P. O., 4, 5, 30, 35, 56, 77, 78, 93, 95, 182
Solem, A. R., 159
Souder, W. E., 163
SPAN, 166, 190
Specialization, and compartmentalization, 130–31
Sphere of discretion, 124
Spray, S. L., 173
Sproat, A. T., 38, 81
Staging, 152, 159
Stagner, R., 7
Standard setting, 71–72
Stanley, J. D., 120, 167
Starbuck, W. H., 49, 56
Staw, B. M., 60, 91
Steffey, J., 63
Steiner, G. A., 138, 147
Stimulated recall, 25, 177
Stock market, 22
Strategic planning, 178
Strategic assumptions, 164, 185
Strategic decisions, 16, 82
Strategic striving, 81–83
Strebel, P., 88
Streufert, S., 25, 63, 89, 118, 146, 147
Stricklin, W. D., 3, 71
Structuring, 180–81
Study of Values, 146
Subjective biases, 95
Subjective probability, 88
Suboptimization, 30
Suedfeld, P., 146
Sutherland, J. W., 75
Swalm, R. O., 74, 185
Synectics, 161–62
Systems view
    of decision support, 191
    of organization, 129

T

Tactical analysis, 82
Tactical and Negotiations Game (TNG), 25
Tactical decisions, 16, 82
Tang, T. S., 95, 190
Tannenbaum, R., 116, 124
Tasks, as constraints, 121–24
Tavis, L. A., 157
Taylor, B. W. III, 97

Taylor, D. W., 21
Taylor, E. A., 89
Taylor, M. L. W., 132
Taylor, R. N., 87, 110, 146, 156, 160, 162
Team theory, 67–68, 153, 156
Technical core, decisions in, 17
Technical rationality, 17
Technological innovations, 58
Technology
  combination and change in, 123
  as a constraint, 121–24
  management's role in, 123–24
Teger, A. I., 140
Teulings, A. W. M., 131
Theory, role of, in studying decision making, 27
Thiagarajan, K. M., 184
Third party intervention, 112–13
Thomas, K. W., 101
Thompson, J. D., 14, 17, 44, 54, 55, 84, 85, 86, 101, 105, 109, 119, 123, 148
Theorêt, A., 5, 7, 8, 26, 35, 41, 58, 59, 70, 93, 159, 172, 173, 180, 186
Threshold studies, 180
Tillman, R., Jr., 137
Timing, 179
Timing delays and speedups, 7–8
Tosi, H. L., 14, 40, 78
Training, impact of, on decision making, 168–69
Trbovich, N., 184
Treddenick, J. M., 97
Tregoe, B. B., 40, 160, 163
Trist, E. I., 117
Tropman, J. E., 61
Trow, D. B., 14, 28, 29, 32, 144
Trull, S. G., 96, 97
Tuden, A., 44, 101, 105
Tullar, W. L., 90
Tversky, A., 22, 60, 64, 79, 89

U

Uncertainty
  absorption of, 87
  adaptation and restructuring, 87–88
  avoidance of, 33, 83
  buffering, 86–87
  coping with, 104
  dealing with, 57–58, 83–89
  instrumental, 84
  isolation, 86
  reducing, 84
  response to, 84–88
  and risk, 83, 88–89
  and subjective probablity, 88–89
  value, 84
Ungson, G. R., 13, 62, 187
Union negotiations, 111

United Fund Boards, 43
Unobstrusive controls, 135
Unprogrammed decision making, 14
Utility functions, 74, 185
Utility theory, 22, 28, 74

V

Vaidya, C., 61
Valenzi, E. R., 145, 148
Value uncertainty, 84
Van de Vall, M., 95, 190
Van de Ven, A. H., 162
Variance absorption, 87
Variance leveling, 87
Vaughan, J. A., 184
Verbal protocols, use of, 177
Vertical integration, 122–23
Videotape, use of, to record decision making, 25, 177
Vroom, V. H., 43, 72, 147, 150

W–X

Wagner, H. M., 155, 157
Waiting line theory, 153, 155
Walker, A., 127, 157
Wallach, M. A., 140, 147
Walters, J. L., 30, 137
Walton, R. E., 101, 109, 110, 111, 111–12
Watergate coverup, 2
Weber, M., 130
Webster, E., 77
Weick, K. E., 83, 126
Weingartner, M., 184
Well-structured problems, 14–15
Wensley, J. R. C., 157
What is versus what should be, 40–41
Whistle-blowing, 167
Whitbread, M., 61
Wilson, C. Z., 30, 36, 37, 54, 57, 62, 65, 95, 108, 121, 124, 125, 153
Witte, E., 8, 26, 27
Woods, D. H., 66
Woodward, J., 122
Work group collusion, 57
Wotruba, T. R., 64
Wright, P., 92
Xerox, 172

Y–Z

Yetton, P. W., 72, 150
Yukl, G., 125, 145, 149
Zander, A., 43
Zeleny, M., 3, 5, 21, 23, 24, 36, 40, 46, 59, 63, 64, 70, 77, 78–79, 80, 92, 94
Zero-sum game, 110
Zimbardo, P. G., 105
Zwicky, F., 161

This book has been set in 10 and 9 point Caledonia, leaded 2 points. Chapter numbers and titles are in Caledonia. The size of the type page is 26 by 46 picas.